Hegel's Theory of Imagination

SUNY series in Hegelian Studies
William Desmond, editor

Hegel's Theory of Imagination

JENNIFER ANN BATES

State University of New York Press

Published by
State University of New York Press, Albany

© 2004 State University of New York

For information, address State University of New York Press,
State University Plaza, Albany, NY 12246

Production, Kelli Williams
Marketing, Susan M. Petrie

Library of Congress Cataloging-in-Publication Data

Bates, Jennifer Ann, 1964–
    Hegel's theory of imagination/by Jennifer Bates.
        p. cm. — (SUNY series in Hegelian studies)
    Includes bibliographical references (p.) and index.
    ISBN 0-7914-6208-0 (alk. paper)
    1. Imagination (Philosophy) 2. Hegel, Georg Wilhelm Friedrich, 1770–1831. I.
Title II.
Series.

BH301.I53B38 2004
128'.3—dc22
                                                              2003063323

IN MEMORY OF MY FATHER, DONALD G. BATES

———————————————

Contents

Preface

THE BASIC CONCERNS OF THIS BOOK

Several years ago I became interested in the fact that although the imagination (*die Einbildungskraft*) is absolutely central to Hegel's predecessors Kant, Fichte, and Schelling, the imagination *appears* to play a relatively small role in Hegel's thought. The word occurs only once in what is perhaps the best known of Hegel's works and that which put him clearly on the philosophical map of the time, the *Phenomenology of Spirit*. Why, when Sensation, Perception, Understanding, and Reason all had chapters devoted to them in that work, did the imagination not likewise appear? My research has shown that the imagination is not only absolutely central to Hegel's thought, it is also one of the central places from which a proper defense of Hegelian speculative science can be made. My argument involves close analysis of the role of the imagination in Hegel's three series of lectures on the *Philosophy of Spirit* from 1803 to 1830, and of its role in his *Lectures on Aesthetics* and in the *Phenomenology of Spirit*.

The Introduction begins with an overview of why the imagination is important. Then I look at why we should look to Hegel's view of it. This involves looking at what the role of the imagination was for Kant, Fichte, and Schelling and then at how the imagination appears in Hegel's first publication, the 1801 *Difference Between Fichte's and Schelling's System of Philosophy*. Following that, in the spirit of Hegel, the book as a whole is divided into three parts.

Part One, "Imagination in Theory," begins (chapter 1) with a look at Hegel's theory of the imagination in the context of his criticism of the philosophies of subjective reflection. I look at his criticism of those philosophies of the period that were based on a subjective ontology as opposed to a substance ontology. The main textual focus of the chapter is Hegel's *Faith and Knowledge*. I also make use of Hegel's *Differenzschrift*, considering Fichte's philosophy for contrast and Schelling's for his influence.

The reason Hegel criticizes subjective philosophies is that, at the time he published his first works (the *Differenzschrift* and *Faith and Knowledge*), Hegel was under the influence of Schelling. Hegel's productive imagination (*productive Einbildungskraft*) is essentially what Schelling calls the "indifference point." The indifference point is a productive self-sundering, and it is at the heart not only of all subject-object relations but of the creative process of the Absolute. Indeed, it is identified as Absolute Reason. In chapter 1, I discuss this sundering imagination. I also discuss the difference between a one-sided reconstruction from that sundering, on the one hand, and a proper reconstruction from that sundering, on the other. I show, in conclusion, why for Hegel the philosophies of subjective reflection are locked within a logic of loss.

The subsequent chapters of Part One deal with how this changes for Hegel, and why. As Hegel's thought moves away from Schelling and adopts (while transforming) a more Fichtean subject ontology, the imagination is specified as a moment within subjective spirit. It is therefore in the Jena System manuscripts, in the two *Geistesphilosophie* (*Philosophy of Spirit*) lecture series (1803–04, and 1805–06), that the imagination turns up in detail. After an introduction to dialectical identity in chapter 2, an analysis of the role given to the imagination in these two *Geistesphilosophie* is given in chapter 3 and chapter 4 respectively.

The role that Hegel gives to the imagination in these works is particularly interesting to sort out, since the relationship between what would eventually become distinct parts of Hegel's methodology—the logical, the phenomenological, and the Scientific investigation of spirit—are not clearly defined before 1807.

Hegel's final discussion of the imagination in his 1830 *Encyclopedia Philosophy of Spirit* (discussed in chapter 5) does not suffer as much from the confusion we see in his earlier versions of the *Philosophy of Spirit*. Hegel's thought on the role of the imagination is clearer by this time and thus "moments" or phases of the imagination are discussed in detail. This clarity is due, I argue, to the fact that by 1830 Hegel has the *Phenomenology of Spirit* behind him. That is, having figured out what work a phenomenology is supposed to do—namely, prepare one for speculative science—he is able to distinguish between a phenomenological account of the imagination and a scientific, speculative account of it. In fact, in 1830 Hegel expects his readers to have done the work involved in a phenomenology of spirit in order to be able to read his *Philosophy of Spirit*. He expects his readers to have thoroughly comprehended the role of picture-thinking in their thinking, or, as I phrase it, he expects his readers to have "thought the imagination through to its end."

Because Hegel's account becomes clearer and clearer, there is a progression in clarity about the imagination's activity from chapter 1 through to chapter 5. I chose to keep the obscurities in my exegesis, in order to avoid explaining the earlier texts through the later ones. I hope in this way to have provided some insight into the development of Hegel's thought about the imagination. Nonetheless, to alleviate some of the obscurity I have indicated, at the end of each chapter, what is most problematic or inadequately or better expressed in the given text. This is done in the light of my understanding of Hegel's thoughts on the imagination as a whole. I have also included a schematic outline (p. xxxix) of the relevant moments of the three versions of the *Philosophy of Spirit*. This schema indicates where the imagination appears in each. So much for Part One.

In order to explain what I do in Part Two, let me remind you of the original question: What role is the imagination playing in the *Phenomenology of Spirit*? None of the *Philosophy of Spirit* texts on the imagination, by themselves, provide the answer. One has to look at the role of the imagination in Absolute Spirit as well. That is, one has to get out of the individual, subjective mind of the *Philosophies of Spirit*, and look at how the mind functions interpersonally. While this process is already underway at the end of chapter 5 in the discussion of sign-making *Phantasie*, the main work of answering the question lies at the start of Part Two, in chapter 6.

Part Two, "Imagination in Practice," concerns the objective authentication of imagination in memory and art. I begin (chapter 6) with a discussion of Memory (*Gedächtnis*). It is the moment following the imagination in the *Encyclopedia Philosophy of Spirit*. In the transition to Memory, the third moment of the imagination, *Sign-making Phantasie*, externalizes its products. In this moment, the inner world of representations is opened to interpersonal, objective communication. It is in this *Phantasie*, and not in any level prior to it, that language and community (Spirit) are actually born.

This leads us to discuss the essential differences between the different kinds imagination, namely *Einbildungskraft*, *Phantasie*, and *Vorstellen*. I take issue with Knox's translation of all of these as "imagination" in his translation of Hegel's *Lectures on Aesthetics*. By the time Hegel gave these lectures these terms meant the following, different things to him: *Vorstellen* (representation or picture-thinking) is always self-reflective, complex, using universals, and *not* always artistic; *Phantasie* (which I keep in the German) is *always* artistic; and *Einbildungskraft* or "imagination," means one or more of three things: (a) the overall notion of imagination which incorporates the three moments explained in the 1830 *Philosophy of Spirit*, namely reproduction, symbol, and sign making;[1] (b) the middle moment of representation; (c) in the *Aesthetics*, the specifically *reproductive* imagination, which can be "passive" but is never creative or artistic. The difference between these terms is crucial for understanding Hegel's *Aesthetics*. I therefore emend Knox's translation throughout my discussion of it.

My discussion of Hegel's *Aesthetics* in chapter 6 concerns in particular the following: Hegel's account of the Artist's *Phantasie*; the Artist's products and how the inwardizing and externalizing activity of reproductive *Einbildungskraft* and *Phantasie* in *Vorstellungen* manifest in the History of Art; Hegel's concept of *das poetische Vorstellen* (the poetic way of looking at things); and finally, the difference between Hegel's concept of poetry as a form of Romantic art and German Romanticism's theory about universal poetry.

By the end of Part Two, we have clarity concerning the context of the single appearance of "*Einbildungskraft*" in the *Phenomenology of Spirit*. The context is that of his criticism of German Romanticism. For Hegel, the German Romantics do not grasp how the Concept works in *Vorstellen*. Our discussion reveals that what this means is that the German Romantics never grasped the role of imagination as the sublating (*aufhebende*), spatiotemporalizing, internalizing, and externalizing activity of a historically developing Spirit. The failure of the German Romantics is therefore a failure of the imagination, a failure to understand its role in thinking and creativity. This is made particularly clear in Hegel's discussion of their concept of irony. With regard to the question why the word only comes up once in the book—we have to look next more closely at the role of *Vorstellen*.

Both artistic *Vorstellen* and phenomenological *Vorstellen* are socially complex representations of experience. After a brief discussion of the difference between these kinds of *Vorstellen*, I move into the final part of the book. In it I discuss how the *Phenomenology of Spirit* teaches us to think them through to their conceptual completion.

Thus Part Three, "Synthesis and Disclosure: *The Phenomenology of Spirit*," concerns the role of *Einbildungskraft*, *Phantasie*, and *Vorstellen* in the *Phenomenology of Spirit*. I begin with an analysis of the only passage in which the first of these terms arises in the *Phenomenology*. Hegel takes issue with the prevailing fascination with genius. I therefore discuss Hegel's critique in relation to two conceptions of genius that had been influential at the time, namely, Kant's and Schelling's.

I then move on to a broader problem with which Hegel is dealing in the passage. The passage in question lies in the preface to the *Phenomenology of Spirit*. One of Hegel's main projects in the preface is to distinguish a proper science of experience, in which reflection is the medium of thought, from ways of thinking that do not reflect experience properly (ironical and 'genius' being among these). I discuss the improper forms of thinking generally in terms of a limited imaginative activity, and I contrast these with what Hegel considers the proper form of reflection in which the imagination is a sublation of its limiting forms. The former have to do with a kind of Fichtean wavering that cannot, on its own, rise above the contradiction within which it wavers. Hegel's form of reflection, on the other hand, is a spiraling up the levels of phenomenological experience. The key to the proper version of reflection is grasping the Concept, which means grasping the sublating, *aufhebende* role of the imagination, its inwardizing and externalizing activity in reproduction, *Phantasie*, and *Vorstellen*.

Since sublation is the dialectic of time and space, sublation happens in pre-imaginative conditions of the soul such as the foetus, and in noncognitive nature in general, as Hegel's *Philosophy of Nature* shows us. But *cognition* of the Concept occurs only with the inception of imagination. The reason for this is that the imagination is the first *cognitive* form of *Aufhebung*. Imagination is the *sine qua non* of our *knowledge* of the Concept in nature and ourselves.

The dialectic of the imagination is a spatiotemporal one, so understanding how the imagination works within the production of representations (*Vorstellungen*) implies coming to grips with the history of Spirit and its self-presentations.

The final section of Part Three concerns how the consciousness that develops in the *Phenomenology of Spirit* arrives at a point where it thoroughly comprehends the role of picture-thinking in its thinking. Consciousness has, as I phrase it, successfully "thought the imagination through to its end." It is in the transition from Religion to Absolute Knowing, the final transition in the *Phenomenology of Spirit,* that consciousness grasps for itself the sublating role of its own imagination. In other words, in the presence and subsequent death of the absolute representation of Absolute Spirit (the God-man; in Christianity, Jesus), consciousness grasps the nature of its own picture-thinking. In so grasping, it attains what Hegel calls Absolute Knowing. Since time is central to all the discussions of the imagination in the *Philosophy of Spirit* lectures, I conclude with a discussion of the time of the Concept. Since time, history, our intentions, and our actions are not separable, for Hegel comprehension of the Concept makes possible the highest form of ethical life.

Chapter 7 thus provides the answer to the question that got me started on this project in the first place: the imagination does not appear as a chapter heading or dialectical moment within the *Phenomenology of Spirit* because the proper thinking through of reflection necessitates the proper thinking through of representation. Imagination, as the central moment of *Vorstellen*, is at the heart of the very movement of the *Phenomenology of Spirit*. The imagination is the moment of synthesis, of comprehension, but as such it is also the moment of difference, of dis-closure. The *Phenomenology of Spirit* does not only make us think through the imagination. It gives us the task of thinking the imagination through fully, to its end. This is the proper reconstruction of thought from difference.

Hegel's System and Modern Subjectivism and Skepticism

One important benefit for us today of understanding Hegel's theory of imagination is that it helps us overcome the deficiencies of modern subjectivism and skepticism. It does so because Hegel argues for a *system* of knowledge. Let us look at this more closely.

One reason for our resistance to systems is that often they prove to be merely conventions or paradigms that in time give over, their apparent necessity only a result of historical or cultural determinations. Furthermore, we tend to rebel against convention and system because of their dogmatic character, because they stifle difference and opposition. But it is precisely the role of the imagination in Hegel's account of system that is therefore so important. The imagination is both at the heart of system, and what keeps it from being mere dogmatism. Let us look at this by discussing the convention of a sign system. The full account of how this works in Hegel is part of what this book is about (see in particular chapter 5). But I can give a summary of the issue here.

Hegelian philosophical psychology bases a linear, horizontal world of time and space and all experiences in it, on an epistemological, vertical ordering of mental capacities. Hegel's levels of consciousness are dialectical; consciousness at each level exhibits the spiraling union of time and space. The lower levels of conscious experience are largely unconscious dialectical reverberations. We, as speculative observers, can follow the logic of those reverberations, but the consciousness experiencing them cannot. But as consciousness develops up the levels of dialectical object-formation, from intuitions to recollections to reproductions in symbols and then signs, consciousness emerges from the night of the mind into the light of communication.

The wedding of epistemology and ontology in Hegel's philosophy means that a conventional sign system is not arbitrarily set up. It is onto-historically developed. It is the result of several levels of the mind, each a dialectic between subject and object, and time and space, developing into communally experienced objects. As I show, especially in chapter 5, convention is a comprehensive folding of the imagination's activity back on the mind's previous dialectical moments. The moment before we have shared signs in a conventional sign system, is the moment where we have only subjective attempts at making meaning. These attempts produce symbols. Symbols are not shared information in the same way that signs are. Signs are systematic, whereas symbols are not. But the sign rises out of repeated uses of symbols. A conventional sign, before it becomes a dogma, is originally motivated by the desire to make a purely subjective symbol intelligible.

The gathering up of experiences that eventually constitute a convention, is therefore, originally an act of a self-conscious effort to communicate and stabilize meaning into a system. The gathering up derives its necessity as much from that self-conscious effort, as from the actual experiences that make up the meaningful, conventional sign. The process of developing a convention is both a subjective and a communal history. It is not an arbitrary exercise of a single or a collective will.

A sign is thus best understood as an organic growth. It develops out of the union of epistemology and ontology, of cognition and its objects. This book discusses that growth in terms of the following. A convention arises from the dovetailing of time and space; since the dialectical imagination produces images that endure and disappear, and since the dialectical imagination is itself a consciousness that endures and disappears, the conventional arises from imagination's *inwardizing,* that is, from its taking in of intuitions, its familiar recollections and its attempts at meaningful reproductions. Through further dialectical reproductions, these first attempts at meaningful reproductions are repeated and gathered into a new form; they become conventional reproductions, signs.

Thus, a conventional sign gets its systematic character from being a comprehensive dialectic. That is, it is systematic because, on the one hand, in its origin, it dialectically takes up the earlier dialectical moments into itself, and on the other, it is thereby determined by them. The system is the necessity and shape of the dialectic. At the heart of this development is the imagination.

If we forget the origination of a conventional sign system, we lose the self-conscious character, and our communications sink back into subjective symbolizings. The imagination gives rise to convention, but its dialectical, negative inwardizing also prevents the system from becoming dogmatic. The truth *becomes.* To understand this fully, the role of imagination in memory is examined closely (chapter 6).

The upshot of this is that system is a good result of developed, communal, cognitive activity. System arises as our memory of our developed experience (that is, both of our history and the way our minds develop). Unlike subjective skepticism, the Hegelian system celebrates its growth. The question is, does it, like all things that have grown, also decay and disappear? Is that part of its changing character as *becoming*?

This question is equally asked of the logic underlying his psychology or his phenomenology. But the clincher question is whether the system of Hegel's *Science of Logic,* a comprehensive ordering of all categories of experience, is subject to decay and disappearance. If it is not, then Hegel's logical system is a dogma. Some philosophers, even those enamored of Hegel's dialectic, find Hegel hard to take because they see Hegel's system as dogmatic.

The key to solving this, I think, lies again with the imagination. Hegel's *Logic* is, for all its structural, systematic comprehensiveness, nonetheless expressed in a conventional system. It does not exist *for us,* outside of the language Hegel or we use to explain it. (As Hegel says, the ineffable is the least interesting.)[2] As a result, even pure speculative philosophy has to be mediated by and for every generation of Hegel students across many cultures and languages. It is necessarily open to its own development. That is not to deny the existence of a logical system. Nor is it to deny that, in Hegel's psychology, there is a logic to the dialectical comprehension of one level of cognition in another. It is to say that the significance of the *Logic* in history, and the significance of those psychological comprehensions in our psychology, will be spelled out differently at different times and places. Which is to say that the *Logic* in history, and those psychological comprehensions, will spell *their* differences out across time and space. There will be logic to those differences. Time will *tell.*

Two Objections to this Work and My Replies to Them

There are two objections to the argument of the book that I would now like to address. The first objection is that I have imposed an externally derived notion of the imagination on Hegel's texts. The objection is supposedly supported by the very fact I have picked up on, namely, that Hegel does *not* discuss the imagination explicitly in the *Phenomenology of Spirit.* The second objection is that there is no reason to privilege the imagination over other necessary cognitive subprocesses whose absence would prevent thought. The objection states further that Hegel explicitly claims that there are no presupposed determinants of our thought process; rather, according to him, thought is completely self-determining. The objection is that I have brought in the imagination as a "hidden hand" that controls thought. I would like to reply to these two objections separately.

With regard to the claim that I have imposed an externally derived notion of the imagination, I answer the following. Let me begin by pointing to the centrality of the imagination for Hegel's immediate predecessors, Kant, Fichte, Schelling, and to how hard these thinkers worked to make sense of the problems to which their theories of imagination gave rise. Given this, the apparent absence of it in the *Phenomenology of Spirit* is conspicuous. It leaves ample room to propose that Hegel may have resolved the issue of the centrality of the imagination in such a way that it permeates the *Phenomenology of Spirit,* rather than making it disappear altogether or relegating it to a less central position. In the light of the tradition out of which he comes, the idea I propose is more plausible. A large part of my introduction is devoted to Hegel's predecessors and the conspicuousness of the apparent absence of the imagination in the *Phenomenology of Spirit.* So I will not say more about that here.

Furthermore, my discussion of the imagination in the three versions of the *Geistesphilosophie* provides ample evidence that the theory of the imagination discussed here is not imported from outside Hegel's works. The larger issue of the centrality of the imagination to Hegel's philosophy as a whole can only be assessed by reading the complete book. However, chapter 3 is particularly helpful in making the case; see especially note 12 of that chapter where I discuss the role of the imagination in Hegel's *Logic.* I also address this issue in my reply to the second objection below.

The second objection states that I have brought out something that does indeed exist in Hegel, but that I have given it more importance than Hegel intended. I agree that there are other capacities without which thought would be impossible. By analogy, I cannot live without a heart or nervous system or any number of other crucial organs. So why privilege, say, the liver? Let me begin my reply using this analogy. No medical book would be complete without an account of the workings of key organs of the body. So despite only being one of many key organs, a medical book must give an account of how the liver works. Similarly, neither Hegel's psychology nor his phenomenology can work without key players in the construction of experience. The psychology lectures show that the imagination is one of the key players. It is no less important to our experience than are the senses, perception, understanding, desire, reason, or spirit. I show that it only stands to reason, that, if the imagination is one of the key players in his psychology, it is also one of several key players in his phenomemology. I show how it works in the

Phenomenology, based on its role in the psychology. Thus, by looking at his psychology, my book shows beyond a doubt that the imagination is a key player in Hegel's philosophy (even in the *Logic*, although showing that is not a concern of this book).

But two important questions remain. Why is there no direct discussion of the imagination in the *Phenomenology of Spirit*? Is the imagination *the* key player of the *Phenomenology of Spirit*? The answer to the first is, as I show, that the dialectic of the imagination is *so* central to picture-thinking (*vorstellen*) that it cannot be isolated as one of the moments to be considered. It underlies all phenomenological moments. Nor can its activity be limited to picture-thinking, for the dialectic of the imagination is the activity that presents objects, even logical ones, to us. The imagination is, therefore, not the same sort of dialectical misapprehension as sense-certainty or understanding or reason is in the *Phenomenology of Spirit*. The dialectic of the imagination, as the basis of representational thought is the fundamental character of those moments. It cannot be addressed in the same manner. Each chapter of the *Phenomenology of Spirit* unravels a one-sided dialectic precisely because consciousness at that stage has not grasped the fundamental character of representation, at the heart of which is the imagination. Each moment of the *Phenomenology of Spirit* moves on to the next until it has thoroughly thought through the nature of representation. Spirit thereby, in the end, comes to know how it appears to itself in space and time, and as space and time. The dialectic of the imagination as the dovetailing of space and time, as the inwardizing and externalizing of intuitions, recollections, and meaningful reproductions, sets the scene for phenomenological existence and its history. Thinking it through, and then thinking through it self-consciously, is what the *Phenomenology of Spirit* teaches us to do. It is, therefore, not only a key player, but *the* key player in the *Phenomenology of Spirit*. This is not to say that it directs experience like a hidden hand. The imagination is an indifferent yet essential foundational dialectic. If we want to know how we experience, and to direct our lives in a self-conscious way, insight into our imagination is essential.

THE BOOK'S CONTRIBUTION TO SCHOLARSHIP

A number of books deal with related topics but none has as its focus Hegel's theory of imagination. Nor has anyone recognized (let alone tried solve) the puzzle of its apparent absence in the *Phenomenology of Spirit*. Kathleen Dow Magnus's book *Hegel and the Symbolic Mediation of Spirit* (Albany: State University of New York Press, 2001) claims that Hegel's philosophy never entirely dispenses with the symbolic, a claim that I find provocative but slightly misplaced. It is the work of the imagination, not its symbolic products, that is essential to Hegel's thought.[3] Paul Verene's book *Hegel's Recollection: A Study of Images in the Phenomenology of Spirit* (Albany: State University of New York Press, 1985) is closest to mine in spirit. However, Verene's book is an analysis of the *Phenomenology of Spirit*, whereas mine focuses on the development of Hegel's theory of the imagination in the *Philosophy of Spirit* lectures and elsewhere, with a view to explaining its role in the *Phenomenology of Spirit*. Also, he stresses the image and the role of recollection (*Erinnerung*) rather than the dialectical moments of the imagination. Furthermore, in Hegel's 1830 lectures, recollection is the moment *before* imagination; my analysis of the *Philosophy of Spirit* lectures shows that it is rather the imagination's sublating activity, its inwardizing (*zurücktreten*) and externalizing, that are central to Hegel's thought and to the *Phenomenology of Spirit*.

Richard Kearney's *In the Wake of the Imagination: Ideas of Creativity in Western Culture* (London: Hutchinson Education, 1988) provides a historical analysis of the use of and theories about the imagination, ending with an account of its role in postmodernism. Hegel is mentioned in a single sentence. Kearney's failure to include Hegel even in his discussion of Kant and post-Kantian idealism is one more indication that while much has been written on Kant's theory of imagination (an excellent example is Sarah L. Gibbon's book by that title [Oxford: Clarendon Press, Oxford University Press, 1994]), very little has reached the academic or general public about Hegel's theory of the imagination.

THE AUDIENCE FOR WHICH THIS BOOK WAS WRITTEN

Hegel's Theory of the Imagination was written for academic readers in philosophy in general, in the history of philosophy and/or Continental epistemology in particular, and for readers in psychology, as well as for nonacademics interested in the activity of the imagination. Philosophically the book fills a gap in post-Kantian philosophy; but its scope is wider since most of Continental philosophy following Hegel cannot be thought without Hegel, and this topic is central to his thought. For example, the philosophies of Jean-Paul Sartre and Jacques Derrida rely extensively on their readings of Hegel; an understanding of his theory of the imagination could change how we read these philosophers. The book also sheds light on the ideals of the Enlightenment and on German Romanticism. The complexity and depth of Hegel's insights makes this book important for anyone seriously interested in understanding how central the imagination is to our every thought.

Acknowledgments

I would like to thank Professor H. S. Harris for his careful reading and comments on earlier versions of this work. He is a model of philosophical humility, acumen, and responsibility. I am also indebted to Professor Kenneth Schmitz. He first introduced me to Hegel and his philosophical prodding has taught me to look deeply into the subject at hand.

I would also like to thank Professor Graeme Nicholson and Professor Joseph Owens at the University of Toronto, and Professor H. F. Fulda and Dr. Harald Pilot (both at the University of Heidelberg) for their insight and help. Two anonymous readers at the State University of New York Press were enormously helpful and I am very grateful for their fruitful challenges and suggestions. I thank the University of Toronto for its support during the initial writing of this work, and the Deutscher Akademischer Austausch Dienst for a year-long research fellowship at the University of Heidelberg. I would also like to thank professor Jay Lampert at the University of Guelph for his helpful editorial suggestions on parts of the final draft.

Why Study the Imagination?

A Brief History from Kant to Hegel

Why engage in a *philosophical* investigation of the imagination? In particular, why a philosophical investigation of what *Hegel* thinks the imagination is? Let me take each question in turn.

The first arises out of reflections such as the following. What comes to mind at the mention of the term *imagination* is fantasy, mental conjuring, pulling together things that normally would not go together (such as a horn on a horse to make a unicorn). Fiction and dreams seem to be the domain of the imagination. So surely, one might argue, the arena for such an investigation is aesthetics and psychology, not metaphysics or epistemology. Again, given the breadth and long history of the role of the imagination in various religions, perhaps such an investigation is more fruitfully carried out in religious studies. (For example, the ancient Hebraic view was that the imagination, *yetser*, was linked to both creation and transgression.)[1] Many religions use visualizations to engender insight into experience.[2] So why do a *philosophical* investigation of it?

The fact is, the imagination has been taken up as a topic by almost every major philosopher in the history of Western philosophy. As early as Aristotle,[3] the imagination was viewed as playing a central role in how we piece together the world. Its role in epistemology has a long and varied history.

When we consider the imagination epistemologically a key opposition emerges: is it mimetic (merely reproductive of what is "out there" for us to sense) or productive (that is, partially or even wholly creative of how the world appears to us)? In the history of Western philosophy up until Immanuel Kant, many philosophers held some version of the Aristotelian view that the imagination is a secondary movement following upon perception of a thing, something like a perceptual echo in the mind. (Some went so far as to say it was decaying sense impressions.) That is, its role was essentially reproductive, and in the service of memory and reason. But despite any helpful, reproductive role it might play, the imagination's ability to combine things that did not go together in our sense experience caused it to be regarded as an inappropriate faculty to rely on for knowledge. It needed the corrective input of sense verification or to be tested for rational coherency, or both.

The view of the imagination as essentially mimetic was rejected in the late 1800s by Kant. According to him the mind is responsible for the way the world appears to us. So understanding the faculties and how they work is critical if we want to establish what we can know and what is beyond the limits of knowledge. The imagination is front and center in Kant's epistemology. Rather than following on the heels of perception, for him it is a "necessary ingredient of perception itself."[4]

According to Kant, the work of imagination is synthesis. It pulls the manifold of sense-impressions together under categories of the understanding, thus giving us objects and judgments about them. As a result, in the modern era from Kant to the Romantics the role of the imagination becomes central and powerful.

Given this change, the view of Hegel is important if we are to understand what is going on during this period, and if we are to adjudicate whether Kantian-influenced philosophers give us a better account of our imagination than their predecessors or successors. Before I go into that story, it is worth returning briefly to the question of why the imagination holds such power over us and thus why it has been a point of such interest for so many philosophers, regardless of their differing views about it.

The imagination is hard to distinguish from opinion and belief. It can inform our opinions and beliefs in ways we do not know. Often, the more visually organized a belief is, the more believable it is; the more imaginatively displayed, the more attractive. From earliest times, stories and parables and visual representations have been the means of passing on history, culture, and morality. Dreams, which are highly pictorial imaginations, have been, long before Freud declared them to be so, the royal road to what lay hidden beyond or beneath conscious experience. The unconscious affects how we perceive and interpret the world. By analyzing dreams we have a way of reading back to ourselves how we are unconsciously putting our world together.

Unveiling the imagination does not only reveal what Freud referred to as our polymorphous perverse nature—the deep web of unconscious drives that make up our id and which can make our behavior neurotic. By trying to understand the imagination and what each of us holds in it, we can come to know our world more profoundly, as well as more artistically and splendidly. Perhaps we can really only come to know the truth about the world by fully knowing our imagination. For the imagination is not merely a reservoir of past experiences which we pull together in dreams and fancies as well as in memories, not even only that limpid surface upon which we see our waking experience when we reflect. It is also the substance of our cognitive shaping of the world.

One of the biggest problems that arises when dealing with the imagination as central to cognitive functions is distinguishing the imagination from other faculties, or for that matter, unearthing it as a faculty at all. For if it is that through which we have a world, even a faculty is imaginatively constructed. The problem becomes one of the justification of any ontology that could support its own creation.

In nineteenth-century philosophy this was the dark problem met at the end of system building, as witnessed in Nietzsche and Kierkegaard, and later in the existentialism of Sartre. In twentieth-century philosophy this has primarily become the problematic of postmodernism and deconstruction: no single take on experience can escape the unraveling of the view from which the picture is taken. Foundations can hold up castles, but insight shows every foundation to be an imaginative web, the strands of which can be individually followed into other meanings, sometimes contradicting the very thing that foundation sought to uphold. In the postmodern era, epistemology seems to have given way to aesthetics. And the ramifications of this change affect not only how we think about the world, but also how we think about each other: it affects our moral views, and therefore how we act.

What we do with our imagination, then, has a great impact on how we experience the world and what we do in it. All the more reason to spend the time to understand what it is.

We can now answer our second introductory question. That question was: Why do a philosophical investigation of what *Hegel* thinks of the imagination? The answer is twofold. By going back to Hegel, we find the historical reasons for some of the developments following out of Kant and the nineteenth-century idealist tradition, developments that reach into the twentieth-century. Secondly, in Hegel we find a system-based, epistemological counterbalance to later claims that philosophy can only be an aesthetic endeavor, without falling back into the problematic Kantian reliance on presumed faculties. Let me address these two points separately.

First, let us look at the historical shift that occurred in the modern conception of the imagination. The story properly begins one step farther back from Kant, with David Hume.

In his *Treatise of Human Nature* (1739) Hume reluctantly grants to the imagination the enormous task of mending the rift in reality which skepticism had revealed. To the skeptic's questions, "How do we know that the objects I see in this room are the ones I saw when I left it last?" "How do I know that I am the same person today as the one who went to sleep last night?" Hume replies that by presenting ideas of things that are no longer immediately present to us, the imagination is the connecting link between ideas from memory and new intuitions. The imagination, according to Hume, thus allows us to see the world as made up of objects that are continuous in time and space and that are independent of us and of each other. Hume repeatedly worries, however, whether the imagination can really perform such a task, writing in one place: "I cannot conceive how such trivial qualities of the fancy, conducted by such false suppositions, can ever lead to any solid or rational system."[5]

Kant's Copernican revolution claimed to have put an end to that skepticism by showing the mind to be the a priori ground of knowledge. This was a turn toward what Kant called critical philosophy, a philosophy that performs a "critique" of the faculties of the mind in order to show their inescapable role in the construction of all phenomena. For Kant, the imagination was analyzed as one faculty of the mind among others, its synthesis operative in the service of the higher faculties of understanding and reason.

The story of the imagination in Hegel begins here. Hegel balances the Kantian critical optimism with the return of a kind of skepticism. But the shape of this skepticism is that it is only one moment in a developing, absolute Concept (also known as absolute knowing). Specifically, it is a negative movement. This movement makes the faculties into moments that are themselves "thought through" in both senses. That is, not only are they that through which we think, but we also think through their definition in a way that reveals their movement in that process. We understand them according to their limited concept. But we can only do so completely once we have grasped how the absolute Concept works. To grasp the Concept is to have complete self-reflection, to reflect fully *on* the act of reflection, *in* the act of reflecting. We cannot accomplish that without understanding the negative movement within the Concept.

For Hegel, as we will see, the negative movement is the middle term of representation (*Vorstellen*). The negative movement is that of the imagination (*Einbildungskraft*). No longer in the service of "higher" faculties, the imagination in Hegel is the key to how we represent what we take to be real. The process of thinking the imagination through reveals how when we do not fully grasp its activity, we go astray or are limited in our reasoning, and our reality is also thereby limited. The developmental story of an individual or community thinking the imagination through in increasing depth and complexity reveals the forms of Reason in consciousness and Spirit. Over the ages, that story is the history of nations; their culture, ethics, art, religion, and philosophy.

So, while Hume was reluctant to give the imagination such an important task as the creation of a rational system, and while Kant placed the imagination inside of and in the service of a rational system, Hegel shows it to be the heart of rationality, outside of which there is no system of reality to be known.

Having briefly sketched this historical shift, let me turn now to Hegel's legacy. Hegel's philosophical system provides the backdrop without which we cannot properly understand contemporary philosophies. To take just two cases: let us look at Jean-Paul Sartre and Jacques Derrida. The negating subject in existentialism, and the moment of *différance* in deconstruction, each has its origin in the Hegelian dialectic. More precisely, each takes as its point of departure the idea that the given is only apparently immediate, and that, under the pressure of inquiry, the true nature of the given reveals itself to be mediated. For Sartre, mediation abuts on the absurd; for Derrida, mediation occurs without a return. Hegel's mediation is the wellspring of these two theories, but also, I think, a challenge to them (if not to Derrida's theories, to many of his deconstructivist followers). It is a challenge to these two views in the same way as it is for Humean empirical skepticism, on the one hand, and for the unconstrained subject of romanticism on the other. That is, it provides a systematic framework for experience, without falling into unconstrained play.[6]

Whether or not one ends up agreeing that Hegel provides the answers we are looking for, the light his philosophy sheds on the main philosophies of his time, and on those of our own, is reason enough to undertake a study of his thought.

The school where we apprentice in the use of the imagination is Hegel's *Phenomenology of Spirit*. That book teaches us the ways we get imagination wrong, and provides the opening onto Hegel's philosophical system. To understand the role of the imagination in that work, however, we need to understand his theory of the imagination in the period leading up to the writing of the *Phenomenology*. And in order to have the proper backing to discuss Hegel's works, we must first look in more detail at Kant and the main players between Kant and Hegel. Therefore, I now complete this Introduction with an analysis of what the main players between Kant and Hegel thought of the imagination.

The following analysis of Kant, Fichte, and Schelling serves to introduce the essential issues and problems concerning the imagination in their thought. I do not provide in-depth analysis or solutions. Hegel is of course another matter: by the end of this Introduction we will be at the starting point of Hegel's engagement with the topic of the imagination, and thus in a position to begin careful analysis of Hegel's theory about it.

ॐ

IMAGINATION FROM KANT TO THE EARLY HEGEL

In the *Critique of Pure Reason* Kant explains that the imagination is that faculty responsible for relating sense perception and the understanding. Its primary characteristic is its ability to conjure an image of something not present to the senses.[7] Its work is that of synthesis.

In paragraph 10 of the first *Critique*,[8] Kant provides a number of propositions about synthesis. Of these, three are of particular interest:[9]

> [I]f this manifold is to be known, the spontaneity of our thought *requires* that it:
>
> (a) (first) be *gone through in a certain way, taken up, and connected. This act I name synthesis.*
>
> (b) Synthesis in general . . . is the mere result of the power of the imagination, a blind but indispensable function of the soul, without which we should have no knowledge whatsoever, but of which we are scarcely ever conscious.
>
> (c) To bring this synthesis *to concepts* is a function which belongs to the understanding, and it is through *this function of the understanding* that we first obtain *knowledge properly so called* (my emphasis)

The deduction of the categories and the Analytic of Principles makes it clear that this product of the imagination includes figurative syntheses and schemata. Just as in figurative synthesis the imagination is a hidden faculty, the "schematism of our understanding, in its application to appearances and their mere form, is an art concealed in the depths of the human soul, whose real modes of activity nature is hardly likely ever to allow us to discover, and to have open to our gaze" (A141/B180–81).

There is an interesting problem which arises in Kant's discussion of synthesis in paragraph 24. Kant begins by asserting that figurative synthesis is responsible for the Euclidean shapes empirical objects have for us; pure figurative syntheses yield pure geometrical intuitions. That is clear enough, but he goes on to define "*figürlich*" synthesis against an "intellectual" synthesis, claiming that the former is a transcendental synthesis *of the imagination*, and that the latter involves no imagination (B155–51).[10] This claim is odd since Kant has earlier said that "synthesis in general" is the product of the imagination. So the problem arises of how intellectual synthesis can be a synthesis if it occurs without the activity of the imagination, or inversely, how the understanding can be thought separately from the imagination.

To understand what intellectual synthesis is, one might appeal to the practical realm: perhaps Kant means that intellectual synthesis is something we can only experience insofar as we are morally free agents, in the act of willing.[11] But if we want to keep the discussion within the epistemological framework, our best bet is to look back to paragraph 10. As we saw there, the synthesis of the imagination is necessary but not sufficient for knowledge: what is still needed is the *bringing* of the synthesis to concepts of the understanding (see citation (c)). Kant claims that this "bringing" is accomplished by the understanding. One might conclude that this bringing to concepts is *synthesis intellectualis*. If our epistemological reading is right, the "spontaneity of our thought" (A77/B102) requires synthesis of the imagination and of the understanding. But it is not clear that this is what Kant means.

H. Mörchen believes that for Kant the imagination and the understanding are one and the same faculty. I am unwilling to settle the matter this way and am also unable to enter further into the debate about the imagination's role in the first *Critique*.[12] We have covered enough of the problem to have a sense of what Hegel is dealing with. Let me conclude this discussion of the first *Critique* by pointing to the clearest articulation in that work of Kant's ambiguous view. In the footnote at B161, Kant writes that the two syntheses are one and the same spontaneity, "there under the name of the imagination, here under the name of the understanding." The phrase "under the name of" hangs like an ambiguous sign above the entrance to critical idealism.

The imagination's central role in Kant's *Critique of Judgment* is in the experience of beauty. In our appreciation of something beautiful, the spontaneity of our thought requires synthesis to be brought under concepts of the understanding.

That requirement does not achieve closure: it is drawn on. It seeks the satisfaction of bringing the intuition under concepts but is unable to do this definitively; its authority is pleasantly captured in the play between imagination's synthesis and understanding the object. The spontaneity of thought is required for the play to continue.

But what prevents the synthesis of the imagination from being brought successfully to concepts? What is so captivating? Is it the sensible object that has that power? Instead of fixing, the mind is transfixed. But by what, exactly?

What draws the spontaneity of thought on in this play is not the direct concern of the aesthetic consciousness. But the critical idealist must answer, and Kant's answer is that we must assume a supersensible power. In the play of the faculties we witness a purposiveness, without a particular purpose. When we are so transfixed, it is "as if" nature itself were purposive. When we make a judgment of taste this disinterested purposiveness arises as a necessary characteristic of that kind of judgment. Thus, the purposiveness is not just "as if" it were nature's. For Kant, purposiveness without a purpose is the basis of all judgments of taste. Furthermore, it is akin to moral feeling. The confluence of purposiveness seeming to be nature's, and yet its being the ground of judgments of taste, means for Kant that when we look at a beautiful rose, we also experience the purposeful, moral character of culture; it appears to be designed in the appreciated, beautiful object (*CJ* ¶59).

Now let us move from his theory of the beautiful to his theory of the sublime. According to Kant, the experience of the sublime reveals our freedom. It does so because the limits of the imagination are exceeded. In the experience of the sublime, the requirement of totality, which is an idea of Reason, calls upon the imagination to comprehend the infinite or the mighty; imagination's inability to accomplish this task causes agitation. But the displeasure aroused in our inability to imagine the infinite gives rise to a different pleasure, that of knowing the supersensible within us. It is the pleasure of knowing that we are somehow more than can be grasped by the senses or the imagination. We sense a purpose beyond our natural life's sense and imagined experiences. As in the experience of the beautiful, it is a sense of purposiveness without any specific (sensed or imagined) purpose. So just as the restful contemplative play of imagination and understanding in the experience of beauty reveal purposiveness, discordance between the imagination and the understanding in the experience of the sublime also reveals purposiveness. When we reflect beyond the agitated imagination, more deeply, into the sublime, we experience a contemplative, pleasurable *accordance* with our deeper nature. We commune with a sense of purposefulness.

Nonetheless, despite the fact that the purposefulness cannot be grasped by the imagination, it is only out of the failure of the imagination that the sublime sense of purpose arises. The imagination is therefore, once again, a central player.

Let us look more closely at the ways in which the imagination's failure points us toward the sublime. According to Kant, there are two ways of arriving at the sublime. The imagination's agitation refers the mind "either to the *cognitive power* or to the *power of desire* . . . . The first kind of agitation is a *mathematical*, the second a *dynamical* attunement of the mind" (*CJ* ¶24, p. 101). In the mathematical sublime the imagination is unable to comprehend. Kant writes of our attempt to think "something not only large but large absolutely [*schlechthin, absolut*], in every respect (beyond all comparison), i.e., sublime" (*CJ* 105).[13] We cannot find an object that corresponds to the absolutely large. So our liking is not of an object. Nor is it a liking of a "purposeful attunement" of our faculties in the cognizing of a beautiful object. Rather, "the sublime must not be sought in things of nature, but must be sought solely in our ideas" (*CJ* 105). What we like, therefore, is "the expansion of the imagination itself" (*CJ* 105).

> [What happens is that] our imagination strives to progress toward infinity, while our reason demands absolute totality as a real idea, and so [the imagination] our power of estimating the magnitude of things in the world of sense, is inadequate to that idea. Yet this inadequacy itself is the arousal in us of the feeling that we have within us a supersensible power; and what is absolutely large is not an object of sense, but is the use that judgment makes naturally of certain objects so as to [arouse] this (feeling), and in contrast with that use any other use is small. . . . *Sublime is what even to be able to think proves that the mind has a power surpassing any standard of sense* (*CJ* ¶25, p. 106; *KdU* ¶25, p. 172.)

Nevertheless, the magnitude of some objects can inspire this appreciation. Kant gives as example an account of standing next to a pyramid. The imagination's struggle is the inability to match up comprehension (*Zusammenfassung*) of the thing's magnitude as a whole, with the practically infinite apprehension of its parts (*CJ* ¶26, p. 108).[14]

The second kind of sublime is the dynamically sublime. Here, it is not our reflective idea of magnitude that exceeds nature. Rather, it is a question of our reflective dominance over the might of nature. "When in an aesthetic judgment we consider nature as a might that has no dominance over us, then it is *dynamically sublime*" (*CJ* ¶28, p. 119). The mighty object of nature must arouse fear in us, but not in a way that prevents us from passing judgment. In other words, it must arouse fear, but not make us afraid (*CJ* ¶28, pp. 119–20). Kant gives as example our appreciation, from a safe place, of "bold, overhanging, and as it were, threatening rocks, thunderclouds piling up in the sky and moving about accompanied by lightning and thunderclaps, volcanoes with all their destructive power, hurricanes . . ." (*CJ* ¶28, p. 120). But, he explains,

> although we found our own limitation when we considered the immensity of nature and the inadequacy of our ability to adopt a standard proportionate to estimating aesthetically the magnitude of nature's domain, yet we also found, in our power of reason, a different and nonsensible standard that has this infinity itself under it as a unit; and since in contrast to this standard everything in nature is small, we found in our mind a superiority over nature itself in its immensity. (*CJ* ¶28, p. 120; *KdU* ¶28, p. 185)

According to Kant, nature itself is called sublime (*erhaben*) only insofar as "it elevates [*erhebt*] our imagination, [making] it exhibit those cases where the mind can come to feel its own sublimity, which lies in its vocation and elevates it even above nature" (*CJ* ¶28, p. 121).

Thus, rather than being transfixed in the zone between intuition and concept as in the experience of the beautiful, in the experience of the sublime we transcend the limits of our representational faculty. But in both the experience of the beautiful and of the sublime, we access the possibility—the "as if"—of nature's supersensible purposiveness, and the possibility that our vocation is one with it.

Two related complaints can be made of Kant's theory of the sublime. First, Kant does not adequately think through how the imagination remains an involved moment in the experience of the sublime. The imaginative representation becomes a superseded, though still agitated, object. What does this mean exactly? Second, we are in the arena of what Kant calls reflective judgments. These judgments do not themselves exhibit the sublating movement of the self. In other words, Kant's reflective, sublime supersession preserves in isolated agitation the faculty beyond which it moves. In this move, the negativity that allows for the *Erhebung* is contained—indefinitely postponed—in the "as if." The sublime itself is thus spared the negation that would reintegrate it into a concrete, natural development. It is preserved infinitely within a projected teleology whose objective reality is forever beyond our reach. Hegel will object both to the ambiguity of the "as if" in the experience of beauty, and to the ideal character of the sublime as something supersensible. But before we look at Hegel, let us look at how Fichte makes steps toward correcting Kant. He does so by making the transcendental ego an *act* rather than a standpoint.

❧

Fichte's *Science of Knowledge* of 1794 was an attempt to bring philosophy through a metamorphosis: not by producing its final form—for Fichte the Kantian critical project was this final form[15]—but rather by going back to and grasping the very first principles of all knowing. Fichte wanted thereby to show the necessity of the Kantian critical system.[16]

The problem with Kant, according to Fichte, was that he failed to properly determine a first principle. This left Kant's system a target for skeptics and dogmatic realists. Reinhold, Schulze, and Maimon among others had attempted to complete Kant's project. After reading Schulze's work the *Aenesidemus* in 1793, Fichte was still unconvinced that Kant's philosophy had reached the level of science. But in the *Science of Knowledge*, published the following year, Fichte asserted that he had found the needed principle that solved the problem and vindicated the Kantian system. That principle states that the *act* of consciousness, *die Tathandlung*, was the ground. The first principle of the entire science was thus, "*Das Ich setzt ursprünglich schlechthin sein eignes Sein*" ("The I posits its being absolutely [primordially]") (*Sc.Kn.* I, 98).

To this first principle Fichte added two more. The second principle is that the self posits a not-self in opposition to itself. The second principle thus gives rise to a contradiction. The third principle resolves the contradiction: "In the self I oppose a divisible not-self to the divisible self" (*Sc.Kn.* I, 110).

The necessity of the second two principles lies in the fact that the first principle on its own cannot yield knowledge. It cannot because there is no opposition, and therefore no possibility of a subject knowing an object. The other two principles provide this opposition. The three principles together are the process of knowing.

Fichte describes the relation between the self and the not-self as a *Wechselwirkung*, a wavering interdetermination. This *Wechselwirkung* between the self and the not-self is the imagination. For Fichte imagination is therefore the centerpiece, indeed the centerpiecing, of the world we know.

> [O]ur doctrine here is therefore that all reality—*for us* being understood, as it cannot be otherwise understood in a system of transcendental philosophy—is brought forth solely by the imagination . . . (*Sc.Kn.* I, 227)
>
> The imagination gives the truth and the only possible truth. (*Sc.Kn.* I, 227)
>
> [T]his act of the imagination forms the basis for the possibility of our consciousness, our life, our existence for ourselves, that is, our existence as selves. . . . (*Sc.Kn.* I, 227)

However, the role of this wavering imagination remains something of a mystery. Let us turn for a moment to his discussion of it in "The Deduction of Presentation" which is found in the final section of the Foundation of Theoretical Science, in the *Science of Knowledge*.

In that Deduction, Fichte investigates the movement involved in the wavering of the imagination. The wavering occurs between the ideal and the real, between the finite and the infinite, between the Self and the Beyond. To explain this, Fichte uses the metaphor of a line extending outward from the self into the infinite. The imagination is for him an act of building—*die Einbildungskraft*—the power (*Kraft*) of building (conjuring) some thing (*Einbildung*). It is also a building-forward, because it goes out beyond what is already, and in so outreaching itself builds the new.

The "going out" happens unconsciously. In order to have cognition we must have opposition. Thus, following the logic of the three principles, the out-going self requires opposition, a check to its unconscious, outward expansion. The check is the positing of the not-self by the self (the second principle of the system). Fichte explains that the check need not be explained in terms of the nature of something "outside" the movement of the self:

> [I]f something is to be determined as subjective with the self, and something else by that determination to be excluded from its sphere as objective, then it needs to be explained how this latter element, that is to be excluded, could come to be present in the self. . . . Our present principle yields an answer to this objection, as follows: The objective to be excluded has no need at all to be present; all that is required—if I may so put it—*is the presence of a check on the self, that is, for some reason that lies merely outside the self's activity, the subjective must be extensible no further.* Such an impossibility of further extension would then delimit—the mere interplay we have described, or the mere incursion; *it would not set bounds to the activity of the self, but would give it the task of setting bounds to itself.* But all delimitation occurs through an opposite; hence the self, simply to do justice to this task would have to oppose something objective to the subjective that calls for limitation, and then synthetically unite them both . . . and thus the entire presentation could then be derived. It will at once be apparent that this mode of explanation is a realistic one; only it rests upon a realism far more abstract than any put forward earlier; for it presupposes neither a not-self present apart from the self, nor even a determination present within the self, but merely the *requirement* for a determination to be undertaken within it by the self as such, or the *mere determinability* of the self. (*Sc.Kn.* I, 211; my emphasis)

The self requires the check, but we need not take the check to be anything other than the limitation of the self's expansion, by the self.

Fichte claims that the entire *Science of Knowledge* is based on intellectual intuition.[17] Understanding this self-positing and self-opposition and self-limiting is central to understanding his project. The problem is that it remains unclear just how the wavering imagination works between the self and the not-self, and what the check is.[18]

I am not concerned here with resolving the issues to which these principles give rise (for example, solving the problem of what the check is). What I want to focus on is the question it raises about the role of the imagination. Are the three principles prior to the imagination or are they the imagination? As central as the imagination is in the creation of content for the mind, is it nevertheless subservient to an a priori self-positing first principle which opposes itself? Is Fichte, like Kant, placing the imagination in the service of the self rather than at the heart of its conception? For Fichte, imagination is absolutely central, but the logic of its activity is not clear.

My brief outlines of Kant and Fichte serve to highlight one important fact. Despite the declared importance of the imagination in their respective epistemologies, both Kant and Fichte leave themselves open to the view that the imagination is a subjective faculty whose product (synthesis) is the *result* of a requirement placed on it by the self. This is not the case in Schelling and Hegel.

Schelling's attempt to complete the project of critical philosophy differed from Fichte's by virtue of his more Spinozistic approach. In 1801 Hegel praises Schelling for this. Hegel writes that, while Fichte presents only a subjective transcendental idealism, Schelling's system develops the Absolute as both subjective and objective. The subjective side of philosophy is presented in a system of transcendental idealism, and the objective side in a philosophy of nature. These two sciences are inseparable, because they are two sides of the absolute, and together make up an organic whole.[19]

Schelling's more Spinozistic approach means that, instead of reflection being a mirroring of the world for the understanding, reflection recognizes in its own gaze the unity and becoming of two perspectival poles.

> The conscious observer of nature is the "center" of an *external* world which he organizes in his empirical knowledge. But as he does transcendental philosophy he discovers himself to be the *internal* center, to be the focus of the life that animates the world. This is the *true* "begetting of the Logos," the discovery of our identity with the eternal Reason. It is a discovery which is throughout a self-*making*. . . . (Harris "Introduction" *Diff* 51)

The story of that making has several "epochs." These constitute Schelling's *System of Transcendental Philosophy*. They are the levels of Reason's coming-to-consciousness or self-making. It develops from original sensation to productive intuition, from intuition to reflection, to the will, and to creative production. The culmination of the transcendental science is the "Deduction of the Art-Product as the Universal Organ of Philosophy," and the imagination is central to it. According to Schelling:

> It is the poetic gift, which in its primary potentiality constitutes the primordial intuition, and conversely, what we speak of as the poetic gift is merely productive intuition, reiterated [repeating itself, *sich wiederholende*] to its highest power. It is one and the same capacity that is active in both, the only one whereby we are able to think and to couple together even what is contradictory— and its name is imagination. (*STI* 230; *Sys. Tr.I.*, 297)

Imagination is that "poetic gift" whereby "art . . . achieves the impossible, namely to resolve an infinite opposition in a finite product" (*STI* 230; *Sys. Tr.I.*, 297).

Hegel's early works take up this Schellingian view and develop it.

❧

Because of the central importance of the faculty of the imagination for Kant, Fichte, and Schelling, and since Hegel comes directly out of this tradition, the question naturally arises: What happened to the imagination in Hegel's philosophy? The word *Einbildungskraft* appears only once in the *Phenomenology of Spirit* as a whole, and this is in the preface.[20] The other "faculties"— Sensation, Perception, Understanding, and Reason—are dialectically thought through.

One might think that the reason for the absence of the imagination is that it is a one-sided notion belonging to Fichtean idealism. But each of the other faculties is brought into the *Phenomenology of Spirit* precisely in order to show their one-sidedness in the dialectic of failure which the *Phenomenology of Spirit* is. So this cannot be the answer.

Ultimately, the solution lies in a careful study of various *Philosophy of Spirit* lectures, and in a comparison of the imagination in them with it in the *Phenomenology of Spirit*. This is what I do in the following chapters.

We can make a general beginning here by looking at Hegel's first major publication—*The Difference Between Fichte's and Schelling's System of Philosophy* (1801). In this work Hegel compares the two philosophies and defends

Schelling's Identity Theory. Hegel rejects the role of imagination's synthesis within a philosophy of subjectivity (like that of Fichte), and adopts instead the Absolute Synthesis of the Identity Theory. The synthesis is not that of a subjective faculty but is rather part of the becoming of the Absolute. These statements require elaboration.

Rather than asserting that the in-itself, of the subject or object, is beyond our theoretical knowledge as in Kant, or infinitely displaced by the check as in Fichte, Schelling and Hegel assert that, in the absolute point of indifference, subject and object are one. The result is that the synthesis cannot be the required product of a self. Synthesis springs out of both subject and object, indeed gives rise to that opposition. Thus, in criticizing Fichte in the *Differenzschrift* Hegel redefines synthesis. It is no longer called the synthesis of the imagination, but rather the synthesis of the Absolute:

> For absolute identity to be the principle of an entire system it is necessary that *both* subject and object be posited as Subject-Object. In Fichte's system identity constitutes itself only as subjective Subject-Object. [But] this subjective Subject-Object needs an objective Subject-Object to complete it, so that the Absolute presents itself in each of the two Subject-Objects, and finds itself perfected only in both together *as the highest synthesis* that nullifies both insofar as they are opposed. As their point of absolute indifference, *the Absolute encloses both, gives birth to both and is born of both*. (*Diff* 155, my emphasis; *Differenz* 94)

According to Hegel in the *Differenzschrift*, realization of this synthesis occurs in art, religion, and in speculative philosophy. Each is an "intuition of the self-shaping or objectively self-finding Absolute" (*Diff* 171). Expressed in Christian terms it is "the intuition of God's eternal human Incarnation, the begetting of the Word from the beginning" (*Diff* 171; *Differenz* 112); expressed in philosophical terms it is "absolute, self-intuiting Reason" (*Diff* 174; *Differenz* 115).

According to Hegel, though the Absolute exhibits itself in art and religion, these two do not satisfy the need for conscious and immediate intuition of the process: only speculative philosophy can do that. Hegel writes:

> In art properly speaking, the intuition appears as a work which, being objective, is enduring, but can also be regarded by the intellect as an external dead thing; it is a product of the individual, of the genius, yet it belongs to mankind. In *religion* the intuition appears as a living (e)motion (*Bewegen*) which, being subjective, and only momentary, can be taken by the intellect as something

> merely internal; it is the single individual. In *speculation*, the intu-
> ition appears more as consciousness, and as extended in con-
> sciousness, as an activity of subjective Reason which suspends
> objectivity and the non-conscious. Whereas the Absolute appears
> in art, taken in its true scope, more in the form of absolute being,
> it appears in speculation more as begetting itself in its infinite
> intuition. (*Diff* 171–72; *Differenz* 112–13)

So far I have scratched the surface by presenting the basic issues. Let me summarize these. Leaving a skepticism that turns reluctantly to the imagination's
synthesis for rational coherence (Hume), we looked at Kant's critical analysis
of the imagination as an a priori faculty whose synthesis is required by the self,
and whose limitation—rather than renewing skepticism—indicates our moral
vocation. Fichte grasped this vocational attitude as a dialectic between the two
poles of self and the forever-beyond of the self's moral completion, with the
imagination as the wavering middle between them. From there we moved to
Schelling's and (the early) Hegel's rejection of this one-sided, subjective
(moral) requirement of imagination's synthesis. For Schelling and the early
Hegel, synthesis is rather the activity of the Absolute; it is the heart, the
"indifference point," of the subject-object opposition, and all truth is the
dialectic of the Absolute's self-revealing.

We have now arrived at our point of departure for discussing the imagination in Hegel's early philosophy. In Hegel, unlike in his predecessors, "[i]t
is as if the concept of imagination were imagining itself into existence: rather
than an object of analysis or *Wesenschau*, it becomes one of the shapers of our
conceptual world."[21] From this idea of the imagination (as the Absolute)
imagining itself into existence, we now must try to think the imagination
through to the end.

Schematic Breakdown of the Imagination in Each
of the *Philosophy of Spirit* Lectures

The Dialectical Imagination: Geistesphilosophie 1803–04

A) Consciousness→   **a) Speech**→   **Imagination:**→   **i) Space/Time**

B) The Negative   b) The Tool   **ii) Universality: Positive & Negative**

C) The People (*das Volk*) c) Possession & the Family   **(bestehende/vergehende**

Consciousness)

iii) Theoretical and Practical

Consciousness (verstehende

Consciousness)

The Inwardizing Imagination: Geistesphilosophie 1805–06

A) Spirit Acc. to its Concept→ a) Theoretical Knowing (i.e., **Intelligence**)→

B) Objective Spirit   b) The Will   **A) Imagination in General:**   **B) Language (Sprache):**

C) The Constitution   c) Objective Spirit **i) Intuition/Imagination (Images)**   **vi) Names (Tones)**

ii) Recollection (The Familiar)   **v) Memory (Order)**

iii) To Mean (bezeichnen) (Signs)   **vi) Understanding (Knowl.)**

The Communicating Imagination: Philosophy of Spirit 1830

A) Subjective Spirit→ I) Anthropology

B) Objective Spirit   II) Phenomenology

C) Absolute Spirit   **III) Psychology**→   **a) Theoretical Mind (Intelligence)**→

b) Practical Mind

c) Free Mind

1) Intuition

2) Representation→   i) Recollection (*Erinnerung*)

3) Thinking   **ii) Imagination**→   **aa) Reproductive Imagination (¶455)**

iii) Memory   **bb) Phantasy: Symbolizing, Allegorizing, Poetic**

Imagination (¶456)

cc) Sign-making Phantasy: Signs, Language (¶457

intro, ¶458 Signs, ¶459 Language, ¶460 Names)

Key German Terms and their Translation as "Imagination" and Related Words

Bildung	*formative education* (Miller)	(e.g., *PoS* ¶33,p
Durchbildung	*formation (of consciousness)* (Miller)	(e.g., *PoS* ¶33, p. 19)
Einbildungskraft	*imagination (faculty of)* (Miller and most others)	(e.g., *PoS* ¶68, p. 42)
Herausbildung	*constructive unfolding* (Miller)	(e.g., *PoS* ¶52, p. 31)

The following two words are often translated as "imagination" or "imagining" by various translators, but are not the same as *Einbildungskraft*.

Einbildung *imagination (as false presentation)* as in the *imaginary*, *illusion* or *conceit* (In common dictionaries it is misleadingly translated as "imagination" as though it could also mean the faculty of imagination)

(It comes up five times in the *Phenomenology of Spirit*: Miller translates it as "conceit" in the preface, ¶51 [*PdG* 50] and in ¶382 [*PdG*

		284]; as "imaginary" in ¶394 [*PdG* 292]; and as "imagination" in ¶758, [*PdG* 551])
Einbilden, *Eingebildet*	It is rightly translated as "*imagining*," "*imagined*" (Miller) as long as one understands it to be limited to a conjuring-up of images; thus in ¶756 it is qualified further as "*visionary dreaming*" (*Schwärmerei*)	(e.g., in ¶756 *PoS* [*PdG* 550])
Phantasie:	*Imagination* (Harris and Knox) But leaving it as *Phantasie* is more accurate: it is the second moment of the imagination in the 1830 *Phil.Spir.*, with Symbolizing, Allegorizing and Poetical Imagination as its moments; *Sign-making Phantasie* is the third moment of the imagination in that work.	(e.g., in *SysEth*) (Cf. *Aesth.* 5, n. 2. and my discussion in chapter 6 page 111)
vorstellen	*imagining,* but it is better translated as *re-presenting*, or as *picture-thinking* (This form is much more frequent esp. in in Miller)	(e.g., Miller *PoS* ¶16, p. 9, and Harris *Hegel's Ladder: The Pilgrimage of Reason*, Vol. I, ¶16, p. 51; also Knox, *Aesthetics*,1001, "The Poetic Way of Imagining Things" and ftn. I) (e.g., Miller ¶764 *PoS* [*PdG* 556]; "*Form des Vorstellens*" = "*form of picture-thinking*," Miller ¶765, [*PdG* 556])

See my discussion of these terms in chapter 6.

Abbreviations

Works by Hegel

Aesth	*Lectures on Aesthetics.* Vol. 1 + 2. Trans. T. M. Knox. Oxford: Clarendon Press, 1975
Ästh.	*Ästhetik.* Bd. 1 + 2. Nach der zweiten Ausgabe von H. G. Hothos, (1842). Hrsg. von F. Bassenge. Frankfurt am Main: Europäische Verlagsanstalt GmbH, 1955
Äst.	*Vorlesungen über die Ästhetik. (Hegel: Werke 13-15.)* Frankfurt am Main: Surkamp Verlag, 1970.
Diff	*The Difference Between Fichte's and Schelling's System of Philosophy.* Trans. H. S. Harris and W. Cerf. Albany: State University of New York Press, 1977
Differenz	*Differenz des Fichteschen und Schellingschen Systems der Philosophie.* Frankfurt am Main: Suhrkamp Verlag, 1974
Enc.Phil.Spir.	*Encyclopaedia Philosophy of Mind.* Trans. W. Wallace. With *Zusätze in Boumann's text (1845),* trans. A. V. Miller. Oxford: Clarendon Press, 1971
Enz.Phil.G.	*Enzyklopädie Philosophie des Geistes* (1830). Redaktion E. Moldenhauer und K. M. Michel. Frankfurt am Main: Suhrkamp Verlag, 1970
Faith	*Faith and Knowledge.* Trans. Walter Cerf and H. S. Harris. Albany: State University of New York Press, 1977
FirstPhil	*First Philosophy of Spirit.* In *The System of Ethical Life (1802/3) and First Philosophy of Spirit (Part II of the System*

of Speculative Philosophy 1803/4), trans. H. S. Harris and T. M. Knox. Albany: State University of New York Press, 1979

G1   *Geistesphilosophie (1803–04)*. In *Jenaer Systementwürfe I: Das System der Spekulativen Philosophie*, Hrsg. von K. Düsing und H. Kimmerle. Hamburg: Felix Meiner Verlag, 1986

G2   *Geistesphilosophie 1805–06* in *Naturphilosophie und Philosophie des Geistes (1805–06)*. In *Jenaer Systementwürfe III*, Hrsg. von R.-P. Horstmann. Hamburg: Felix Meiner Verlag, 1987

GW   *Glauben und Wissen, Jenaer Kritische Schriften*. Hrsg. von H. Brockard und H. Buchner. Hamburg: Felix Meiner Verlag, 1986

PdG   *Phänomenologie des Geistes*. Redaktion E. Moldenhauer und K. M. Michel. Frankfurt am Main: Suhrkamp Verlag, 1970

Phil.Rel. *Lectures on the Philosophy of Religion—the Lectures of 1827*. Ed. Peter C. Hodgson. Trans. R. F. Brown, P. C. Hodgson, J. M. Stewart, with the assistance of H. S. Harris. London: U. of California Press, 1988

PoS   *The Phenomenology of Spirit*. Trans. A. V. Miller. Oxford, New York, Toronto, Melbourne: Oxford University Press, 1977

SPR   *System der Sittlichkeit*. In *Hegels Schriften zur Politik und Rechtsphilosophie*, Hrsg. G. von Lasson. Leipzig: Verlag von Felix Meiner, 1913, 418–503

SysEth   *System of Ethical Life*. In *The System of Ethical Life (1802–03) and First Philosophy of Spirit (Part II of the System of Speculative Philosophy 1803–04)*, trans. H. S. Harris and T. M. Knox. Albany: State University of New York Press, 1979

Works by Fichte

Sc.Kn.   *The Science of Knowledge*. Ed. and trans. P. Heath and J. Lachs. Cambridge: Cambridge University Press, 1982

WL   *Grundlage der Gesamten Wissenschaftslehre (1794)*. Einleitung und Register von Wilhelm G. Jacobs. Hamburg: Felix Meiner Verlag, 1988

Works by Kant

CJ   *Critique of Judgment*. Trans. W. Pluhar. Indiana: Hackett Publishing Company, 1987

CPR	*Critique of Pure Reason.* Trans, N. Kemp Smith. London and Basingstoke: MacMillan, 1983
KdU	*Kritik der Urteilskraft.* Hrsg. von Wilhelm Weischedel. Frankfurt am Main: Suhrkamp Insel Verlag, 1957
KrV	*Kritik der reinen Vernunft.* Hrsg. von R. Schmidt. Hamburg: Felix Meiner Verlag, 1990

Works by Schelling

STI	*System of Transcendental Idealism (1800).* Trans. P. Heath. Charlottesville: University Press of Virginia, 1993
Sys. Tr. I.	*System des transzendentalen Idealismus.* Hrsg. von H. D. Brandt und P. Müller. Hamburg: Felix Meiner Verlag, 1992.

PART ONE

Imagination in Theory:
"Subjective Authentication"

CHAPTER 1

The Sundering Imagination of the Absolute
(Hegel's Earliest Works)

———————— ✠ ————————

Hegel's earliest published works, *Faith and Knowledge* and the *Differenzschrift*, offer an imperfect account of the imagination, but one that nevertheless gets us beyond some of the problems present in Kant's and Fichte's view of the role of the imagination. Hegel's account is couched in his adoption of Schelling's Identity Theory, and in his critique of, among others, Kant and Fichte.

The thesis of the Identity Philosophy that concerns us is that the imagination is a sundering activity that creates the opposition between subject and object. This thesis is argued for by Schelling and the early Hegel, in opposition to the "one-sided" views of Kant and Fichte, who make the subject the original principle. In order to adjudicate the benefits and failures of this view, we have to look at how this thesis of the originary sundering imagination takes shape. We begin with Hegel's assertions against the philosophies of subjectivity (Kant and Fichte among others). Then we look at some problems with the theory of original sundering.

IMAGINATION AS THE SUNDERING ABSOLUTE

In *Faith and Knowledge* Hegel writes triumphantly that

> the metaphysic of subjectivity has run through the complete cycle
> of its forms in the philosophies of Kant, Jacobi, and Fichte . . .
> [and it] has brought this cultural process to its end. Therewith the

3

> external possibility directly arises that the true philosophy [i.e.,
> Speculative Philosophy] should emerge. . . . (*Faith*, Conclusion,
> 189; *GW* 133)

It is in this work, in his criticism of Kant and Fichte, that the imagination's role as Hegel perceived it starts to become apparent. In both this work and the *Differenzschrift*, Hegel contrasts grasping truth through the intellect (the wrong way of grasping truth) with the recognition of Reason's self-making through Speculative Philosophy (the right way of grasping it). Kant and Fichte belong to the first kind. According to Hegel, Kant fails to recognize the Speculative Idea in the transcendental imagination; Fichte fails to see the Speculative Idea in the practical ends of Reason.[1] Let us look at these criticisms more deeply in order to understand what role Hegel attributes to the imagination. Since Hegel developed these ideas in close association with Schelling, our analysis here involves Schelling's account as well.

According to Kant, there is a difference between reason and the imagination. They are distinct faculties, with different products. The products, respectively, are ideas and the syntheses of the imagination.

All knowledge for Kant is based on the latter. The syntheses of the imagination under concepts of the understanding provide us with empirical and pure judgments about the world. The former, ideas of reason, can never lead us to true knowledge because for Kant ideas are pure intuitions: "Ideas are not concepts, rather they are pure intuitions, not discursive, but rather intuitive representations."[2] Only a divine mind could be capable of true ideas (intellectual intuitions). As a result, any attempt to prove the truth of ideas leads to antinomies and paralogisms.

This epistemological division in Kant between reason and imagination, and between ideas and syntheses, means that there can never be an absolute reconciliation between our ideas and our experience, or between thought and being. We may postulate the existence of a divine mind in whom true ideas exist, but we can never know it or its inner possibility. Likewise, we may postulate a future world in which our moral worthiness to be happy corresponds to our actual happiness, but that world image remains necessarily an ideal. This failure to unite thought and being, and this alienation from the absolute were unacceptable to Schelling and Hegel.

For Schelling and the early Hegel, there can be no question of a hypostatized intuitive understanding. Kant's division between reason and imagination does not hold: according to them imagination *is* reason. In his *System of Transcendental Idealism* Schelling explains this view. Using the language of Fichte but to a different end Schelling writes:

[W]hat is commonly spoken of as the imagination is in fact such a wavering between finitude and infinity; or, what comes to the same, an activity mediating the theoretical and the practical. . . . This power, therefore, which we refer to meanwhile as imagination, will in the course of this wavering also necessarily produce something, which itself oscillates between infinity and finitude, and which can therefore also be regarded only as such. Products of this kind are what we call *Ideas* as opposed to concepts, and *imagination in this wavering is on that very account not understanding but reason;* and conversely, *what is commonly called theoretical reason is nothing else but imagination in the service of freedom.* . . . [O]nce they are made objects of the understanding, they lead to those insoluble contradictions which Kant set forth under the name of the antinomies . . . these Ideas must assuredly be mere products of imagination, that is, of an activity such that it produces neither the finite nor the infinite. (*STI* 176, my emphasis; *Sys. Tr. I.,* 228–29)

Schelling defines the imagination as a wavering between the finite and the infinite. We see here a shift from the Kantian notion of synthesis, to what in Hegel will be a dialectical motion. This wavering is at the heart of identity. So all identities are in fact moving, in flux. The wavering is between the finite and infinite, so there is no question of a fundamental incommensurability between the finite and the infinite: they are united in and through the imagination's wavering between them. In fact, the conceptual identity of "finite" and "infinite" is purely a function of the wavering imagination's having appeared to stop at a point that in actuality is not a static point but is rather itself a wavering between finite and infinite. There are different levels or kinds of these nodal points, but they all share this characteristic of being a wavering of imagination. There are no entities outside of thought, but thought is nothing other than the generation of entities. Thought does not lie in waiting, it is those creations. And thought's activity is a wavering imagination.

For Schelling, there is no question of ideas existing beyond the wavering, or of a divine mind in which ideas reside, existing beyond the wavering: any idea, including that of a divine mind, is produced by the wavering imagination. Ideas are higher forms of the wavering between finite and infinite than occur in empirical and pure intuitions. Only when fixed does an idea generate seemingly unsurmountable contradictions with other ideas. So it is the fixing of the wavering that is the cause of the (false) division between ideas and experience. The true relationship to ideas is the one that views them as forms of the imagination's wavering.

Now, there are clearly problems with this view, problems that Hegel will eventually recognize and try to solve. Let us look at the problems first. One of them is clear in Hegel's version of what Schelling says above. In *Faith and Knowledge*, Hegel claims, like Schelling, that the imagination is not separate from reason; like Schelling he claims that, in fact, it is the same as reason:

> [W]e must not take the faculty of [productive] imagination as the middle term that gets inserted between an existing absolute subject and an absolute existing world. *The productive imagination must rather be recognized as what is primary and original, as that out of which subjective Ego and objective world first sunder themselves into* the necessarily bipartite appearance and product, *and as the sole In-itself.* This power of imagination is *the original two-sided identity.* The identity becomes subject in general on one side, and object on the other; but originally it is both. And *the imagination is nothing but Reason itself.* (*Faith* 73; my emphasis)

The problem becomes clear in a qualification Hegel goes on to make: ["I]t [imagination] is only Reason as it appears in the sphere of empirical consciousness." The imagination is reason, but not the "absolute, *self-intuiting* Reason" (*Diff* 174); it is self-shaping, but not the "*intuiting* of th[is] self-shaping or objectively self-finding Absolute" (*Diff* 171). In other words, there is a difference between the sundering imagination and reason's consciousness of itself as this sundering. The problem is that the latter is also supposed to be the action of the imagination. Thus, there appears to be a contradiction: the imagination is the "sole-in-itself," the Absolute, and yet it is also only one moment of the Absolute. Reason and imagination are the same, and yet they are different. How are we to reconcile these two claims?

In the move from Kant's view to Schelling's and Hegel's, we appear to have merely shifted from one kind of rift to another. In Kant there was a rift between the syntheses of the imagination and the ideas of reason. Schelling and Hegel try to move beyond this by saying that in both syntheses and ideas, what is operative is the sundering imagination. But we fall into another rift in that there is still a difference to be accounted for between the sundering of imagination into empirical, finite entities and the self-knowing sundering of the imagination as the Absolute, infinite entity.

Schelling and Hegel's problem seems to go away if we turn it on its head and say that the real problem is thinking in terms of entities at all: what we should be focusing on is the common factor of the imagination's sundering. But this still leaves us with the problem of accounting for the distinction between the different kinds of entities that the imagination produces in its wavering. It also leaves us with the problem of distinguishing the imagination in its empirical guise from the imagination as the self-knowing absolute, which is not empirical.

The problem is provisionally solved by looking at the development of the sundering absolute from its originary moment up through varied levels of being. This is what Schelling and the early Hegel advocate. For them the genetic history of self-consciousness is the natural history of the Absolute's coming to be self-conscious. Schelling's *System of Transcendental Idealism* gives the stages of development: his ideal reconstruction is the account of the various graduated powers (*Potenzen*) of consciousness.

Kant's hidden (*verborgene*) imagination, is therefore mistakenly viewed by Kant as a subjective spontaneity in the service of an already present understanding. According to Schelling and Hegel it is hidden, yes, in the sense of being, at its deepest level, unconscious. But it is an originary sundering of the Absolute into subject and object. Intuition is the first division of this absolute, epistemological genesis. The understanding is a second, more differentiated level of the Absolute's self-reflection. Both have the same principle—the sundering into opposition. Thus, Hegel writes:

> This original synthetic unity [the Absolute] must be conceived, not as produced out of opposites, but as a truly necessary, absolute, original identity of opposites. As such, it is the principle *both* of *productive imagination, which is the unity that is blind,² i.e., immersed in the difference and not detaching itself from it; and of the intellect, which is the unity that posits the difference as identical but distinguishes itself from the different.* This shows that the *Kantian forms of intuition and the forms of thought cannot be kept apart at all as the particular, isolated faculties* which they are usually represented as. One and the same synthetic unity—we have just now determined what this means here—is the principle of intuition and of the intellect. (*Faith* 70, my emphasis; *GW* 17–18)

As we have seen,⁴ Schelling says much the same in his *System of Transcendental Idealism* of poetry making, which is the concluding, highest *Potenz*:

> What we speak of as the poetic gift is merely productive intuition, reiterated to its highest power. *It is one and the same capacity that is active in both,* the only one whereby we are able to think and to couple together even what is contradictory—and *its name is imagination.* (*STI* 230; my emphasis)⁵

This principle means that the intellect, although creating difference, is nevertheless creating a difference that is a level of the Absolute's self-reflection, and it only ever generates the difference as a result of the originary indifference point sundering itself. Thus, the subject's positing at the level of intuition, or at the level of intellect, *is* Being. The view is of Being.

This view distinguishes itself not only from Kant's, but from Fichte's as well. According to Schelling and Hegel, the Absolute's sundering is not (as in Fichte) the action of a self striving toward its infinite completion. Let us take a moment to look at this more carefully.

Fichte's subject suspends the imagined perfection in front of itself, and thus the view is never of absolute Being. For Fichte

> the idea of an infinity to be thus completed floats *as a vision* before us, and is rooted in our innermost nature. We are obliged, as it enjoins us, to resolve the contradiction [of realizing the infinite]; though we cannot even think it possible of solution and foresee that in no moment of an existence prolonged to all eternity will we ever be able to consider it possible. But this is just the *mark in us* that we are destined for eternity. (*Sc.Kn.* I, 270; my emphasis)

As we have seen in our introduction, for Fichte, the principle of the intellect is the check that the subject imposes on its own activity, thereby initiating the wavering of the imagination between the self and the beyond toward which the self strives. In that opposition there is no reconciliation with the infinite, only a striving to reach beyond the finite. It appears, therefore, as though the self both posits itself and exceeds itself. The consequent history is therefore an ongoing construction required and motivated by the intellect, an intellect that is never able to cash in its check.[6] The self is never one with the world. In one of Hegel's more sardonic criticisms of Fichte he writes:

> [W]hat is most horrifying and saddening for Fichte's I is being one with the universe, having the universe live and act in me, being obedient to the eternal laws of nature and to the hallowed necessity. Since difference, or the bad, is so incorrectly conceived, the reconstruction cannot be authentic either. For the infinite is posited as originally un-unified and un-unifiable with the finite: the Ideal [*das Ideelle*] cannot be united with the real or pure Reason with existence. (*Faith* 182; *GW* 126–7)[7]

If, on the other hand, the foundational principle is an originary sundering, then what evolves out of it is the history of that self-reflective Being, a history of the infinite. Rather than Fichte's line, which extends from the subject out toward infinity, for Hegel the Absolute's history is an infinite cycle of sundering, opposition, and self-conscious return, each return being a new level.

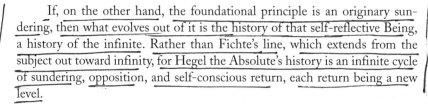

This difference between Fichte on the one hand and Hegel and Schelling on the other can be seen in terms of categories. According to Fichte, the category that underlies all the other categories in Kant's table is the third category of relation—that of *Wechselwirkung* (interdetermination). This *Wechselwirkung* is the wavering of the imagination between the finite and the infinite. It lies at the basis of all the other categories because all the other categories presume opposition. (For example, quantity: one cannot isolate a quantity without having an object over against one.) Furthermore, in Fichtean epistemology, the imagination is the *subjective* synthesis at the heart of all the categories.

For the early Hegel, since the imagination is the indifference point's sundering, it gives rise to subject and object. Thus, the imagination is the basis of all thought. It is not only subjective synthesis. The basis of all categorial determinations is *substantive*. According to Hegel, the imagination is not causal in the Fichtean sense because, as we saw, the self does not require synthesis but rather itself arises out of the synthesis. The primary category for Hegel, at least at this point in his thinking, is therefore not that of interdetermination. Rather, "the true relation of speculation" is that of substance and accident (*Diff* 116 and cf. 161).[8] As a result, for the early Hegel, "Both art and speculation are in their essence divine service—both are a *living intuition of the absolute life* and hence *a being at one with it*" (*Diff* 172).

ONE-SIDED RECONSTRUCTIONS

What I want to look at now is why Fichte and Kant got it wrong. First, let me explain the title of this section. Why "reconstruction"?

In Schelling's and Hegel's conception of the Absolute, the fact that we have experience at all is evidence that the sundering has always already happened, for we could not have a subject on the one hand, and an object of knowledge on the other, without that sundering having occurred. So their account of the different levels of the absolute sundering imagination is a reconstruction of experience. Schelling and the early Hegel, and according to their view, anyone else who was seeking the truth in this matter, had to go back to the original sundering and to conceptually reconstruct what experience is in terms of how it came about, from the original sundering forward.

According to the early Hegel, a reconstruction along Fichtean lines is "one-sided" because Fichte does not recognize a particular preponderance that consciousness has when it is making reconstructions. The preponderance is consciousness' tendency to suspend the truth outside as something beyond what is available to consciousness. According to Hegel, this is what both Kant and Fichte do, the former by referring to a thing-in-itself and the latter by setting up the check, and by making absolute reconciliation something for which practical reason can only ever strive. The preponderance prevents the reconciliation of thought and being.

Schelling and Hegel believe that their speculative philosophy fully recognizes and overcomes the preponderance, and therefore does achieve the reconciliation. Thus, in the *Differenzschrift*, Hegel explains:

> [T]hough speculation certainly conceives the Absolute as becoming, it also posits the identity of becoming and being; and what appears to speculation as self-begetting is at the same time posited as the original absolute being which can only come to be so far as it is. In this way, *speculation can rid itself of the preponderance that consciousness has in it; the preponderance is in any case something inessential.* (*Diff* 172, my emphasis; *Differenz* 113)

The preponderance to one-sided reconstructions is a result of viewing things from the point of view of an understanding that has not been thoroughly, critically thought through and thereby recognized as only one level in the development of the Absolute's self-cognizance. According to Hegel, both Kant and Fichte make the mistake of privileging the understanding and determining the Absolute conceptually from that intellectual standpoint.

Having looked at the one-sided nature of Fichte's reconstruction, it is easier to see how one-sided Kant's reconstruction of the intellect is for Hegel.

The One-sided Reconstruction into Faculties

We recall Kant's statement in *The Critique of Pure Reason* that the two syntheses—that of the imagination and that of the intellect—are one and the same spontaneity "there under the name of the imagination, here under the name of the understanding."[9] As we saw, what Kant means by "under the name" is not clear. One might try to clarify the matter by asserting generally that the two names are proper to some one thing, and that in this case the thing is a faculty. But this is a far cry from explaining *how* the thing falls under two different names.

The problem is more complex than just finding out how something can be called two different things at different times and yet still be the same thing. *What* we are trying to get a handle on (synthesis) is the very thing responsible for our ability to make such a distinction between two names, as well as being that whereby we can name at all. One can't *give* a name (or names) to something and hope that that will tell us something about it or about how the process allows us to distinguish things by naming them. That which acquires the name *imagination* or *understanding* does so as a result of synthesis; synthesis cannot simply be said to exist under those faculty names. Synthesis *is* in the very production of the names, but in a still unrevealed way. The names alone don't tell us anything.

Giving an account of the way each synthesis *is* (assuming that there is in fact more than one kind), is the task of proper reconstruction. For Hegel, not only names, but "faculties" are products of synthesis. Insofar as we have isolated them, we abstract ourselves from the absolute as becoming, thereby reifying cognitive activity. To remain contented with this is to end up with what Hegel later calls a "bunch of powers" and a view of the mind as a "skeleton-like mechanical collection."[10] While reification is part of the self-determining process of the Absolute (as witnessed in consciousness' propensity), to fix on the abstracted products is to slip into a point of view that itself is abstract. It is to slip into a dualism that takes the place of becoming.[11] Kant's critical perspective suppresses the actuality of the synthesis in favor of unreflected nomenclature. His view thus suffers from intellectual one-sidedness.

Kant's Beautiful Reconstruction

Hegel does not deal with Kant's *Critique of Judgment* in his *Faith and Knowledge*, but it is worth looking briefly at this reconstruction too.

In Kant's explanation of the experience of the beautiful, and in the section on teleology in the same book, Kant discusses the notion of regulative ideas. These ideas are contrasted with constitutive ideas. While the latter constitute objects, the former are used to regulate our experience of objects. For example, according to Kant the real nature of the universe in itself is unknowable to us. If we are to think about that supersensible structure, we must somehow regulate our reasoning. In the *Critique of Pure Reason*, Kant asserts that any attempt to explain the supersensible leads to antinomies of reason. But in the *Critique of Judgment* Kant attempts to use ideas to regulate our thinking about what we cannot know for sure. Thus, in that work Kant asserts that nature appears to act *as if* it were purposeful. The *as if* is regulative, not constitutive: it regulates how we experience natural objects when we think beyond what reason can know for sure; it does not play a role in constituting the objects of nature. But it does, somewhat underhandedly, let Kant entertain a relationship between thought and being.

According to Hegel, though Kant did not always fully understand them to be such, these ideas are intellectual intuitions of the absolute sundering indifference point.

Let us take an example. According to Kant,[12] when we look at something beautiful, a rose, say, we become aware of the fact that though we can isolate different aspects of the rose (the shape of a petal's curve or the intensity of the color; the relation of the petals to one another; the necessity of the rose being as it is or the possibility of its withering), we are aware of how none of the isolated concepts are adequate to explain why the rose is beautiful. Beauty is the play between the imagination (which synthesizes the sensory input) and the understanding (according to whose categories the synthesis occurs). The play is a sustaining of the failure to conceptually grasp beauty, and this play of our powers is pleasurable to us.[13]

According to Schelling and Hegel, Kant was on the right track when he recognized the play as one between the finite understanding and the infinite possibilities producible in the contemplation of beauty.[14] But Kant wrongly maintained the antithesis between subject and object. He did so, first, by asserting that in the experience of the beautiful it is *as if* nature were purposive; second, he intellectualized the product of that difference—the regulative Idea of nature as purposive; and third, he asserted that such an idea can never be complete precisely because it is (merely) an intellectual idea.[15] According to Hegel, Kant was mistaken in asserting that this Idea could only sit on the side of the intellect. That is, Kant was mistaken in asserting that the Idea could never really be about the object in any knowable, true way. This one-sidedness was a result of Kant's holding to the antithesis between subject and object.

For Hegel, that antithesis is not structurally absolute (in the sense that the epistemological machinery won't work without it). Rather, the antithesis is *apparent*, a result, and something that can be superseded. It is the result of synthesis, and that synthetic activity is not just on the side of the subject. It is the very activity of being. Thus, the regulative Idea that nature is purposive need not be held strictly as arising on the side of the intellect. Any idea, like the apparent antithesis of subject and object, is *itself* a product of synthetic activity.

The irony for Hegel is that Kant's idea *is* true. But because Kant designs his epistemology in terms of fixed structures of the mind, rather than in terms of the purposiveness, he fixes that purposiveness as an idea of nature, an idea that can only be regulative, not constitutive, and one that is therefore never complete. For Hegel, to cling to the intellectual idea as fundamentally incomplete is to miss how it arose in the first place, and to miss how it is merely a product and not an a priori truth of consciousness. Thus, Hegel asserts (rather cryptically) that "the sole Idea that has reality and true objectivity for philosophy, is the absolute suspendedness [*Aufgehobensein*] of the antithesis" (*Faith* 68). For further insight into what this means, we must move beyond one-sided reconstructions and look at what he writes in *Faith and Knowledge* about proper reconstruction.

PROPER RECONSTRUCTION

Let us return to the question that inspires any reconstruction: How does the absolute, through its sundering, go from being unconscious to being empirically conscious to being self-conscious? And what role is the imagination playing throughout?

Faith and Knowledge offers a murky set of propositions about what the reconstruction is. Hegel writes that to be authentic

> this reconstruction would have to unveil the essence of the spirit and [first] expound how nature reflects itself in spirit. Nature takes itself back into itself and lifts its original, unborrowed [*ungeborgt*] real beauty into the ideal realm, the realm of possibility. Thus nature rises as spirit. . . . [Secondly the reconstruction would have to expound] how the essence of nature, in the form of possibility, i.e., as spirit, has enjoyment of itself as a living Ideal in the visible and active reality; and how it has its actuality as ethical nature in which the ethical infinite, that is, the concept, and the ethical finite, that is, the individual, are one without qualification. (*Faith* 182; *GW* 127)

Though sketchy, this passage is important because it contains within it the seeds of the reconstruction as Hegel viewed it. These seeds are contained in his implicit criticism of Kant's notion of beauty: Hegel writes that "Nature takes itself back into itself and lifts its original, unborrowed real beauty into the ideal realm, the realm of possibility." Notice that it is Nature that does this, not the mind. It is not some epistemological machinery that, ordered to do so by the subject, lifts beauty from the rose; and the supposition that nature acts *as if* it were purposive is not, therefore, merely a regulative Idea. Rather, nature reproduces itself at the ideal level, in the mind. The implication is that in Kant what is really happening is that beauty is not generated by the subject, it is merely borrowed. In Hegel's reconstruction, on the other hand, it is not the subject per se that causes the experience of beauty, but rather Nature which "lifts *its original, unborrowed real beauty*" into the realm of the subjective, the ideal realm in which what is, becomes what is possible.

In the *Differenzschrift* and in *Faith and Knowledge*, the imagination is depicted as originary, as the point of indifference, as the unconscious original sundering into subject and object, as the "sole in-itself." For the answer to how reason becomes self-conscious one would have to go beyond these works to works in which Hegel develops the notion of Spirit. Spirit starts to take shape in Hegel's subsequent Jena works, in *The System of Ethical Life (1802/3)* and in *First Philosophy of Spirit (1803/4)*. Ultimately, how reason becomes self-conscious Spirit will be what the 1807 *Phenomenology of Spirit* teaches us.[16]

But the *Differenzschrift* and the end of *Faith and Knowledge* do provide the key to proper reconstruction. The propensity of consciousness to create a one-sided view is overcome by a demise of abstraction in(to) original sundering.

For the self generated by the one-sided reconstruction, this demise, however, means its own negation. It is a fall into the night. Let us therefore look at this fall into darkness.

THE LOGIC OF LOSS

In "*Das Absolute als Nacht, Nichts und Abgrund*,"[17] Bonsiepen claims that in Hegel's early writings negation is connected more to destruction and death than it is in his later texts. Indeed, Hegel asserts that to become one with the imagination as Speculative Idea (i.e., to stop understanding it and to be [one with its] becoming), the self must throw itself into "the abyss," into the night. However, the night is not just a death. It is also the birthplace of truth. The loss is also originary. The relationship between loss and creation is like the perpetual circular turning of night into day. The night is the birthplace of truth, and the necessary ground to which all must go in order for birth to occur. Hegel writes soberly that "[t]he manifoldness of being lies between two nights, without support. It rests on nothing—for the indeterminate is nothing to the intellect—and it ends in nothing" (*Diff* 95; *Differenz* 26).

Although the night is one of the three moments of an absolute whole, in these early texts it is the predominant moment. "The Absolute is the night, and the light is younger than it; and the distinction between them, like the emergence of the light out of the night, is an absolute difference—the nothing is the first out of which all being, all the manifoldness of the finite has emerged" (*Diff* 93–94; *Differenz* 24–25).

For the subject, the night is the negation of the antithesis of reflection, and therefore the negation of consciousness itself:

> [I]n its highest synthesis of the conscious and the non-conscious, speculation also demands the *nullification of consciousness itself. Reason thus drowns itself* and its knowledge and its reflection of the absolute identity, in its own abyss. . . . (*Diff* 103, my emphasis; *Differenz* 35)

The "demand" of Reason here is entirely different from the demand in Kant and Fichte. For them the demand was made by reason of the imagination:

it was the requirement that there be synthesis. Here, the demand is that reason throw itself into an abyss, that reason submerge itself in the movement of synthesis. Only out of that loss can something be created, just as the day arises out of the night.

Negation is therefore not a return to unconsciousness, *point final*. It is a return that, in negating the antithesis, is the condition of Spirit's becoming. The negation happens within the circular movement of the Absolute's self-development. Instead of mere negation, one must speak of the *suspendedness* (*Aufgehobensein*) of the antithesis.

This is a substantial *as well* as subjective movement. Like any reflection, the "reflection of the absolute identity" implies the subject-object antithesis. In the negation of this antithesis which is reason drowning itself in its own abyss, what is given up is the singularity of the negation. In other words, the act of a single will is given up and becomes simply the negative moment of self-becoming substance.

It was this substantial side of things that Fichte missed. Fichtean negation (the *Anstoss*) is that without which we could have not have an object. Negation for him is also necessary if we are to feel morally compelled to exceed our limitations. But Fichte mistakenly thinks that it is we ourselves who, for the purpose of moral completion, propel ourselves beyond what is, toward the future. Had Fichte seen the *Anstoss* as a moment of being instead of appropriating it as a requirement which the self places on itself, if he had seen completion as reconciliation with being *through* negation (through the giving up of our finite selves into being from which we only appear to be separate), he would have been asserting what Hegel is asserting here. For in Hegel, despite being mere appearance, the horizon that has *become* abstract, mere appearance, is the material expression of the Absolute. The future beyond it is a projected object, an intellectualized figure of the negative moment of the Absolute. *That future* does not hold our moral completion; we mistakenly strive after it if we believe this to be so. Our moral completion lies rather in the "death" of the self—in the *mise en abyme* of any finite self-certainty.

Just as the understanding in Fichte is the *fixed* wavering of the imagination,[18] in Hegel "mere reflection" establishes a fixed absolute opposition. That "antithesis" must be sublated, since that antithesis is a generated abstraction. It is like saying that day and night are the unreflected, empirical concepts of day and night, when in fact day becomes night and night day: one is defined by the other. Such a concept—even of what is immediately the case—is immediate but not actual. It is not actual unless the conceptualizing shares in the becoming. How that works remains to be clarified in Hegel's later works.

Through the *mise en abyme,* the immediate is mediated; the abstracted self becomes actual. For Hegel, "the task of philosophy consists in uniting these presuppositions [night and day], to posit being in non-being, as becoming; to posit dichotomy in the Absolute, as its appearance; to posit the finite in the infinite, as life" (*Diff* 93–94; *Differenz* 25).[19] Positing being in non-being means mediating what has become immediate. Non-being is that which has no movement.

Because the night is equally the birthplace of all appearances, the night—as past, as potential, and as determining—is always already (full of) appearance. Absolute negation is absolute determination.

Hegel continues his sober thought: "Reason thus drowns itself and its knowledge and its reflection of the absolute identity, in its own abyss: and in this night of mere reflection and of the calculating intellect, in *this night which is the noonday of life, common sense and speculation can meet one another*" (*Diff* 103; emphasis).[20] Like Kierkegaard's Knight of Faith, we are finitely infinite.[21] The apparent incommensurability between the finite and the infinite is overcome, "suspended."

For Hegel the night is "the noonday of life." We can, therefore, assume that in the following cryptic passage, it is the night that is the "irradiating focus." "To speculation, the finitudes are radii of the infinite focus which irradiates them at the same time that it is formed by them. In the radii the focus is posited and in the focus the radii" (*Diff* 111).[22]

In his conclusion to *Faith* Hegel writes similarly:

> Infinity is the pure nullification of the antithesis or of finitude; but it is at the same time also the spring of eternal movement, the spring of that finitude which is infinite, because it eternally nullifies itself. Out of this nothing and pure night of infinity, as out of the secret abyss that is its birthplace, the truth lifts itself upward. (*Faith* 190)[23]

For Hegel, that which underlies all opposition is equally substance and subject. *Aufhebung* is substantial *and* rational. In *Faith and Knowledge* and the *Differenzschrift,* Hegel's view of that rational whole takes Christian form. The dialectic of night and light and their becoming is referred to on occasion in the *Differenzschrift* as the Trinity. The original sundering of the imagination is the night, the Father; the product is the Son, the Logos; and the figurative reconstruction, the reconstruction of "nature as possibility," is the Holy Ghost.[24]

But for Hegel, the religious casting is not the final "form" of the sublation. What has gradually emerged in these early texts is Hegel's early view of the Speculative Idea. It is the *philosophies* of subjectivity that have been the object of criticism in *Faith*. In the concluding section of *Faith and Knowledge* the *religious* expression of loss is raised to philosophical understanding.

> [T]he pure concept or infinity as the abyss of nothingness in which all being is engulfed, must signify the infinite grief [of the finite] purely as a moment of the supreme Idea, and no more than a moment. Formerly, the infinite grief only existed historically in the formative process of culture. It existed as the feeling that "God Himself is dead," upon which the religion of more recent times rests. . . . By marking this feeling as a moment of the supreme Idea, the pure concept must give philosophical existence to what used to be either the moral precept that we must sacrifice the empirical being (*Wesen*), or the concept of formal abstraction [e.g., the Categorical Imperative]. Thereby it must re-establish for philosophy the Idea of absolute freedom and along with it the absolute Passion, the speculative Good Friday in place of the historic Good Friday. *Good Friday must be speculatively re-established in the whole truth and harshness of its God-forsakenness. . . . the highest totality can and must achieve its resurrection solely from this harsh consciousness of loss. . . .* (*Faith* 190–91, square bracket additions are Harris's, italics mine; *GW* 134)

Had Kant used the metaphor of the night it probably would have referred to the inaccessible noumenal world. Had Fichte, it probably would have referred to the intellectual intuition as the basis of all knowledge,[25] and to intellectual intuition of the beyond toward which we strive. Each allows for a failure of their respective versions of the self to achieve completion. Nonetheless, neither Fichte nor Kant point to an *experience of loss*. The experience of the sublime in Kant, while an experience of the loss of the ability to comprehend, is rather an opening onto the supersensible, and so is not really an experience of the loss of reason. And Fichte's experience of never arriving is appropriated representationally: Fichte writes that it "is just the mark in us that we are destined for eternity" (*Sc.Kn.* I, 270).

But for Hegel, the experience of loss is the logical conclusion of the subjective attitude. A proper critique of subjective philosophies must therefore bring about the consciousness of such loss.[26] Since for Hegel, "the True is the whole," (*PoS* 11),[27] loss is part of the whole. The failure of Kant and Fichte to know this loss is a sign of their failure not only in the critical enterprise, but also therefore, a failure to know the whole, or in other words, to reconcile thought and being.

CONCLUSION

I mentioned earlier that the solution offered by Schelling and Hegel was only provisional. This is because *Faith and Knowledge* and the *Differenzschrift* leave us several difficulties. By way of conclusion, I want to focus in particular on the difficulties that Hegel's early writings present for a theory of the imagination.

The Identity Philosophy claims that the imagination is an absolute original sundering. One problem with this is that the original identity of subject and substance is too baldly asserted to make much sense. We must adopt their starting point if we are to follow their development from it. But the starting point is not adequately argued for. This gives rise to a second problem. Hegel never clarifies how the intellect develops out of substance.[28] Hegel shows why one-sided—merely intellectual or subjective—reconstructions must suffer the logic of loss: the loss is a plunge of reason into the abyss of the sundering imagination. But his adoption of the Identity Theory in *Faith and Knowledge* does not yield an account of how that loss is related to the genesis of the intellect or to the history of Being. This makes the role of reflection in the reconstruction unclear. It remains unclear until Hegel develops the concept of Spirit over the next few years in Jena. The first account of the genesis of intellect occurs two years later, in Hegel's 1803–04 *Geistesphilosophie* lectures, and then again in a further developed form in his *Geistesphilosophie* lectures of 1805–06. In 1807 Hegel's labors do yield the reconstruction of both intellect and the history of Being as the *Phenomenology of Spirit*. The *Phenomenology of Spirit* presents the dialectical history of speculative reflection.

To understand this development, let us turn to the first of the two *Geistesphilosophie* lectures.

CHAPTER 2

Dialectical Beginnings

(Fragment 17 of *Geistesphilosophie* 1803–04)

In his *Geistesphilosophie* lectures of 1803–04, Hegel offers a more involved account of the imagination. This change was the effect of a profound shift in his thinking. In the time between his early works of the *Critical Journal* (the *Differenzschrift* and *Faith and Knowledge*) and the *Geistesphilosophie* 1803–04 lectures, Hegel shifted from the Identity Theory to a dialectical theory of identity. Out of this change, a new form of the imagination emerges: a *dialectical* imagination. Before trying to understand what he asserts about the imagination as a dialectical identity, we have to understand what Hegel means by dialectical identity. This chapter is therefore devoted to an analysis of Hegel's new dialectical thinking. An exegesis and discussion of the role of the dialectical imagination in the *Geistesphilosophie* 1803–04 lectures is offered in my next chapter.

The chapter is organized in the following way. I begin with a discussion of the context of the *Geistesphilosophie* 1803–04 lectures. I then discuss the significant changes that occurred in Hegel's thought since his earlier works of the *Critical Journal*. Of these changes I focus on one in particular: the change from viewing logic as something concerned with finite determinations, to viewing logic as reflective of thought as *infinite*. This involves a lengthy and difficult, but very worthwhile discussion of Fragment 17 of the 1803–04 *Geistesphilosophie* lectures. The Fragment helps us to get a clear sense of

Hegel's emerging dialectical thinking. Without that, we would not be able to understand what he goes on to say in that work about the imagination.

Let me make a brief note about the text of Fragment 17 (and of the *Geistesphilosophie* as a whole). Because the text under analysis consists of Hegel's lecture notes (published posthumously), the normally difficult task of understanding Hegel is even more difficult. Hegel often uses dashes rather than full sentences, and the dialectical moments are not always clearly marked. Nevertheless, because of this complexity it can be said of both *Geistesphilosophie* lecture series that they are more interesting than the clearer, later works.[1]

CONTEXT: THE SHIFT FROM THE EARLIER JENA WORKS

Hegel was reportedly not particularly good in the classroom at Jena. Among others is a report in a letter from a British student, Henry Crabb Robinson, who wrote: "I once heard the poor Hegel. You cannot imagine how pitiful his lecture was. He coughed, cleared his throat, stuttered, he couldn't even articulate two sentences clearly."[2] Lecturing at the same university as the great Schelling was a difficult task and Hegel even had to cancel a number of courses for lack of attendance.[3] The course for which the *Geistesphilosophie* fragments of 1803–04 were written was, however, well attended.

Despite Hegel's rather mediocre success in Jena, his manuscripts over the seven years are evidence of deep and prolonged philosophical development. As Klaus Düsing writes:

> In the balance with such modest outward accomplishment were
> . . . the content of his speculative lectures and the development of
> Hegel's thought. The latter could not have been more original,
> richly variable and sweeping as it was in Jena. The decision for a
> Metaphysic of the Absolute as Science occurred during the tran-
> sition from Frankfurt to Jena and it was definitely original. During
> the Jena phase Hegel succeeded in moving—and this is evident in
> particular in his lectures—from the Metaphysics of Absolute
> Substance, which he first held, to the Metaphysics of Absolute
> Subjectivity; he also moved from a negative Dialectic—as he first
> conceived it in Jena—to a speculative dialectic. Furthermore, he
> formulated a complete system in detail, trying out multiple alter-
> natives. So it was in Jena that the ground was laid for Hegel's
> mature system.[4]

The most important shift during this Jena period from 1801 to 1807 was in Hegel's concepts of logic and metaphysics. As Troxler's notes from Hegel's lectures in 1801–02[5] show, initially for Hegel, logic was the science of the finite, metaphysics that of the infinite. For the early, Schellingian Hegel, metaphysics concerned the indeterminate, and logic concerned finite, determinate units of thought. The Identity Theory was essentially a privileging of the metaphysical over the logical in the sense that the metaphysical was the ground of the logical. For the early Hegel, in order to do metaphysics one had to let go of logic by submerging reason in the abyss. The finite must be submerged in the infinite, the determinate units of thought must be submerged in the indeterminate. Out of that death the new day is born; the finite radiates forth. Reason mediated by its own death is thus the ground of knowledge. According to the early Hegel's version of the Identity Theory, logic, which is about finite determinate units of thought, could not be the method of science. It could not be because logic did not involve the necessary *mise en abyme* of the Identity Theory. That *mise en abyme* was required of logic by the Identity Theory in order to do metaphysics.

The change between 1801 and 1807 was that, for Hegel, logic ceased to be about the finite alone, and became the science of the infinite. Part of what this means is that he began to equate thought with the Absolute. Thought determinations (logical determinations) are no longer superficial units needing to be submerged in the abyss of the absolute indifference point. Rather, the determinations of logic are moments of infinite thought, moments in the movement of thought. Thought is (the movement of) the Absolute,[6] and logic is the science of that movement.

This shift seems to be one in the direction of Fichte. One would therefore assume that the role of the imagination would switch back from being caught up in the category of substance and accident as it was in the Identity Theory, to being again a wavering interdetermination between finite and infinite. In other words, the shift ought to be from viewing the imagination as the fundamental sundering (absolute creative act) of the Absolute, to being the creative act of thought as subject. But Hegel's shift is not completely to Fichtean subjectivity. Hegel's story is more complex, if, at this stage, still imperfect.

To see just how the Hegelian imagination shapes up in this shift and how it differs from Fichte, we must examine the logic involved more closely. We can do this by analyzing one of the opening, introductory paragraph of the *Geistesphilosphie* of 1803–04. That is, we must look at a section of Fragment 17 of the *Geistesphilosophie*.

THE *GEISTESPHILOSOPHIE* OF 1803–04 IN GENERAL

First, a few words about the 1803–04 *Geistesphilosophie*. This work belongs to one of Hegel's first attempts at a complete system of philosophy. In it, Hegel states[7] that there are in fact three parts of this system of philosophy, of which the *Geistesphilosophie* is the third part. (The first part is a kind of logic, the second a philosophy of nature.) Only the second two parts are extant.[8] The extant manuscript therefore begins with fragments from a philosophy of nature, and moves on to the *Geistesphilosophie*. So the part on logic itself is not available for scrutiny. Nevertheless, in what is left to us lies Fragment 17. From it we can glean what sort of logic is at work. We can also see, more specifically, how that logic is essential to the movement of consciousness.

The *Geistesphilosophie* begins at Fragment 15 and ends at Fragment 22. Fragment 17 is part of the introduction to the *Geistesphilosophie*.[9]

FRAGMENT 17

Fragment 17 begins as follows:

> The simple essential multiplicity is the thus determined concept, the single [being] immediately taken up into positive universality, the single [being] as self-identical, or its other-being, its non-identity made identical with itself. What is opposed to it is *unity as absolutely unequal* [or] *as absolutely exclusive* [i.e.,] *numerical one*; this is indeed self-identical but in its self-identity it is the direct other of itself as absolutely negating [itself], or the absolute singularity. (*FirstPhil* 208)[10]

While nothing short of tortuous, this passage is nevertheless a dialectical tour de force. Hegel attempts to describe not only that over against which consciousness finds itself, but also how there is an identity between that and consciousness. The passage appears to be a series of contradictions: multiplicity is unity; the single is the universal; the self-identical is other-being; the non-identical is identical, etc.. The moments are excruciatingly difficult to follow. Part of what is going on is that Hegel has abandoned descriptive adequacy in order to reflect a dualism, which, it would appear, is what consciousness *is*. But has Hegel thereby given up reason? Is he speaking in tongues? Are we to grant Hegel that "martyrdom of unintelligeability" so prized by the Knight of Subjective Insight?[11]

I believe that Hegel is trying to *do,* in words, Fichte's three originary principles of the self. That is, he is trying to bear witness to Fichte's claim that consciousness is made up of the following three activities: "[T]he I posits its being absolutely [primoridially], the self posits a not-self in opposition to itself, and thirdly in the self is opposed a divisible not-self to the divisible self" (Sc.Kn. I, 110). Hegel is trying not to describe or explain, but to *exhibit* consciousness' nature as these three principles. As Hegel will put it years later (in his *Encyclopedia Logic*):

> It is precisely the business of the Logic . . . to exhibit the thoughts that are merely represented, and which as such are not compre-hended nor demonstrated, as stages of self-determining thinking, so that these thoughts come to be both comprehended and demonstrated. (addition, ¶121, "Ground," p. 189, Harris et al. trans.)

To make sense of Fragment 17, let us define the terms Hegel uses, and then see how they stand in relation to each other.

Identity

Simple Essential Multiplicity

Tempting though it is to consider the "simple essential multiplicity" as Kant's manifold of intuition, it would be wrong to limit the multiplicity to intuition: Hegel gives no indication that we are looking at a specific kind of multiplicity (i.e., a manifold of *intuition*). Therefore, it is better to assume that the multi-plicity is that of consciousness (the latter being as yet undefined). In other words, the multiplicity is *whatever* stands over against one.

I am consciously equivocating on the word *one* here—it is both episte-mological oneness, "one's" unified "view from nowhere"—as well as numerical identity (which, granted, may be an aspect of our subjective unitary view, but how that is, has yet to be sorted out). The multiplicity is also ambiguous. It is both that over against the unified self, and that which stands categorically in opposition to unity. One can develop the logic along either interpretation of the ambiguity, but for the purposes of the present discussion I will develop only the interpretation involving the subjective view and its "other." Thus, the view from nowhere is that assumption with which we begin.

The Determined Concept

Hegel goes on to say that the simple essential multiplicity is the "determined concept." What does "determined" mean here? When we say, for example, "the universe," we can mean the universe with all of its complexity (even if we can't thoroughly comprehend that complexity). We articulate it as one thing. The variously clear and distinct or confused content of our view of the universe is not what is being considered when we speak of the "determined concept"—we are simply concerned with the multiplicity as "determined" by our view. Our view makes it unified, even if we could count a number of different things that fall within that view. So when considering the expression, "the determined concept of the universe," we are not thinking of the universe as determined in this or that way; it is "determined" in that we view it. All we are looking at is the fact that it is this way, and not some other way.

To clarify what it means to say that the existent universe stands over against one, one can think of the Leibnizian simple monad: its self is this immediate view of the universe.[12] While each monad is not sufficient in terms of the view other monads have of the universe, each is the sufficient reason for the universe as it is determined by that monad's view.

But to remain with this monadistic "determined concept" of the universe would be to have only one side of the story. The other side of the story is that there is in fact the *universe* which is viewed. Kant would say that we can never know what the universe is in itself, and so we can never know what it is that we have determined phenomenologically. But, unlike Kant, in acknowledging the "thereness" of the universe, Hegel does not posit a universe *in itself*: we don't have to have a new concept for *what* is determined, (that is, we don't have to have a determined concept of the *universe in itself* over and above the determined concept of the universe). That problem only arises when we take up the one-many opposition along the lines of interpretation that we left aside, where the one is categorically determined in relation to a plurality. For Hegel, the determined concept which we already have is adequate evidence that the universe is. What is under consideration is the nature of that identity, of that "is." In this example, we are concerned with the identity of the multiplicity that is the universe.

Single Being and Positive Universality

The next line in Fragment 17 states that the determined concept is "the single [being] immediately taken up into positive universality, the single [being] as self-identical, or its other-being, its nonidentity made identical with itself." Let us deal with the first part of this sentence. It states that the determined concept is the single being immediately taken up into positive universality. How did the determined concept become a single being? What does it mean to "immediately take up" a single being? What is positive universality?

To answer these questions one might be tempted to adopt a Schellingian view. In that reading, the determined concept is of the Absolute. For the Absolute is a single being. According to this Schellingian reading, the arising of the determinate concept would result from the Absolute sundering itself into subject and object. It is the objective side of the Absolute which is then taken up into the subjective side as a concept, as a positive universality. By "positive universality" one would mean that the concept of the single being (that is, the concept which the Absolute has of itself), has the character of unity to which any future (determined) being will be conceptually indebted.

Thus, to recapitulate this Schellingian view, the very fact that we have a concept of the universe is a result of the universe having generated a part of itself (at least one reflective agent) such that it can reflect upon itself as a unity, as a single being. And the determined concept of itself is the positive universality for any determinately conceptualized being thereafter.

This answer is not a convincing explanation of what Hegel means in Fragment 17. It is not, principally because one has to accept the assumption of an Absolute that does this self-sundering and self-cognizing. Hegel is trying to exhibit what conscious experience is at its most basic level without making any assumptions, including this one. By 1803, Hegel has moved away from the ontology of the Absolute and its sundering. In the absence of any other candidates, therefore, we are left to conclude that the simple being that is "immediately taken up into positive universality" is for Hegel, here, *any* identity. So, Schelling's Absolute would just be an instance of identity: lost in a moment of deep metaphysical contemplation, the identity one had "taken up" might indeed be the Absolute. But Hegel is not being ontologically monistic here. We must not begin with any assumptions about our object, even if we do begin from the fact of there being something there for one. Hegel is talking about any identity. We have to draw from our experience; there are things in our experience, whether we have before us the concept of the universe, of the Absolute, or of a pencil.

That said, however, the character of that identity qua positive universality is the same as in the Schellingian account we gave. That is, whether the Absolute, the universe, or a pencil, this single being (this identity) is "immediately taken up into positive universality," and that determined concept is then the generic prototype of identity. Positive universality is the (still unreflected) concept of identity, the identity and the difference of the single being taken up into the mind. And whatever identity it is that we have thus taken up is a universal in the sense of being both unity and multiplicity in the same way as any other identity that gets so taken up.

What has been taken up is, however, not the immediate content of the view. For example, we cannot take up the universe itself. Rather, it is the determinate concept *universe* or *pencil* that is taken up. And that determinate concept is both the one and the multiplicity—the "one" of the view of it, and the "multiplicity" which it is. Both sides of the equation are divided, but the single being is the representative of the unity of identity and difference. Thus, Hegel goes on to qualify the single being that is positive universality: "the single [being] as self-identical, or its other-being, its nonidentity made identical with itself." The identity is nonidentity because the universal is not the same as the singular that is meant.

It is not just the simple being that is generated in this process. In the sundering, object *and subject* are generated. Consciousness is the being conscious of something. So this is the process whereby consciousness itself arises. Identity (any identity) *is* consciousness. Now we need to clarify what the difference in identity is.

Philosophers variously and erroneously "take up" this difference conceptually. They call it, for example, *noumena* or "material substratum" or the "radically alterior" or "you in yourself" or "me as I am in myself." That kind of "taking up" is erroneous because the identity of that difference is not questioned. In other words, the process of *identifying* such "objects" of thought, that is, the difference as *noumena* or as another consciousness or simply as the noun *difference,* is not recognized. To understand this, we have to look at how identity arises. More specifically, we have to look at the process of identification.

Identification

We have started with the most primitive of experiences, that of one's view and that of the view's content. This is a determinate concept, the simple being, which is taken up into positive universality. In a way, we have all we need in these two actions to define the process of identification. Yet the moment of contradiction, of difference, has not been made explicit. Only when the moment of contradiction has been made explicit can we begin to understand consciousness.

This contradiction is what the remainder of the sentence helps us to see. For the single being is a unity of identity and difference. The remainder of Hegel's sentence shows consciousness *to be* the generation of identity through contradiction and the suppression of that contradiction: "the single [being] as self-identical, or its other-being, its nonidentity *made* identical with itself."

Let me explain further by appealing on the one hand to the difference between analytic and synthetic notions of identity, and on the other by introducing the notion of time. In the expression $A = A$, it is not merely analytically true that the first term is identical to the second, it is *also synthetically true.* This means not only that we bring two things together in a synthesis; it also involves time. We must take the *time* to move through the equation, and to compare one term with the other (or, to compare the being under consideration with itself). There is a temporal lapse. This might be expressed as the mind holding the one moment in which A is present in memory over against the new, second moment in which A is present. The second A is not just the *still present* first A, it is also that first A *again*. One must say "again" because for a moment there was at least the *possibility* that it was not self-identical, and it is only the second term in relation to the remembered first term that annuls the possibility that the two terms are different.

The gap was correctly recognized by Fichte to be the wavering imagination. So it is of no small import to our investigation of the imagination to understand this gap and to see how Hegel might differ from Fichte.

One might dispute that the possibility that it is not self-identical is not in any way necessary to identifying something.[13] Here I would borrow the Aristotelian notion of our being potentially cognizant of the object prior to our being actually cognizant of it. We cannot cognize something unless we are capable of cognizing it. So, we move from being capable and having the possibility of cognizing it, to actually cognizing it. If we do this only once, we don't have an identity, we just have a view. It is when we do it a second time that we cognize an identity. But if we do it a second time without reflecting on the process, we don't raise the viewing up along with the term, and thus we don't see the epistemological character of the identity. It is when we raise the A to "positive universality" and say that it is what it is, that we have an identity. That means moving through the space of potentiality again on the way to the second viewing of the A.

To return to the first term for a moment, in the Aristotelian reception of the form without the matter we receive a unity. This is also the case in Hegel. But while we have a unity, we don't have an identity until we reflect on the object of perception. The thing is initially only a determined concept, not something taken up into positive universality. Only as taken up into positive universality is it properly identified as selfsame. And that taking up is what takes time. Judgment takes time.

The process involves returning to a momentary state of potentiality with regard to the object in question. Difference is possibility, potentiality. We become habituated to think what we actually know. But the ability to know comes first, epistemologically speaking.

Thus, as is well known, for Hegel there is a moment of nonidentity in identity. The nonidentity is annulled, sublated in the final picture. Depending on what one wants, in the final picture one either has a new potentiality toward knowing, or one has a self-identical object. Clearly, if one wants to be a knower, the smart way of viewing any conclusion is as a new set of actual and potential habits of thought. In this way we can see that Hegel's consciousness is not an appropriating tyrant.

If one were trying to be a witness to this *process*, articulating, one after the other, the three moments of identity, nonidentity, and then identity *again*, one would utter something like what Hegel has in Fragment 17. That is, one would speak of "the single [being] as self-identical (1), or its other-being (2), its nonidentity made identical with itself (3)." (We can now recall Fichte's three principles, too: "the I posits its being absolutely [primoridially]," the self posits a not-self in opposition to itself, and thirdly, "in the self is opposed a divisible not-self to the divisible self" [Sc.Kn. I, 110].) But, unlike Fichte, according to Hegel, the "view" with which we started is not necessarily a *subject* identity in the process of identity construction. It is *any* identity.

The remainder of the paragraph is now understandable, since Hegel is repeating the movement. "What is opposed to it is *unity as absolutely unequal* [or *as absolutely exclusive* [i.e.,] *numerical one*; this is indeed self-identical but in its self-identity it is the direct other of itself as absolutely negating [itself], or the absolute singularity." Stated in terms of our example: what is opposed to consciousness is the unity of a multiplicity, the universe conceived as an absolutely exclusive, numerically one thing. The concept of "universe" is indeed self-identical but in its self-identity it is the direct other of itself as absolutely negating itself, in the sense that one has to blink, as it were, to know that it is really there. That "blinking," or moment of negation, is the production of identity, and consciousness of that blinking is what differentiates analytic from synthetic identity. Only with that consciousness does one have an absolute singularity, the simple being that is positive universality.

Were we to take the original contradiction of the determined concept (e.g., the universe as being both one and a multiplicity), we would not have negation or absolute singularity fully in the picture. In raising the determined concept (which includes the contradiction) to positive universality—i.e., identifying it by taking the time to assure ourselves of its self-sameness—absolute singularity is exhibited. And the character of absolute singularity is a state of potentiality in the copula, the absolute negativity of the moment between the A and A in the our identification of A = A.

In conclusion, therefore, for Hegel, the principle of identity *is* consciousness. But this principle is not some a priori transcendental subject. It is a process of making identity. Furthermore, consciousness (identity) relies on not-being in order to be. I have characterized the "not-being" as both temporal and potential. I have also implied that knowledge is nothing without that potentiality, even in its result. This is not the platitudinous claim that all knowledge is open-ended. The claim is much more radical: consciousness is only possible insofar as its object in part does not exist. Identity is the unity of identity and difference. This is not to be thought only laterally extending out within the scope of conscious view: it must be thought as the ground of consciousness.

Hegel states this view clearly in *The Science of Logic* of 1831 (in the following citation I include the paragraph preceding his statement of it, since it shows how the *Phenomenology of Spirit* will ultimately be related to Hegel's logic):

> The Notion of pure science and its deduction is therefore presupposed in the present work in so far as the *Phenomenology of Spirit* is nothing other than the deduction of it. Absolute knowing is the *truth* of every mode of consciousness because, as the course of the *Phenomenology* showed, it is only in absolute knowing that the separation of the *object* from the *certainty of itself* is completely eliminated: truth is now equated with certainty and this certainty with truth.
>
> Thus pure science presupposes liberation from the opposition of consciousness. It contains *thought in so far as this is just as much the object in its own self, or the object in its own self in so far as it is equally pure thought*. As science, truth is pure self-consciousness in its self-development and has the shape of the self, so that the absolute truth of being is the known Notion and the Notion as such is the absolute truth of being.[14]

CONCLUSIONS FOR OUR UNDERSTANDING OF THE IMAGINATION IN HEGEL SO FAR

This tour through Hegel's dialectic is all fine and well, but what does it tell us about his theory of the imagination at this stage in his thinking? A more in-depth account follows in Fragment 20, which I discuss below. But so far, what can be said?

We have moved from Hegel's earlier view, which he shared with Schelling. That view was of the imagination as the Absolute's sundering of itself into subject and object, a sundering that happened at different levels or *Potenzen*. Now we are to understand the imagination as the ground principle in any identity, without asserting any identity to be that of the Absolute. Furthermore, Hegel has moved closer to a Fichtean view by asserting that any identity is inseparable from consciousness. It is *consciousness* that gives rise to identity. This would lead us to think that we are back with Fichte's notion of the imagination as a wavering movement, a repeating movement of extending out from the subject and being checked. But Hegel differs from Fichte's view in that Hegel does not begin with an absolute Self that posits itself absolutely.

Rather, *identity* is posited. And identity has difference within it. Hegel also differs from a Schellingian view in that he characterizes the difference in identity as nonbeing and temporal change. Neither subject nor object, nor the sundering of the absolute into subject and object, is primary. Hegel's notion of identity therefore avoids slipping into Fichte's absolute Self or into Schelling's Absolute Indifference Point. The truth about identity is that it is dialectical. Since imagination is the core of both Fichte's and Schelling's notion of identity, we must conclude that Hegel's alterations of their view of identity changes the character of imagination. It is neither the activity of the absolute Self as in Fichte, nor the sundering activity of the Absolute as in Schelling. It is the dialectical imagination inherent in identity formation. What that means, exactly, remains to be worked out.

So while Hegel's account avoids a pure subjectivity on the one hand and a pure Absolute on the other, it leaves the role of the imagination still quite unclear. Before we try to give that more clarity, let us look at some potential problems with Hegel's dialectical identity theory so far, and how he might answer them. Then we will go to Fragment 20 to see how the imagination fits into the picture.

PROBLEMS WITH HEGEL'S DIALECTICAL ACCOUNT
IDENTITY SO FAR

Three problems appear to arise from this analysis of Fragment 17. The first problem comes out of the claim that identification requires two temporally distinct moments, such that the assertion can be made that at time two, the object in question is the same as it was at time one. Hume would interject here that there is no way to get beyond the skepticism that this difference in time allows; that the only way we can know the identity is through holding the *memory* of the object as it was in time one before our mind's eye and comparing it to the object in time two. (Derrida's notion of *différance* is the assumption that it is never the same the second time.)

Hegel's account of identity here does not try to solve that skepticism, it tries to show what is going on that allows that skepticism to take place. And what allows it is the difference in time. So on the one hand, Hegel is unwilling to solve the problem of skepticism by simply adopting an analytic notion of identity, in which all temporal change and the opposition of subject and object are irrelevant. On the other hand, he is unwilling to take the critical idealist position that the object is "phenomenal," mind-dependent, and that its identity is a result of an a priori unity of apperception operating categorically upon the manifold of intuition.

Instead, Hegel wants to witness the process of identification, to get underneath the structures that otherwise explain away contradiction. He wants to be a witness to the contradiction inherent in identity, to exhibit how identity is always a suppression of difference. Fragment 17 shows consciousness *to be* the generation of identity through contradiction and the suppression of that contradiction: "the single [being] as self-identical, or its other-being, its nonidentity made identical with itself."

Secondly, it might be asserted that, in our description, we have assumed the existence of an epistemological structure, and that memory is central to identity formation. The objection looks something like the following: We have seen that "being identified" involves suppression of potential differences. We have also seen that the suppression of difference presupposes favoring unity over difference. We can only conceive the unity over against the differences because we *remember* and compare the past with the present. So, without memory there would be no identity. But "memory" is itself an object of consciousness in that we isolate its activity, determine its identity as that activity, over against other activities. Insofar as memory is self-identical, it has identity in so far as it is *identified*. But we have shown that any identity can only be identified through the use of memory. Thus, the very "object" (memory) that we use to explain the process is itself a product of the process. It would seem, therefore, that we cannot get outside of the structure by which we identify the elements of that very structure, and therefore we really don't have any reliable explanatory tools. We just have end products that characterize the world and our mind's activities according to their own imaged activities.

Before I answer the second problem, let me introduce the third one, since it is related to the second. The third problem is the following. The rawness of Hegel's exhibition of consciousness as identity maker, does not save him from the criticism that his account of consciousness is cooked up. It is cooked up in a logic, the identity of which has not been accounted for, even on Hegel's own terms. After all, Hegel's logic of identity suppresses an important difference, namely, the analytic view of identity. Any account of consciousness that suppresses that difference will be one-sided. Hegel's epistemology is therefore circular.[15]

Now let us try to answer these problems. The solutions to the second and third problems lie within the objections themselves. What these objections cannot deny is that Hegel's logic of identity is self-identical by virtue of suppressing difference, and this act of suppression is exactly what Hegel says is necessarily involved in identity making. In the analytic view of identity, change is not viewed as contradiction. In the analytic view, change is viewed rather as an inessential property of the object. The changing properties are accidental to the object's identity. But that view suppresses the view that change *is* essential to the object's identity. So the analytic *identification* of identity suppresses differing views of what identity making is. The advantage of Hegel's view is that it recognizes suppression of difference, and it recognizes it as the cornerstone of anything of which we are conscious.

The first objection (skepticism) is right in that it is not enough to say that consciousness *is* the principle of identity, nor is it enough to witness the process of identity construction as Hegel does in Fragment 17. There must be an investigation of the kinds of identities we have assumed are at work in that process. And Hegel does give those needed, dialectical exhibitions of the epistemological structures (including memory and imagination) in the fragments that follow Fragment 17. Hegel also develops them in his later *Geistesphilosophie* lecture series. Those investigations should solve the problem of skepticism by refining the dialectical structure to the point where skepticism itself is included in the process. In doing so, those investigations also solve the two other problems: the problem of what the faculties are, and the problem of the circularity of Hegel's argumentation. We must therefore move onto those investigations to assess them.

At this point we can conclude, however, that the advantages of having understood Fragment 17 are enormous. Because of Fragment 17, we henceforth never escape *knowing* that, according to Hegel, whatever we investigate will be self-identical because of its movement as consciousness. Further, when we investigate so-called "faculties" of the mind, we cannot escape bearing witness to the process of identifying such faculties: that is, according to Hegel, we never get out of the circle of consciousness, even when it is the structures of consciousness that we are analyzing. Fragment 17 is, therefore, an essential lesson in identity. It is within its logic that the rest of Hegel's philosophy of spirit takes place.

Our labor so far has been necessary in order to get into the "spirit" of Hegel.[16] Hegel is trying to (get us to) *think* identity, to go through the movement of identity. It is passages such as Fragment 17 that highlight how much more involving Hegel's dialectic is than Fichte's descriptive one.

Fragment 17 has helped us see in what way thought is no longer simply about determinate concepts, but is itself an infinite process of identification. The determinacies are not themselves finite objects of thought a priori, they are fixed into being such by thought, and that is part of the *logos* that thinking is: the *logos* that thinking is, is a dialectical process of identification.

Fragment 17 is worthy of attention for another reason: it goes on to provide us with the condensed development of an absolute singularity (*absolute Einzelnheit*) into *das Volk*. In other words, it renders explicit that it is *consciousness* that develops into *Geist*:

> In so far as we are cognizant of the *organization* of the spirit, we do not regard consciousness as the merely inner aspect of the individuals. . . . Instead, because we recognize consciousness generally, according to its concept, as the absolute union of singularity and the determinate concept, we take cognizance of its organic (*organisierenden*) moments too, in the way that they are on their own account as moments of the absolute consciousness, not as something which is merely, in the form of the individual, one side of the absolute consciousness. (*FirstPhil* 209; *G1* 188)

CONCLUSION

Fragment 17 helps us to see a transition that has taken place in Hegel's thinking between 1801 and 1803. Instead of a sundering absolute identity, we have a dialectical identity which cannot be separated from thought. Identity is not static, nor is it merely an act of some preexisting conscious self. It is a judgment that involves time, and that is constitutive of the self. It involves raising intuition to positive universality. Higher levels of cognitive functioning than intuition are involved, namely, memory and imagination.

Now we need to see how these dialectical beginnings play themselves out as the dialectical imagination in the *Geistesphilosophie* 1803–04 lectures. We will see that the negative moment I have described above and that is central to the process of identification, is the imagination. I will offer my conclusions about the successes and failures of this dialectical imagination, as well as some reflections on the shift in Hegel's thinking I have discussed so far, at the end of the next chapter.

CHAPTER 3

The Dialectical Imagination

(*Geistesphilosophie* 1803–04)

In this chapter I continue to look at the *Geistesphilosophie* of 1803–04. Instead of focusing on Fragment 17, I want now to turn to his discussion of the imagination in later fragments of that work. In this 1803–04 lecture series, Hegel has advanced to a dialectical view of identity. This allows him to offer a better account of the imagination than he could in his two earlier works. The central advance is that Hegel looks at the role of the imagination in our conscious experience, and thus as a function of our dialectical identity making, rather than as the sundering act of the Absolute. The problem, however, is that he muddies his description by not clearly differentiating between a dialectical account and a descriptive one. That is, because of his dialectical account, he is unable to get outside of the imagination enough to describe it adequately; and his attempt to describe it compromises the clarity of his dialectical method.

In this chapter I examine the dialectical imagination in detail and highlight its advantages and problems. After that we can advance to the solution to these problems and to Hegel's most successful account of the imagination in his later works.

First let me outline the significant contents of the fragments leading up to Hegel's discussion of the imagination.

The Dialectical Imagination: _Geistesphilosophie 1803–04_

A) Consciousness→	a) Speech→	Imagination:→	i) Space/Time
B) The Negative	b) The Tool		ii) Universality: Positive & Negative
C) The People (_das Volk_)	c) Possession		(_bestehende/vergehende_ Consciousness)
	& the Family		iii) Theoretical and Practical Consciousness
			(_verstehende_ Consciousness)

The outline in the second part of Fragment 17 indicates the place of the imagination within the grand picture. That is, the imagination is located within the development of consciousness from a single mind into the spirit of a people (_das Volk_). The next fragments either help us to understand the method of that development or give us an overview of it. Thus, Fragment 18 provides insight into the process of _Aufhebung_ (sublation). That process is the movement of consciousness throughout the entire development. Fragment 19 gives the overview of the _Geistesphilosophie_.[1] In Fragment 20 we enter the development itself. The first power (_Potenz_) indicated in Fragment 20 is the dialectical development of the primary dialectic (consciousness in general) into tool-using consciousness. The first tool is speech. It is in Fragment 20, within this first _Potenz_, just before his discussion of memory and speech, that Hegel introduces and discusses the imagination.

The development in Fragment 20 of the moments of the first _Potenz_ might appear, in a general way, to be a compressed version of Kant's "Transcendental Aesthetic" and "Transcendental Deduction of the Categories" in Kant's _Critique of Pure Reason_. As in Kant, Fragment 20 begins with Sensation (_Empfindung_) and moves to intuition (_Anschauung_). As with Kant, the discussion about intuition is a discussion centered upon consciousness as space and time. Then, like Kant, Hegel discusses the reproductive imagination (_die Einbildungskraft_). But this comparison with Kant does not take us any farther. First, memory, which follows upon imagination in Hegel's text, does not get discussed by itself by Kant; and second, the nature of consciousness and its medium—reflection—is profoundly different in Hegel and in Kant. For Hegel, as we saw in Fragment 17, consciousness is generated out of the opposition of a primary dialectic that in itself does not stabilize into a fixed schema for the understanding. We must move through the practical trial of really being the temporally changing consciousness of a given identity. Kant, however, by taking the position of critical appraisal, investigates the components of the intuitive consciousness theoretically, without the practical trial of really being such a (temporally changing) consciousness.[2]

Alongside this development of sensation-intuition-imagination-memory is the development of the products of consciousness: signs and names. Signs are the product of the reproductive, imaginative consciousness, and names are the product of the consciousness that has memory. These products are important not only for understanding the necessity underlying the transitions from sensation to memory, but for understanding how language arises. If language is to arise, consciousness must develop from the mere *aufhebende Begriffe* (superseding concept) of space becoming time becoming space and so on, through a series of increasingly complex *Aufhebungen*.

According to Hegel, consciousness is that which can reproduce individual moments and spaces from a previous time and a different place.[3] Its activity in so doing is the imagination. While this echoes Kant's view that the imagination is that which can call forth images of sensible objects that are not present,[4] it is unlike Kant's imagination since the conditions of the image being there in first the place differ in Hegel by virtue of their arising dialectically.

Now we can turn to the details.

EXEGESIS OF THE PASSAGES ON THE IMAGINATION IN THE
GEISTESPHILOSOPHIE

One can divide the text into two sections. The first section concerns intuition and the transition to the imagination. As we will see in more detail in a moment, in this first section the imagination is both theoretical and practical, both enduring and disappearing, its object both universal and particular, both time and space, both universally positive and universally negative, both being and not being. In other words, we see the emergence of what I call Hegel's dialectical dovetailing imagination. In the second section, we see how the imagination's dovetailing leads to a loss of objectivity, a kind of spiraling downward into complete subjectivity. That spiraling is only turned around later, through another transition.

Section One

I begin with the first division in the first section. It concerns intuition and the transition to the imagination. Hegel introduces the imagination in this first division as follows. I have divided the citation according to the main propositions.

> It [consciousness] does not intuit Space and Time as such,
> 1) they [Space and Time] are universal and empty, higher idealities in themselves, concepts

A 2) but it intuits them only as both being and not being qua universal; [being] when it posits them as singular particularized [contents] as filled [time and space];

B 3) [not being] because even while space and time are the positive universal [side] of consciousness, it makes them at the same time immediately and formally the opposite of themselves[5] and particularizes them;

A+B 4) that being of consciousness [i.e., its positing space and time] is just as much theoretical, passive, as it is practical;

5) the theoretical side consists in its being in the form of positive universality, and the practical in its being simultaneously in negative universality, and particularizing this universality itself.

6) *This form of consciousness is empirical imagination*;

7) *as positive universality, intuition* is in the continuity of time and space generally; but at the same time [empirical imagination is] breaking it up, and turning it into determinate singular beings, that is making it into filled pieces of time and space. (*FirstPhil* 219)[6]

The first thing that should be said of this obscure passage is the following. Hegel is offering a description of this process of consciousness, rather than a practical experience of it as in Fragment 17. This, however, does not make it easier to understand. Since his description is so difficult, let me summarize what I think is going on, and then rewrite the passage more clearly.

To begin with, Hegel has indicated that the object under investigation is consciousness qua empirical imagination. It is also clear that this form of consciousness involves time and space.[7] Now let us look in detail at the passage.

Empirical consciousness is "filled" times and spaces. But it is also the positive and negative universalities of Time and Space. So on the one hand, consciousness has the experience of times and spaces. For example, this time in which I am writing and this space which my computer takes up. On the other hand, these filled times and spaces are the "positive universality of times and spaces." The way to get from positive universal times and spaces to the particulars, involves what Hegel is calling "negative universality." Stepping back for a moment, we note that it is not hard to understand time and space in terms of experienced particular times and spaces. What is difficult is understanding them as positive and negative universalities. What are they and what is the difference between positive and negative universality? How are universal time and space related to the particular times and spaces?

One answer might be that time and space are recognized by empirical consciousness, at a theoretical level, to be universals, but that, practically, consciousness experiences time and space positively, that is, *through* their positive universality, *as* particulars. This answer blends both inductive and Kantian perspectives: the positive universalities are arrived at by induction, and yet they are also the forms through which the particulars are seen. This explanation, however, does not work.

It does not work, for in 1), Hegel specifies that empirical consciousness does not cognize the idealities of Time and Space. So empirical consciousness is not concerned with an induction of multiple times into the universal notion of time (or multiple spaces into the universal notion of space). Instead, he writes that consciousness intuits time and space each as both "being and not being." What could that possibly mean?

To answer that question we can recall our discussion of it in Fragment 17. There we saw that positive universality is the unreflected concept of identity. That is, it is a single being that is taken up into the mind. In that process there is no awareness of the dialectic between being and nonbeing that that "taking up" involves. Whatever identity it be that we have thus taken up, it is a universal in the sense of being both unity and multiplicity.

Thus, if a time is taken up into the mind, it thereby has become a positive universality. Time as positive universality is both a unity and a multiplicity. It is a unity insofar as it is the universal of multiple times. It is a multiplicity insofar as it is actually particular, filled times. The same is true of space.

But how does this translate into the being and not being of time?

The being of time is the particularized time. It is also any particularized time taken up into positive universality. But the being of any particular time depends on the not being of itself qua positive universality of time, for that time qua positive universality stands for all times and therefore is not the being of the time qua particular. The time qua particular has its being only insofar as it is not itself as a positive universality. Furthermore, the particular, filled time also only exists as particular by not being other times—both in the sense of not standing for them, and of not being them. It negates them. What gives being to time is therefore a suppression of positive universality and of other particular time-identities.

For a particular time to be time, it must both be positive universality and yet negate that aspect of itself as well as all other times. If it is not a positive universality, it is not conceptually unified, but is rather an indiscernible part of an undifferentiated stream; on the other hand, if a particular time is not differentiated from its positive universality and all other possible or actual times, the particular time is not determined. Therefore, there is a necessary negative activity by which the time becomes a particular time. Positive universality is necessary. So is what Hegel calls negative universality. Negative universality is inherent in the work of positive universality insofar as positive universality negates the particularity of the time, and negative universality is inherent in the work of the particular time insofar as the particular time, to be particular, negates its self as positive universality and negates all other times. In this latter sense, negative universality is the breaking apart or suppression of positive universality in order for a particular time to exist.

But the story does not end here. Positive universality requires the not being of particularity, since as particular limited being, that particularity threatens the unity of the universal structure. That "not being of time" is the positive universality that threatens the reality of the particular time. Thus, positive universality's negation of particularity must be negated by time qua particular. Either way we look at it, the negation of the other is necessary. Since both are *what time is*, both negations are necessary. Yet, again, since both are *what time is*, they contradict each other and make time impossible.

Part of the reason for this apparent impossibility is that so far we have isolated time from space. In the dialectical dance, that cannot be done: space and time determine one another. Let us look at how this occurs.

The dialectical contradictions I have just expressed are not experienced by consciousness as theory in the way that I have just expressed them. Rather, they are experienced as a movement between universal and particular through being and not being. Their dovetailing becomes evident when we realize time and space as the not being of each other, that is, as mutually limiting and determining antitheses, the spiraling dance of empirical imagination. I will explain this more in a moment.

Standing back for a moment, I think that what makes Hegel's sentences so hard to understand is that Hegel is confused in his method of exposition. He is both explaining and bearing witness. Were he to merely bear witness as an empirical consciousness, we would get the first chapter of the *Phenomenology of Spirit*. That is, we would be entrenched in natural consciousness' certainty about its apparently immediate sense experience of "here and now." On the other hand, were he to give merely an explanation, we would get a *dialectical* version of Kant's two forms of intuition in the "Transcendental Aesthetic," not unlike the one I just gave. At this point in Hegel's thinking, he has not sided on one or the other of these methods, so his writing is hard to follow.

Returning to the text, let us go through the moments more carefully. We know from 1) that consciousness does not think of time and space as idealities. In A) Hegel announces the positive universality—the "being"—of times and spaces, which for empirical consciousness arises as appearances. Consciousness experiences singular beings, or filled, particular times and spaces. This makes up one half of the equation. The second half of the equation is that empirical consciousness intuits times and spaces as not being. The two halves are joined as the transition from positive universality to negative universality, from being to not being and back. This is the process that involves what I call dialectical dovetailing. Let us look at the second half of the equation and how the dovetailing starts.

Hegel writes (at B3) that consciousness intuits times and spaces as "[not being] because even while space and time are the positive universal [side] of consciousness, it makes them at the same time immediately and formally the opposite of themselves and particularizes them." There are two ways of reading these lines, and they dovetail.[8]

One is to say that any given time and any given space becomes the opposite of itself. That reading is based on the discussion I have given so far. The second reading is that a given time becomes a given space as its opposite, and vice versa. I'll discuss the two readings one after the other.

On the first reading, Hegel's line B3 means that any given time and any given space becomes the opposite of itself. To explain this we can draw on what we learned in Fragment 17 as well as our discussion above. In B3 it is difference, originally suppressed in the identification of a time or a space, that is at work. Thus, this time in which I write is only the time in which I write to the extent that I suppress all other times or even the changing character of the "now" in which I presently write. Similarly, this space that my computer takes up is identified because all other spaces are negated, including the changing placement of subatomic particles at its limits. On this reading of B3, that suppression, that moment of possibility, is what is introduced when Hegel speaks of time or of space becoming its opposite. The difference is the not-A in between A. This time is only itself because another time—not this time—is not. The same is true of space.

When we cognize positive universality, we suppress difference in favor of the identity. When we cognize those differences (which, in favor of identity, we formally suppressed), then we see the not being in the identity of time or of space. By raising the not being of identity to universality, we cognize negative universality.[9]

It might be argued that we cognize this negative difference only by negating positive universality, and thus that our cognition of negative universality relies on positive universality; it relies on the suppression of difference in favor of a positive cognitive concept—even if it is the concept *of negation*. This is true on an abstract level. Negative and positive universality are the same insofar as each has been identified over against the other. Negative universality can be identified, and as such, it is no other than positive universality. Insofar as it *is* (even if it is only a concept) it has being, which is the character of positive universality. But they have different, if inseparable, functions.[10] Each has one side of the truth: positive universality is the sine qua non of identity; but without negative universality there would be no differentiation, and therefore no identity. A consciousness that can see the two as inevitably intertwined can rise above the immediacy not only of this apparent conceptual contradiction, but also of empirical contradictions. But we are getting ahead.

Positive universality, whether of time, space, of positive universality or of negative universality, implies difference and the negation/suppression of that difference. But it is not only difference in the sense of the multiplicity of times that is suppressed when we consider the unity of time as positive universal. Difference in the *definition of time* as an identity, *for example, how time is not space,* is suppressed. This brings us to a second way to understand B3.

A second reading is that times and spaces become the opposite of themselves in the sense that time becomes space, and space becomes time. Time and space are opposites. This can be seen by looking at the role of change in Hegel's notion of identity.

Change keeps us from the purely analytic notion of identity. As we saw in our discussion of Fragment 17, for Hegel, that change cannot be merely analytically identified. Change is a process inseparable from consciousness. Even in the tautology A = A there is a movement through not-A. That moment of change is a radical contradiction and then a suppression of contradiction in favor of the identity. While it is true that what constitutes our judgment "in favor of identity" is the recognition that the thing is selfsame, that A = A, and while it is true that it is an analytic truth that we are recognizing, the cognitive process by which we arrive at that truth cannot be separated from the moment of change. There has to be movement and comparison, otherwise there is no judgment. Even though the contradiction always appears spatially as a comparison between this here and that there, the actuality of contradiction is fundamentally temporal. All a priori truths for Hegel are synthetic a priori *as well*. Let me explain.

According to Hegel, space is the *Bestehende* (enduring) and time is the *Vergehende* (disappearing). The filled times and spaces both are and are not.[11] Consciousness cognizes each as it does any identity—that is, as both being and not being. But in each changing from being to not being and vice versa, space becomes time, and time becomes space: space as the *Bestehende* (enduring) gives over to time insofar as space is also *vergehende* (disappearing) that is, insofar as space changes. And time as the *Vergehende* is also space insofar as it stands still in the identification of this time (i.e., it is *bestehende*).

What Hegel means in B3 by "becoming their opposites" is that time and space fold into one another, become each other. The enduring disappears, and the disappearing endures.

This second way of understanding B3 brings with it a further dialectic. Were we to privilege an analytic reading here, we would say that it is time and space as ontological entities, apart from consciousness, that become their opposites. But this is only half the truth. It is also true that it is consciousness *as* time and space that processes in this way. For Hegel, the identified time or space is an object of consciousness, but also, each is that by which consciousness comes to be at every moment. Thus, we not only have *bestehende* and *vergehende* moments which turn into each other. We also have consciousness as either *bestehende* or *vergehende* (enduring or disappearing), depending on how it identifies itself in the process. We also have consciousness as changing from being *bestehende* into being *vergehende* and vice versa.[12]

As the *Bestehende* (the enduring), consciousness takes itself to be self-identical, and its attitude is theoretical: times and spaces appear to be changing apart from it. As the *Vergehende* (the disappearing), consciousness is practical; it is the demise of the *bestehende* consciousness. The disappearing is what *determines* positive universality, thus creating time(s) and space(s). Hegel therefore writes of consciousness that "the theoretical side consists in its being in the form of positive universality, and the practical in its being simultaneously in negative universality, and particularizing this universality itself." The enduring, the disappearing of what endured, the enduring of what disappeared, and the disappearing of that, and so forth, is what makes time and space. The process is both theoretical and practical; theory and practice are inseparable.

The dovetailing is thus of four different dimensions: positive universality, negative universality, theoretical consciousness, and practical consciousness. Returning to the citation and my margin indicators there, we get the result: A+B. That is, "that being of consciousness [i.e., its positing space and time] is just as much theoretical, passive, as it is practical." In one way, theoretical consciousness is the spatializing consciousness, and practical consciousness is the active, temporalizing consciousness. In another way, theoretical consciousness is the temporal stream of consciousness, and practical consciousness is the spatializing, breaking up of that temporal stream by determining (submerging itself into) a particular time and space. Put in these terms, we can see all four moments of the dialectic dovetailing.

Hegel concludes that "[t]his form of consciousness is empirical imagination." There is some question in the text as to whether by "this" Hegel means only practical, negative universality, or the whole gambit from the beginning (both positive and negative universality). Since our concern is to understand exactly what the imagination is for Hegel in this text, we must spend some time on this ambiguous comment.

The problem arises because in the German text one must ask whether "*diese* Form" refers to the "latter" (to consciousness as practical, negative universality), or to the whole of what has been described in this passage. Had Hegel used, as the translators do, a semicolon after the word *imagination,* rather than a comma, the second would appear more likely, for what follows is then the fleshing out of the statement in terms of positive and negative universality.

But it is tempting to interpret the empirical imagination along the first line, that is, as only being the practical (*negative universality*). This seems justified given that in 7 Hegel speaks of the *positive universality* as "*intuition*" and not as imagination:

> 7) *as positive universality, intuition* is in the continuity of time and
> space generally; but at the same time [empirical imagination is]
> breaking it up, and turning it into determinate singular beings, i.e.,
> making it into filled pieces of time and space. (*FirstPhil* 219)

Furthermore, while intuition is needed by the empirical imagination, what characterizes the imagination is that it is the negative, limiting (*besondernde*) consciousness.

But finally, I think that there is more reason to understand empirical imagination to be the whole of what has been discussed, rather than just negative universality. Since every new moment contains the previous moments, imagination also contains intuition and its dialectic. The imagination's concept (its dialectical moments taken together) must be the whole dovetailing dialectic, and not just the negative universal moment of practical consciousness.

I conclude, therefore, that empirical imagination is both positive and negative universality: "*diese*" refers to all the moments described in the passage so far. This is not to say, however, that the empirical imagination is aware of what "we" are in its own working. We have made sense of the shape of empirical imagination from an expository distance. So while we can see the dovetailing dialectic, empirical imagination's experience is a dovetailing confusion.

Although the imagination is the whole of the dialectic in that passage, the accent of the imagination clearly falls on the negative. That is, of the two sides of the empirical imagination described above (positive and negative universality, theoretical and practical) what is characteristic of the imagination, and that without which we would have only intuition, is negation, the practical side of consciousness. This is the case in all subsequent versions of Hegel's philosophy of Spirit lectures. This accentuation is clear here when we look more generally at the dialectical movement from intuition to imagination to memory: the imagination is the middle term, and the middle term is always negative. Let us look at the three-part movement from intuition to recollection, and then discuss it in terms of the next phase involving memory.

We recall that in the identification equation A = A, we move from A to not A, and on to A again. If we replace the A with the identity in question in this section of Hegel's philosophical psychology, that is, with theoretical consciousness, then we get the following equation: (1) theoretical consciousness is intuition, (2) is not intuition, (3) is (recollected) intuition. In other words we get (1) intuition, (2) imagination, which is the "not being" of intuition, and (3) the recollection of the intuition as practically and theoretically determined. In the movement of the identity in question, imagination is the practical, negative moment. It breaks up interiorized intuition and reproduces them.

At this point, we have a clear picture of the dialectic involved in Hegel's account of the empirical imagination. The story, however, is not finished. While the passage shows us that empirical consciousness is dependent upon empirical imagination, empirical imagination does not provide all that is needed for empirical consciousness. Without the further process of memory, empirical consciousness is unstable. The confusions that arise in consciousness as a result of not having memory are made clear in the subsequent passages of Hegel's text. There, Hegel describes how imagination without memory is like a dream-state, or insanity.[13] Let us turn to those passages now.

Section Two

The first section has been about intuition and the transition to the imagination. There we saw how the imagination is both theoretical and practical, both enduring and disappearing, its object both universal and particular, both time and space, both universally positive and universally negative, both being and not being. In other words we have seen the emergence of what I am calling Hegel's dialectical dovetail imagination.

In that first section, the practical attitude arose as dominant in the imagination. This only happens at the end of the development. Until then, the dominant side of these experiences is theoretical. The second section is the development of the practical attitude.

In this section, the practical subsumes the theoretical within it. Despite the fact that there is recollection (the ability to recall what has been negated), the character of recollection is not what is dominant. There may be recollection, but there is no memory. What is dominant is the character of negation and change. The result, for consciousness, is a loss of objectivity. There is no stability. In this second section, therefore, Hegel describes how the empirical imagination, when predominantly practical, is lost in subjectivity. Let us look at this in more detail.

We recall that the moment of the *positive universal* is the enduring, theoretical side of consciousness (the *Bestehende*). Our new moment, in which consciousness is subjectively determining, is the disappearing (*Vergehende*) moment of consciousness. Consciousness is free but out of control—there is no abiding unity. It is merely subjective reproduction, without grounding in any unitary principle.

> The determinacy of the sensation, the *this* of time and space, is abolished *in it*, [in subjective reproduction] and their succession and coordination appears as a free one, it is quite contingent (*gleichgültig*) for the universal element; [it is] an active reproducing, since it is this universal element that is particularized.
>
> This *formal being* of consciousness has *no genuine reality, it is something subjective*, it does not exist externally; it only is as the form of the abstract, pure *concept* of infinity, as space and time, the concept of infinity as it immediately is as consciousness; and consciousness as this empirical imagination is a waking or sleeping dream, *empty* and *without truth*, [occurring in human experience] either as permanent derangement, or as a transient state of sickness, when consciousness falls back into the animal organism, and only is as its concept.
>
> This *dumb consciousness* is its *formal being* in its own universal element of infinity . . . (*FirstPhil* 285; *G1* 199)

From a commonsense point of view, Hegel is not saying anything particularly revealing. He is asserting that consciousness locked in imagining is a purely subjective, dreaming, or deranged consciousness. Nevertheless, there is a subtle problem here. Hegel has attempted to derive the moments thus far from a dialectic, without ever falling back onto commonsense notions of space and time, or onto commonsense notions of what is internal or external to consciousness. Indeed, he has been trying to show that these commonsense concepts are fundamentally dialectical. He has shown that commonsense notions of time and space are not self-explanatory and cannot be taken as presuppositions behind or independent of the dialectic.[14] So in the above passage, when Hegel distinguishes "genuine reality" and "external existence" from the consciousness which is "empty . . . without truth" and purely subjective, we cannot simply acknowledge this distinction from a commonsense point of view as one between external time and space, and a deranged internal ordering of time and space. We have to ask what "genuine reality" is, and what the standards for the objective and the "external" time and space are.

No doubt, from the psychological standpoint, the subjectivity we are witnessing is simply a consciousness with an inner world of images, images it can reproduce even if, for now, there is no recognized principle guiding that reproduction. Such a consciousness is the result of the progression from being merely intuitive to being imaginative. Times and spaces are being reproduced such that "their succession and coordination appears as a free one" (*FirstPhil* 285). But the problem remains: What is it free of?

One answer might be, (a) that it is free of the necessity that bound the spaces and times together in the original intuitive consciousness of them. But what is that binding necessity? We cannot simply use commonsense notions of external time and space. Another answer is, (b) that it is free of an internal principle guiding the reproduction, such as a will. But then again, (c) it might be considered free precisely because it is determined only by a will. Or, (d) one might say that the succession and coordination of images appears to be free of *any* guiding principle, whether internal to the mind or external.

The second option seems more likely than the third, since the state is "dream-like," and, normally, we don't attribute free will to our dream states. In fact, we would sooner say that the dream state is *free* precisely *of* our conscious will. One might follow a theory such as that of Freud, whereby the unconscious has a kind of will of its own, a will that is often best understood by analyzing one's dreams. But even if one did subscribe to such a view, it is not likely that one would describe unconscious willing as "free." The term *free,* when applied to subjects, is associated with conscious willing, but here we are dealing with a dream-like state. I think, therefore, that we are better off viewing the term *free* as meaning "free *from*" constraints, rather than being a free will of some sort.

What we will end up uncovering is that the constraints from "outside" are not separable from consciousness. It is one-sided to speak of the freedom as being a freedom *from* something separate from the mind. As we saw in our analysis of Fragment 17, there is no identity separate from consciousness. So if this is an apparent freedom from external constraints, it is in fact a false freedom, since there is no "externality" to consciousness that could singly be constraining it. But we must go through the steps in order to see how this is so.

In order to make the moments clear, we need to make an assumption that in the end will be proven untrue. It is a pragmatically justified assumption because it makes up the false dialectic of this confused consciousness. The false assumption that we need to make is that "free" does mean the absence of an *external* coordination and succession of times and spaces that gets intuited by consciousness. In support of this assumption we could appeal to an earlier passage in the work, in which Hegel writes of intuitive consciousness that its "particularization is just those primary sensible representations" (*FirstPhil* 219).[15] The difference between consciousness as predominantly theoretical and its condition here as predominantly practical, then, would be the difference between the "primary sensible representations" and the imagined ones with whose apparently free succession we are now concerned. So to understand what it means to be free of an external principle, we would figure out this difference between the primary sensible representations and the imagined ones. We could do this by comparing the two sections.

In the first section, what was being determined were times and spaces; these were the filled moments of consciousness. Empirical consciousness was not reflecting on positive universality, it was just using it. *For empirical consciousness*, times and spaces were external to it. The latent or ideal moment was the empty infinity of consciousness (the "*leere Einfachheit*"). It was that which gave unity to the spaces and times. Only "we" were aware of the nature of positive universality (and its inseparability from the activity of consciousness). Empirical consciousness was not aware of this empty infinity. In the second section, in reproductive, imagining consciousness, the empty infinity, the "Universal element of consciousness itself" is what is being determined (*FirstPhil* 219; *G1* 199). In the second section, the latent moment, this element of consciousness, this infinity, is the medium being particularized. Hegel writes, "[t]he *universal* [Form] *that is particularized* is the *universal element* of consciousness itself, its empty infinity as time and space; the recalling *within itself* of intuitions had previously or in another place" (*FirstPhil* 219).[16]

In this folding in upon itself, consciousness is folding back upon objects it had already "taken up" into positive universality; it is folding back on previously, intuitively delimited objects. And it is determining them apart ("freed") from (we assume) their original context. Empirical consciousness (common sense) takes that original context to be external space-time, which it intuited and now freely plays with. But that original context was equally *consciously* organized immediate intuitions. So we are really just seeing an overlap of the process onto itself, only now the material being carved up is *recollected* space-time rather than intuitively "new" space-time. And that recollected space-time is being carved up into imaginatively new space-time, and thus is free of the way in which it was (made into) context the first time around in intuition. But really, all that is being generated are new intuitions, just more heavily mediated by negation and difference—more "imaginative." But as we have seen, that is not to say that the work of the imagination was not present in the first intuitional context making—it was, for both positive and negative universalities must dovetail in the creation of a context. But let us go back to what the experience of this predominantly practical consciousness is.

The subjective imagination experiences conflations and collisions of old intuitions with new ones in its "present" space-time. There is no order that is self-consciously made. The associations are random. One assumes that for such a consciousness there is not even a sense of time passing linearly. So it is not necessarily a question of being "free" of new intuitions. It is more a question of being free of the original contextual constraints on old intuitions, and free of any willful or "rational" processing of those old ones in a new context of intuitions that are also organized. The freedom is really only the beginning of freedom. Neither original space-time intuitions nor imaginatively mediated ones are really free. They are just two levels of complexity and mediation.

This completes our exegesis of the sections on the empirical imagination in the *Geistesphilosophie* of 1803–04. But one must ask whether rising up the phenomenological ladder really does make one any more "free," or just more complex. But according to Hegel, consciousness does not necessarily only get more sophisticated dream states as it goes up the ladder of complex space-time folds. It can and indeed eventually does develop reason. There is something specific that is causing the "dream-like" state at this and other levels of consciousness: it is the lack of consciousness of difference. The lack at this dream-like stage is a result of, and a further cause of, unconscious suppression of difference. By difference I mean both context difference (e.g., this time is not that time) and definitional difference (e.g., time is not space). Without reflection on those differences (which is essentially a reflection on the process of identification) consciousness is not self-consciously aware, which is the same as saying that it is not open to possibility. It persists in dream states. Without that openness, it is hard for reason to develop. But the more complex consciousness gets, the harder it is to keep the fact of differences out of reflection. For Hegel, in the long run, reason prevails because its essence has difference in it. We first see this in the dialectical imagination.

Looking ahead in the text, we find that what allows consciousness to have insight into difference is another empirical consciousness. It is in the effort to *communicate* that objectivity is formed. Ultimately, objectivity is expressed and understood information; it is language. The reflective determinations become *interpreted* moments of time and space.

According to Hegel, consciousness can only raise itself out of the merely subjective by making use of its reproductive power to "indicate" something that is understood by another person in his/her linguistic community. At first it fails, because it uses only signs. (Unlike in the later works, in the early *Geistesphilosophie* a sign is a product of the imagination which has not been reflected into itself through another person, so the sign does not break out of the subjective entirely.) The two sides of consciousness—the *Bestehende* and the *Vergehende*—only occur properly developed and together once time and space are externalized again in such a way as to be both objectively and subjectively taken up, that is, once consciousness is language. At that point we have not only the *Bestehende* and *Vergehende* but these two sublated and preserved as the understanding—the *Verstehende*. According to Hegel, the first *true* universal is the name of an object, and communication is the basis of "genuine reality."

We can see from this discussion that reason, for Hegel, is not a correspondence of theory with external time and space, nor is it a purely practical determination of times and spaces according to will. As we have seen, time and space are dovetailing, phenomenological developments of the dialectical imagination. Reason develops as a sophisticated insight into, and development of, this conscious, historical, material process.

CONCLUSION

By way of conclusion I would like to do three things. I want to take up again the discussion of chapter 2 concerning Hegel's shift in his view of logic. I do this in the light of the above investigation, and in relation to Fichte. Secondly, I want to comment briefly on the shift by comparing the starting points of the 1803 *System der Sittlichkeit* and the 1803 *Geistesphilosophie*. Finally, I note some of the problems with which the latter work leaves us.

The shift from Hegel's Shellingian phase in *Faith and Difference* to his view in the 1803 *Geistesphilosophie* can be characterized in terms of a new view of Fichte's project.

The move that Hegel made completely by 1807 is one from the more substance-based ontology of Schelling's Identity Philosophy, to a kind of Fichtean subject ontology. It is almost as if, even in this first 1803–04 *Geistesphilosophie*, Hegel began trying to rewrite the "Deduction of Presentation" section of Fichte's 1794 *Wissenschaftslehre*. In that work Fichte had shown how movement, or more precisely time, must be not only *recognized* in a critical deduction of representation: it must be *actual* in it. That is, for Fichte, the self *posits* itself and also *limits* itself by positing something beyond the self, thus being (generating) the three moments of time. We can see in the *Geistesphilosophie* dialectic that Hegel has taken this up: he wants us to *experience* the moments of consciousness' development. Hegel agreed with Fichte's view that "the moments must rise before our eyes."[17]

But as we noted earlier, Fichte is blinded by his picture of the future: the future for Fichte is a line extended *infinitely* outward. The self's striving to complete itself in that future is misguided, and, perhaps more importantly, the content presented in the here and now is rendered inessential. Hegel offers a more adequate model.

Hegel adopts Fichte's logic, but he rejects the loss of content in Fichte's casting of that logic. In the long run, what Hegel succeeds in realizing (and what Fichte did not) is, first, the *degree* to which the self must lose itself in its posited other, and second, that a fully dialectical account of experience is therefore also a *history* of it. While Fichte introduced time into critical philosophy, Hegel introduces history.

For Fichte, the imagination's wavering creates space and time.[18] But Fichte's reconstruction is only ever in the service of moving beyond that present condition. We might say that Hegel's final "version" of Fichte's "Deduction of Presentation" is the phenomenologically rich *Phenomenology of Spirit*. Hegel eventually writes a pure logic in 1812, but not before he reconstructs the *content* of experience (its history) in the "Science of Experience" (as the original title of the *Phenomenology* was given) in 1807.

Fichte's account of the movement is both descriptive and dialectical. His overlaying of description onto the dialectic is confusing. Hegel's dialectic is based on a more profoundly dialectical movement of thought in and through its other. Initially this is equally confusing: we see quite early on the degree to which Hegel is willing to forgo descriptive eloquence and clarity in order to follow the movement of thought (witness Fragment 17). And when Hegel writes his lectures on *Geistesphilosophie* in 1803 and in 1805, the logic-phenomenological division is still not yet completely clear in his mind. To the extent that during that time Hegel remains unclear about the difference between explanation and the way one gets the reader to think dialectically, he falls short just as Fichte did.

The shift from viewing logic as finite to viewing it as infinite is, as noted already, a step away from Schelling in the direction of Fichte. It is a shift away from the view expressed in *Differenzschrift* and in *Faith and Knowledge*—both works in which he was critical of Fichte. In other words, Hegel is no longer satisfied with getting beyond the standpoint of subjective reflection by submerging subjective reflection in the absolute abyss of indifference. He has shifted toward a view, clearly expressed later in the preface of the *Phenomenology of Spirit*, that reflection is the *medium* of consciousness; that determinate reflection is always already infinite. The risk of ontologizing the indifference point, the abyss, is thereby sublated. The Absolute Night is sublated as much as—and no more than—Fichte's infinite future.

We see the shaky beginnings of this view in the *Geistesphilosophie* of 1803–04. Here Hegel's genesis of consciousness is dialectical *from the start*. We cannot posit the indifference point as a singular sundering absolute *in separation from reflection*. Consciousness is from the start the "concept of the union of the simple with infinity" (*FirstPhil* 206).[19]

So while Hegel's reconstruction, which is the present's rational self-superseding (its process of *Aufhebung*), sounds close to what Fichte was saying about the *Anstoss*, there is an important difference: in Hegel, completion occurs in the process, not in some unattainable future. The *Anstoss* is not a call to the self to limit itself and then reach beyond that limit: that picture of things only arises if one takes a certain moral view. Rather, the *Anstoss* is the negative determination *of* Being. The "of" here cuts both ways. The genitive is generative: "genitive" comes from the Latin *genetivus* which comes from the Greek *genesis*. It is the originary process of being speculative—indeed of Speculative Being. The moral call to strive after speculative completion is only one shape it can take.

Furthermore, Hegel's subjective consciousness does not succeed in attaining objectivity merely by virtue of this unconscious genitive within it: it must be checked by another consciousness. Although some commentators have tried to argue that the *Anstoss* in Fichte has to do with another consciousness,[20] in Hegel it is explicitly the case that consciousness cannot move from a merely subjective (even sign-making subjective) position to objectivity without communication with another consciousness.

Our focus has, so far, been on the beginnings of that story. We have stayed with an analysis of the empirical consciousness. And we have seen that, while the grand picture may be easily summarized, the details are, in 1803–04, still murky.

Part of the murkiness has to do with the shift in Hegel's thinking which we have been discussing. In other words, it has to do with the collapse of the difference between the logic of reflection and Being. On the one hand that collapse has been a good one, for it is no doubt what gives rise ultimately to the possibility of phenomenological *system*. Our knowledge is, for Hegel, *of* the real. As Hegel later writes: "[W]hat is rational is actual and what is actual is rational."[21] But on the other hand, it is predominantly the initial confusion of that collapse (of reflection and Being) that we experience in the 1803–04

Geistesphilosophie fragments. We experience the collapse in the not-quite distinctly phenomenological, not-quite distinctly logical, not-quite distinctly "philosophy of spirit" account of the forms of consciousness. The "wavering" of the imagination is all too often a waffling. But the essential shift has been made: Hegel henceforth begins with *consciousness*.

This completes our analysis of how Hegel's shift has been a shift toward Fichte.

The shift in Hegel's thinking is also marked by a difference in the starting point of two of Hegel's 1803 writings on spirit. We recall Hegel's passage about "reconstruction" in *Faith and Knowledge*, in a section in which he criticizes Fichte's ethics. We noted in passing that for Hegel this reconstruction was not separable from the ethical, from Spirit. We can now look at the difference between the starting point of Hegel's first attempt at a reconstruction in the *System der Sittlichkeit* of 1803, and that of the 1803 *Geistesphilosophie* reconstruction.

The central difference between the two works has to do with the role of consciousness. In the *System der Sittlichkeit* it is not mentioned. That work focuses first on natural ethical relations and then on the development of that into the levels of government and classes (*Stände*). The focus in the *Geistesphilosophie*, however, begins with consciousness and develops *that* into *das Volk*.[22] Hegel is concerned with ethical forms as dialectical developments arising from the concept of consciousness as the ground of Spirit. The *Geistesphilosophie* 1803–04 is thus a progression from consciousness (the most fundamental form of *Geist*) to social forms of *Geist*, such as the family. So despite the fact that both works develop through three moments, the second moment being the negative one, the two have very different starting principles.

H. S. Harris notes the fact that "the 'concept' of spirit is *consciousness*, is not mentioned in the *System of Ethical Life*."[23] This absence of consciousness in the *System der Sittlichkeit* suggests that it is only with these lectures on *Geistesphilosophie* that Hegel begins to think in the Fichtean terms we have discussed above. Furthermore, after this work, Hegel is unwilling to abandon the standpoint of consciousness.[24]

I would like now to turn to some of the problems left unsolved by what I have called the dialectical imagination of the 1803 *Geistesphilosophie*. First, in this work Hegel begs the question: How can we have a speculative genesis of imagining consciousness when we cannot get to a point in consciousness that is free of the very reflective determination for which we are trying to account?

Part of the problem is that, though Hegel succeeds in separating out the dialectical moments and in showing their movement, the dialectical moments still lack clarity. Part of *that* problem is due to the fact that Hegel has not given an adequate account of the negativity involved in this genesis of the imagining consciousness. In this 1803–04 work, Hegel is so keen to develop the Concept (consciousness) in its progress toward the universality of language, that he carries us into the night of the ideality of reflection and tries to show us from inside how the filled times and spaces of intuition are reproduced in it. But then he switches from this phenomenological perspective into that of the philosophical observer of consciousness, inviting us to see how subjective that level of consciousness is. The objectivity that makes our switching over possible is the very objectivity that is missing in the subjective imagination consciousness. But it is also an objectivity that makes a genuine taking up of that earlier subjectively imagining standpoint difficult. Without more clarity about the nature of objectivity, "we" the readers are at risk of only *apparently* being able to take *either* standpoint—of the subjective, reproductive imagining consciousness, or of the philosopher looking at how crazy such a consciousness is. Thus, while the right way to understand the imagination may be to understand it as a dialectical identity maker, Hegel has not figured out how to give a clear account of it. The Hegel of 1803 has not yet achieved Speculative Science, nor has he developed the method of getting us to it that will be called *The Phenomenology of Spirit*.

In the more reflective-oriented account of the 1805–06 *Geistesphilosophie* we will see a more powerful account of that inwardization—the first negative moment which gives rise to externality in the first place, and which thereafter works its way through the moments. In Hegel's later working-through of these moments, the negative is given more definition as the Night, and later still as the nightly mine (*nächtlicher Schacht*) of reflective determination. Hegel thereby defines more clearly the dialectical moments involved. Despite this, however, the tension between, on the one hand, our phenomenological following of the moments, and on the other, the logic of the genesis, persists within the structure of his *philosophy* of Spirit, even in the 1830 version. The only place it is ever really overcome is in the *Phenomenology of Spirit*.

Let us move on now to a discussion of the 1805 Inwardizing Imagination.

CHAPTER 4

The Inwardizing Imagination

(*Geistesphilosophie* 1805–06)

Hegel's 1805–06 psychology lectures[1] develop the role of the imagination more clearly. He discusses the imagination in terms of time and space, the animal (body), and subjectivity. Most importantly, he identifies time with "inwardizing" (*zurücktreten*). Inwardizing is the negative moment in the dialectic of identity making. From here on in Hegel's thought, this negative moment is a central characteristic of the imagination.

The negative moment is a temporal one. This has two implications for his theory of the imagination at this stage. One is that the spatial aspect is not essential yet. The spatial aspect is identified with the lateral spread of the meaning of a word, its intention. It does become essential later (see next chapter). But here the spatial is not predominant, the temporal is. The second implication of this predominance of the temporal, is that we are dealing again with a kind of plunge into the night. It is reminiscent of the *mise en abyme* of the Sundering Absolute. But rather than an ontological indifference point vaguely operating at the heart of being and cognition, here we have a dialectical negative. This night-time is the sine qua non of the intellect's dialectical development: it is determined by and determining of the increasingly complex levels of cognition from intuition to the ability to communicate.

The lectures are divided into a discussion of intuition, recollection, and the beginnings of language. Hegel refers to these three moments as "Imagination in General." But it is not surprising, given the role of the night-time here, that he

55

also refers to them as "the dreaming spirit," and contrasts them with the awakened, fully articulate, communicating spirit.

In this chapter, I begin by discussing the place of the imagination in the text of the *Geistesphilosophie* of 1805–06. Then, to clarify Hegel's view, I compare it with Aristotle's notion of imagination. This focuses on time as the negative, inwardizing movement of the mind essential to producing images. Recollection is the next stage of development. For Hegel, recollection is of "the familiar." But recollection lacks the externality needed for there to be language. It is signs that allow for transition to language. A sign, for Hegel, is an image that stands for its history, stands for its recollections. Developed through memory, signs indicate a transition to shared sign *systems*. My analysis as a whole shows that for Hegel, communication systems require the negative movement and stored images of "the dreaming spirit" for their constant awakening.[2]

OUTLINE OF THE STRUCTURE OF THE TEXT AND THE PLACE OF THE IMAGINATION IN IT

Let us begin by situating our discussion within the text of the *Geistesphilosophie* of 1805–06. The basic triadic development of Hegel's notes are given in bold headings by Hegel. For clarity I have isolated them schematically here:[3]

The Inwardizing Imagination: *Geistesphilosophie 1805–06*

A) Spirit Acc. to its Concept→ a) Theoretical Knowing (i.e., <u>Intelligence</u>)→			
B) Objective Spirit	b) The Will	**A) Imagination in General:**[4]	**B) Language (*Sprache*):**
C) The Constitution	c) Objective Spirit	**i) Intuition/Imagination (Images)**	**vi) Names (Tones)**
		ii) Recollection (The Familiar)	**v) Memory (Order)**
		iii) To Mean (*bezeichnen*) (Signs)	**vi) Understanding (Knowl.)**

Our concern with the imagination places us in the first overall moment, Spirit according to its Concept.[5] The discussion of the imagination, or "dreaming spirit," occurs in the transitions of the Intelligence. The section on Intelligence is Hegel's development of theoretical knowledge, which, as in his 1803–04 lectures, is for him the development of the epistemological foundations of language.

Let me say a few words here about the general structure and problematic of the intellect. In the intellect we have two subtriads: A) Imagination in General (*die Einbildungskraft*; dreaming spirit/*traümende Geist*), and B) Language (*Sprache*; awakened spirit/*erwachende Geist*). These correspond to two powers: the representing power of the imagination[6] and the name-giving power. The name-giving power is the "first creative power which spirit uses."[7] A third power is that of the Understanding, and it brings in the transition within language to Will.

The problem being worked out in the first of these subtriads (Imagination in General) is that of creating an inner world of representations (images) that are meaningful (to oneself). The problem that *leads to* Language is that of making that meaningfulness universal in the sense of communication (with others). The problem addressed *in* Language (the second triad) is how that order comes about which is required for something to make objective sense: in other words, Hegel tries to develop necessity in communication. This necessity gives rise to the understanding, which is the conclusion to the section on the intellect and the beginning of the section on the Will.

The main focus of the present investigation is the first moment of the first triad Imagination in General ("the dreaming spirit"). Hegel's thought in these discussions reveals the importance of spirit's depth and traces to the process of awakened communication. Before I begin an investigation of these moments, a general comparison of this text with the 1803–04 *Geistesphilosophie* is in order.

THE 1805–06 NOTES IN CONTRAST WITH THE 1803–04 *GEISTESPHILOSOPHIE*

Hegel uses a different procedure in 1805–06 than in his earlier *Geistesphilosophie* lectures of 1803–04. Not only are Hegel's lecture notes on the *Geistesphilosophie* much clearer, many of the divisions established here—including some of the ways in which the imagination is handled—are kept twenty years later in the *Encyclopedia Philosophy of Spirit*.[8]

Hegel moves more quickly in the 1805 notes to a discussion of imagination: the first overarching development is not intuition but rather "the representing imagination in general" ("*[die] vorstellende Einbildungskraft überhaupt*" [*G2* 171]) with intuition as *its* first moment. It may be safely assumed, I think, that Hegel chose the imagination as the first development because it is the first reflexive movement of consciousness and thus what properly makes it conscious. This may also be an explanation as to why the derivations of consciousness with which he began in the fragments of the 1803–04 *Geistesphilosophie* are missing. In other words, in 1805 the first development is premised on how we relate to the things we sense, rather than how we might unravel the basic categories operative in any action of consciousness. It may be, therefore, that he has realized that the first movement is best characterized not by the oppositions of the understanding (of its categories) such as unity and multiplicity, but by the oppositions constitutive of the imagination (images in space and time, inwardizing and externalizing into recollected familiarity, and through that process the generation of significations). It is tenable given the general character of his speculative philosophy subsequent to this work: the beginning of the 1807 *Phenomenology of Spirit* is "Sense-certainty," the 1812 *Logic* begins with "Being pure Being,"[9] and the 1830 *Geistesphilosophie* begins with intuition and its first moment, which is feeling—something immediately present to us, not an abstract category such as unity.

The negation that makes for the mediation of such immediate starting points first arises in the moment of the imagination. So it is ultimately the truth of the imagination that is revealed and brought forward through the other moments. How this is so will become clearer as we go.

Also absent here in the 1805–06 notes is the elaboration in the 1803 manuscript of the productive imagination as a merely subjective (deranged or dreaming) consciousness. Hegel mentions that such a consciousness is "*träumende*" but he does not develop it as such. His concern in the 1805 notes is more with the logic of the moments, so in his discussion of the imagination proper he spends less time looking at the world through the glasses of the imaginative subject. He moves quickly to his general goal of showing how we get from immediate consciousness to consciousness of the truth and consciousness in truth or "*Geist*."[10]

INTUITION AND THE PROBLEM OF THE BEGINNING

The general problematic of subjective spirit—moving from immediate consciousness to consciousness of the truth—is articulated in the opening paragraph of the notes. Hegel distinguishes between intuition, in which what simply is there (*das Seiende*) is immediate, and *Geist* or the truth of that perception. "Spirit is this [knowledge of a being] through mediation with itself; spirit is only in suspending and superseding what (it) immediately is—in the retreat (return, *zurücktretend*) from the immediate" (*G2* 171). Spirit is only in this inwardizing.

The truth of the perception is Platonic to the extent that the intuited object is the last, not the first thing to occur, even though what appears is at first taken to be what is there prior to any thinking about it. But it is not Platonic in the sense that, for Hegel, the result is also the beginning. *Geist* is not separable from the making of an intuited thing: the merely immediate *Anschauung* is what is there when we have forgotten how we got (it) there. It is only through *Geist*—the suspending and superseding of being—that we experience something apparently immediate. To see the mediation—the spirit—in the thing (that which went into making the object), we must take the object as the first thing and investigate it.

Hegel chooses the imagination as the first development because, as we will see, he recognizes it to be the first reflexive movement of consciousness and thus what properly makes consciousness what it is. It is the imagination's negative moment, the return into itself, this inwardizing—what Hegel calls the Night—which is at the heart of the apparently immediate starting points of intuition in the first triad. Hegel's failure to see this in 1803 was the main problem in the first *Geistesphilosophie* lectures.

Our concern is thus with what Hegel calls moving from Being to truth: "Being (*Sein*) is the form of immediacy, but it should come to be (*soll*) posited in its truth" (*G2* 171). The move is from the *Allgemein* in form only, to the true universal (*wahrhaft allgemein*).

EXEGESIS OF THE TEXT

The word *imagination* only comes up three times in this section. It comes up once at the beginning in the first moment defining the general realm we are working in, then twice in the third moment: first as clarification again of its general power, and then in a comparison of how the two powers (imagination and name-giving language) differ in taking up their objects.[11]

Imagination in General

Just as in the first *Geistesphilosophie*, Hegel develops intuition in terms of space and time. In the two-paragraph introduction, before we get to the first division, we find ourselves on one side of the dialectic of Space and Time. "I and the thing are in Space" (*G2* 171). Space is "[t]he enduring of the object ... Being .... the abstract pure concept of enduring Being (*des Bestehens*)" (*G2* 171). The word we are translating as "enduring Being" is *das Bestehen*, "that which stands in place." It is upon this stable "over-against" that intuition apparently rests. It is the truth of that over-against that must be thought through and revealed. We know from the last chapter that the stable thing is just as much something that does not stay in place, that it is temporal as well as spatial. That is why, despite Hegel's initial discussion of space here, in the first proper division of the text, (a), Hegel begins with the other side of the dialectic: time.

As we noted already, time is the movement of *Geist* inward. Any movement (away from what is) means a breach in the immediate "nowness" of the enduring object. Such a breach, while establishing spatial difference, is movement and therefore temporal. This negative moment is, as we saw in the earlier *Geistesphilosophie*, that proper to the imagination.

(i) Intuition and the Inwardizing Imagination

As with his earlier lectures, intuition has to do with the dialectical dovetailing of time and space.

Inwardizing as the Space and Time of Intuitions.   In simple intuition, the object has immediate Being, *Sein*. But *Geist* "returns out of this immediacy [of *Anschauung*] into itself, and is for itself" (*G2* 171). It is in the description of this return that Hegel introduces the imagination:

> [I]t sets itself free from this immediacy, distances itself from it at first, it is, like the animal, time, which is for itself, and just as much the freedom of time; this pure Subject, which is free from its content; but also master of it, unlike time and space which are selfless; it goes from this Being out, and sets the latter in itself as a non-being,[12] as a something superseded in general, and in so being it is the representational power of the imagination in general—It is the Self against itself. (*G2* 171–72)

Hegel refers to a space and time as selfless. Selfless space and time would, like any immediate intuition, seem to be independent of our self, to precede cognition in the sense in which the realist takes space and time to be independent of thought. But Hegel is concerned with moving from general universals to the true universals. The *truth* of space and time is a temporal-spatializing dialectic. Without that dialectic, we could not have the general concepts of space and time, let alone the developed cognitive functions that allow us to synthesize such concepts as "selfless space and time."

Let us compare this with Kant's difficult footnote in the *Critique of Pure Reason* at B161 (*CPR* 170–17). Kant distinguishes between the *form of intuition,* which "gives only a manifold," and the *formal intuition,* which "gives unity of representation." He writes that the latter "presupposes a synthesis which does not belong to the senses but through which all concepts of space and time first become possible." One might think that the latter synthesis belongs to the understanding, expressed as or through the transcendental unity of apperception. But Kant writes that "the unity of this *a priori* intuition belongs to space and time, and not to the concept of the understanding." He notes that for clarification we should turn to his ¶24, the paragraph in which the imagination is defined and discussed. But his discussion of the imagination there does not clarify his comments just discussed from B161. The confusion is that Kant has made the synthesis *the condition* of concepts of space and time, and yet he has also made that synthetic a priori unity of intuition *belong* to space and time. Kant's incomplete insight here about the relation of synthesis to time and space is clearly what Fichte and Hegel try to complete, the former with the wavering imagination (which originates space and time), and the latter with the *bestehen/vergehen* dialectic of the Night (which also originates space and time).

So while the passage in Hegel that we are dealing with now is a reworking of the relationship between the commonsense understanding of time and space on the one hand, and a true, dialectical understanding on the other, it is also a reworking of Kant's unclear discussion at B161 of a formal intuition that unifies time and space, and forms of intuition that give us a multitude of times and spaces. By rethinking the activity of the imagination as a dialectic of time and space, a dialectic that is just as much one between theoretic apprehension and practical determination, Hegel is able to clarify that a formal unity of time or space is inseparable from the dialectical multiplicity of times and spaces: the formal unity aspect just privileges the spatial, *bestehende*, theoretic side of the dialectic. It is nothing other than the holding in place of time or space. But that holding in place is none other than the inwardizing, negating activity that gives rise to any time and space in the first place. Then, once the held object is a set of times and spaces that have already been inwardized, what emerges as the changing object inside of the stable form is the play of times and spaces.

The role of the self as a unifying dialectical principle is also central to this discussion. In other words, the difference between Kant's, Fichte's, and Hegel's models of how synthesis, space, and time are related, determines what the self is at this level of cognition. But we must wait until later for that discussion.[13]

Keeping in mind, then, the dialectical nature of time and space for Hegel, we return to Hegel's text. The predominant dialectical moment in the text at this point is the *temporal* side of inwardizing. As we have seen, Hegel identifies this return with the animal state, time; the "freedom of time"; and the pure subject. Let us look at each individually.

Temporal Inwardizing: Inwardizing as the Animal State.   We are in the arena of "the representing imagination in general" (*G2* 171). I once thought that we could explain Hegel's identification of the return with the animal state by looking to Aristotle. I believed this was justified by the fact that in his 1830 *Philosophy of Spirit* Hegel states a clear indebtedness to Aristotle.[14] But Hegel also indicates there the importance of reinterpreting Aristotle's lesson, of "reintroducing unity of idea (*den Begriffe*) and principle into the theory of mind." Therefore, the return which typifies the imagination and which is identified with the animal state, cannot be fully explained by turning to Aristotle. Nonetheless, Hegel's position is clearer if we return to Aristotle and perform the Hegelian reinterpretation.

According to Aristotle, all animals possess imagination since they can (or appear to) dream, and imagine desired food.[15] Hegel seems to hold generally to the view that what distinguishes humans from animals is not the ability to have inner representations. Rather, it is thought that distinguishes us.[16] One might therefore believe it safe to interpret Hegel's identification of the imagination with the animal state along these Aristotelian lines.

There is, however, a significant difference between Hegel and Aristotle's views on the *immediacy* of intuition. Essentially, the difference is the kind of Platonic moment in Hegel that we mentioned earlier. More specifically, Hegel writes of an inwardizing that makes Being (*Sein*) into the possession of the self (it becomes *sein*). For Aristotle, imagination is a second movement following from sensation.

> [The] imagination must be a movement produced by sensation actively operating. Since sight is the chief sense, the name *phantasia* (imagination) is derived from *phaos* (light), because without light it is impossible to see. (*De Anima* 429a)

The role of light in this citation fits in well with the kind of immediacy Aristotle attributes to perception: for him "the activity of the sensible object and of the sensation is one and the same" (*De Anima* 425b26, p. 147). But this formulation alone does not work for Hegel, for in imagination, actuality is not only the light (*Sein*) of sensation, it is also the darkness (negativity, possession, *sein*) of the soul. Indeed, the presence of the imagined content arises as a result of the movement inward of the light, *because* of the inward movement of consciousness into its Night. "In intuition consciousness is first in itself; it complements this with the for-itself,—through the Negativity, separation from the in itself and goes back into itself" (*G2* 172). The inwardizing makes Being (*Sein*) into the possession of the self (it becomes "his"—*sein*).

We can see as well, incidentally, why Hegel cannot be identified with Fichte. Fichte's imagination moves outward as the primordial act of the subject, whereas Hegel's act is an inward move, drawing Being inward. Fichte writes of the "check" whereby the self is made aware of a not-self, whereas Hegel's not-self must always already be there in the apparently given. The Aristotelian *physis* is a part of the Hegelian dialectic. The darkness takes the light (Being) inward. There has to have been *Sein* in order for it to be *sein*. Hegel differs significantly from Fichte, therefore, in that his dialectic of Night and light take the matter of Being seriously.[17]

What is missing in the Aristotelian account, however, is precisely the inwardizing movement of *Geist*. What is missing is the *für sich,* the grasping, or, in the language of the *Encyclopedia,* this "unity of idea (*den Begriffe*)."[18] Inwardizing is the condition for the preservation of intuitions. In drawing itself inward, consciousness not only sets its intuitions over-against itself—it also draws them into itself, into its Night.[19] The very power of difference is also a drawing in and a possession. It is determination.[20]

The dialectical truth of this return is thus that it creates intuitions as property, as internal to consciousness. As such property, the object is no longer intuition but Image (*Bild*). "This image belongs to consciousness, it is in possession (*Besitz*) of it, consciousness is master (*Herr*) over it; it is held in its treasure (*Schatze*) in its Night—the image is unconscious" (*G2* 172).[21] What is missing in the Aristotelian account, is this account of the soul's activity of moving inward, the ideal moment of the dialectic.

If we cannot appeal to Aristotle, how then, one might now ask, do we account for the identification of this return with the animal state? The answer lies in that, for Hegel, at the level of the imagination, there is no knowledge of the inwardizing, no reflection of it for the self, indeed no self yet for which it would be reflected. "The image is unconscious," and so is the inward movement. The movement is like the body itself, prior to subject-object distinctions. Thus, it is like the animal. What gets produced at this stage are images, *Bilder.* The imagination "bodies forth" as Theseus says in *A Midsummer Night's Dream.*[22]

More needs to be said before we can understand what this means. Let us turn, therefore, to the second thing with which Hegel identifies this inwardizing.

Temporal Inwardizing: Inwardizing as Time.   There are two sides to this identification, corresponding to two sides of property. On the one hand, the movement inward is Time as pure movement. It is the pure activity of taking something in. There is no consciousness of the enduring nature of what has been inwardized. It is just a grasping determination, a halting of the flow of time. On the other hand, the inwardizing creates for consciousness something *for consciousness itself.* Property reflects this two-sidedness: on the one hand we normally say that something belongs to me (consciously) insofar as I take it as mine. But I can be in possession of images without being conscious that I am in possession of them. Indeed, the advertising industry counts on the unconscious taking in of their advertisements to stimulate desire for real possession of what they sell. (In this latter case, it is really the advertising industry that is, through images we have internalized, potentially in possession of us. But that is another story for a more developed dialectical moment.) So on the one hand, something is taken in, and on the other, the image, through this inwardizing, is now stored in the mind and belongs to the mind.

The two sides of property are captured in Hegel's ambiguous identification of inwardizing with the "*Freiheit der Zeit.*" On the one hand this expression means freedom *of* time, on the other, freedom *from* time. Let us look at each separately, and then at how they intertwine.

Consciousness is the freedom *of* time in the following sense. Like time, consciousness is the boundary between the present and the open future. That boundary is a limit of consciousness, not in the face of something else, but simply, in the face of what is not (yet). Freedom of time is inwardizing as the free negation of something's otherness, the free taking of it, the isolating of it and inwardizing of it; the making-mine of it. That is what we do when we say "now": we create and hold the otherness at bay, we keep the moment from spilling into its own future. We prevent it from being other than what we say. At an unconscious level this is what is happening with any inwardizing of any thing. The movement of time is Fichtean limitation: it is negation and determination at the same time. Time in this sense is the causal character of consciousness. The difference from Fichte is that, in Hegel, this is an inward movement, whereas for Fichte it was a line moving outward that was checked.

In Hegel, this inward motion gives rise to the other side of this dialectic of time, namely the freedom *from* time. This freedom is the *result* of the inwardizing of representations. That is, once in the Night, an image is not bound by the temporal order of the original intuition. It is free from the times and spaces within which it was originally tucked. We recall this from the *Geistesphilosophie* of 1803–04. Any reproduction of the image is therefore free from those temporal (and spatial) constraints. Without the inwardizing, we are not able to generate higher forms of cognition based on more complex orderings of space and time.

Freedom of time makes it possible to have freedom from time, since if there had been no inwardizing, there would be no temporal and spatial images in the mind. If there were no dovetailing of time and space in the first place (in intuition) there would be no possibility of a further fold of time and space onto themselves in the second place (imagination).

To conclude, the inwardizing as time and as "*Freiheit der Zeit*" means that we begin with a determination, a free inwardization. This is a temporal and spatial determination. *Re*production (of an image) requires a further determination of that original determination. It implies being free of the original temporal-spatial context.

Let us move on to the final characterization of inwardization: namely, that it is a pure subject.

Temporal Inwardizing: Inwardizing as Pure Subject.   Freedom of and from time explains in turn how we have before us a pure subject: only time, this *"für sich,"* could be a pure subject. It is hard to reconcile this with the previous claim that it is a return to an animal state, for we are reluctant to call animals pure subjects. However, the subjectivity in question here is not that of a person, which for Hegel is to say that it is not that of an interpersonally connected identity. Rather, the subjectivity in question is that of the body.[23] Its purity lies strictly in the initial unconscious freedom that this inwardizing moment of the imagination is.

Hegel can talk about this stage as both pure subject and animal stage because, although an animal's imagination can freely combine and separate different images despite the order and is therefore a *pure* subject, it is not a *free subject.* What is free about consciousness at this level is not its subjectivity, but its imaginative activity. We recall that Hegel refers to it as a dream state. So while there is freedom (of and from time) and while there is pure subjectivity, there is not yet pure, *free subjectivity.* The reason for this in this text, as it was in the 1803–04 *Geistesphilosophie,* is that a free subject, unlike a merely pure subject, involves mediation in language.[24] I think it is safe to conclude that for Hegel animals are pure subjects in the sense that they create a reflected inner world, but they do not have knowledge of this reflectedness per se. It is only known to be freedom when we can communicate. Only then is it freedom as we *know* it.

A further clarification about pure subjectivity is needed. Inwardizing as time and as pure subject is not sheer negation. Inwardizing is a drawing in of the light into the Night; it embodies in the sense that it creates bodies (images). An image is "the object taken up—superseded but preserved (*aufgehoben*)—as being" (*G2* 172). Each image is "taken up (stored) in the self's treasury, in the self's Night." (*G2* 172). Because it is not sheer negation, but equally determination, ("just as much substance as subject," as Hegel would later say) inwardizing creates property. In the first dialectical round, in intuition, *Geist* is identified with the object ("its first self is the object for it"). But in the next dialectical round, the sublated image (*aufgehobenes Bild*) *belongs* to *Geist.* These two movements of inwardizing—the taking up and the storing in the mind (intuition and imagination)—create property. "[T]his image belongs to it, the self is in possession of it, is master over it." These two moments make up the representing imagination in general ("die vorstellende Einbildungskraft überhaupt.").

So far, we have focused on the inwardizing as the taking in; the time of inwardizing and of storing up as mental property. Now we need to look at what the image gets taken into; the "self's Night." But what is the Night? The answer to this question involves the other side of the dialectic, the spatial side of inwardizing. Thus, we turn now to what this Night is, to this storehouse and its contents.

Spatial Inwardizing.   Hegel's description of the Night is wonderfully rich. It echoes the Aristotelian notion of the soul as the place of forms,[25] drifts midway into a kind of Goethean *Walpurgisnacht*,[26] and in the last lines prefigures existentialism:

> Man is this Night, this empty Nothing, which holds everything in its simplicity—a kingdom of endless representations, images, none of which appears immediately to him—, or which are not immediately present. This is the Night, Nature's inner, which here exists—pure self,—phantasmagorical representations are surrounded by Night, here shoots out a bloody head,—there another white figure suddenly comes forward, and disappears just as suddenly—One catches a glimpse of this Night when one looks others in the eyes—into a Night which would be frightful,—here hangs over against one the Night of the world.

In a note on the side of his manuscript Hegel writes, "Night of safe-keeping/storing up" (*Nacht der Aufbewahrung*, G2 172, note 2). The Night is the subjective space of representations because what is *aufbewahrt*—held in the mind—is held in the grey area between already fixed representations and their being fixed within an infinite set of possible constructs.

One might again be tempted to identify this Night as Kant's a priori form of Space. But Hegel gives a more complex account. The Night is the space of representations *and* the negative power of determination. The movement of consciousness that gives rise to the Night as space, is also the movement of consciousness that negates. As Night, it is considered spatially. But the Night is equally time, negation. The two together are the Concept, the "grasping of" that generates property. So the Night, though considered here as spatial, implies negation. The Night is not simply the possibility of relation in space. Hegel is indebted to Fichte for this dialectical character of cognition. For Fichte, the primary category is not relation, as in Kant, but interdetermination. This was a result of his theory of the imagination as "*Wechselwirkung*" and as central to cognition of any kind (See *Sc.Kn.* 193).

Because the image in the Night is thoroughly mediated by the dialectic of space and time, any image is a manifold as much as a unity. Hegel writes that "[t]he image is a manifold—the Form is to it as determination, and through its being defined as an object different from others, [it is] plurality in general" (*G2* 173). The form that gives it intuitive unity is the self. But it is not the Kantian unity of apperception *tout court*. According to Hegel, "'I' is the form not only as simple Self, but rather as movement; the relationship of the parts of the image,—the Form, relationship posited as the self's own" (*G2* 173).

This passage makes sense if we back up a step and move forward from the start. Taken together as temporal and spatial, the Night is the condition of representations. It is this because on the one hand it is the negative power of determination, and on the other hand, it is the subjective space of representations. The self holds a plurality in the Night as a whole, and yet is itself the movement between of the parts of the whole. The movement is constitutive of the relationships between the parts. So on the one hand, we have Kant's unity of apperception, but on the other, because it is dialectically generated, the self is nothing other than the movement constitutive of the relationships between the parts, and indeed, it is constitutive of the parts as well. The self is nothing other than the dovetailing dialectic of space and time, folded back on itself, considered in terms of space.

When we speak here of the self, we do not mean a developed notion of self. According to Hegel, at this level of cognition, caprice or arbitrariness governs the moving determination of relations. Hegel is careful to define what he means here by caprice. He does not mean what the English at the time called the associations of ideas. That English version is based on the passive receptivity of things in the order in which the objects come to be known to us. It is a passive form of arbitrary determination. The general arbitrariness to which Hegel is referring is rather an active form of capriciousness in the sense that it is consciousness building and taking images apart. The reason it is not organized (and is therefore capricious), is that consciousness at this stage is not actively aware of what it is doing. Another way of putting this is that the Night is the freedom of time as the freedom from (original-context) time. But the Night is not yet the self's freedom to put things together according to some rationally decided-upon order. In this Night as space, the self's movement is free from the constraints of intuition. Its movement is "a completely other movement from the one of Space and Time, remaining free from the movement of mere being (*seienden Bewegung*)" (*G2* 173, note 3). This gives rise to the illusion of freedom, but it is closer to what Freud would later call unconsciously motivated association.

Thus, *Geist* is both aspects of the Night, the negative and the storehouse in which images are held. But two illusions arise at this level. The first, as we just saw, is that the self is freely operating; the second is that the self is free from its operations. With regard to the second illusion, *Geist* as the Night appears to endure as something separate from its shifting and changing images.

The truth, however, is as we have seen: the Night is inseparable from the production of determinate form. This means that the self's active (capricious) determination of images is determining the self. And this means that the self does not endure as a separate entity or self-space within which these changes occur. As Hegel's analysis goes on to show, the seemingly self-consistent time-movement that goes from one image (or part of an image) to another and thereby actually defines the representations, is itself defined spatially by the differentiations of the images. There is no atemporal (*bestehende*) self. There is no atemporal, Kantian unity of apperception.

Thus, the self that is capable of taking times out of temporal order (and spaces out of their places) is only the appearance of freedom, for in fact this arbitrariness with regard to times—this freedom *from* time—contains a contradiction. Hegel calls this arbitrariness "*die leere Freiheit*" empty freedom—since *Geist*, though it is the determining movement, is determining with only *immediate* consciousness of its determining activity. One shape of this immediacy is the plurality of images that seem to play before the mind, the other side of this immediacy is the mind as a stable entity before which the images play. Both immediacies are in fact mediated by the other. If consciousness is to have any truth about itself, immediacy has to be seen to be mediate.

The process of making the immediate activity of the self appear in its truth as mediated, is a long one, and ultimately involves communication with other consciousnesses. The passive, *bestehende* self must become active and a giving-over or disappearing (*vergehende*) one. But this is not just a return to the *mise en abyme* of the reason which we saw in Hegel's early works. For we do not lose sight of the plurality of images. Rather, the plurality of images, and the process by which they arise in the mind, is kept in play in the turn of the dialectic. But as with every new moment of the dialectic, the previous shape of things is that against which negation is applied. That against which negation is applied determines the next shape of things as much as the negative act does.

This concludes our section on the inwardizing imagination. One problem that Hegel does not address in this text but should have, is where the original intuitions come from and what time and space they are in to begin with. That is, if negation is what determines an intuition in the first place, and is what instantaneously lifts the intuition into the mind for storage as an image, it is either the case that there are objects out there that are passively received in a given time and place, or it is the case that consciousness determines these and creates time and space. I have argued that Hegel is saying the latter and I have gone considerable distance to show that this is the only viable way of clarifying Kant on this matter. But if I am right in reading Hegel this way, Hegel ought to have made my case more clear. He could have done so by making clear just what the images and the capricious play among them in the mind are free *of.* As a result of Hegel's failure to provide clarification, Hegel commentators have differing views on what Hegel might have meant.[27]

In any case, the advantage of this discussion of the inwardizing imagination is enormous. We now have a dialectical account of the imagination that gets us into the mind and on the road to more and more complex forms of (thinking about) objects. We next see that the inwardizing as a negative movement continues to be active up to the next levels of cognition, from recollection through to language.

(ii) Recollection (Erinnerung)

Recollection is a repetition of inwardizing, not in sequence but rather on top of the previous inwardization and its products. Thus, recollection is an inwardizing that presupposes both the first inwardizing of intuitions into the Night as images, and the appearance in the Night of an object. The object of recollection is a repetition and has the quality of being familiar to us.

Though *Erinnerung* is translatable as "remembering" or "recollection"[28] the force of the German meaning is rather the going-inside-of, *Er-inner-ung*. In this moment, the thing not only is, but it is mine (*das Mein*): the object is "already familiar; or I remember it. Or I have the immediate consciousness in this procedure that it is mine."[29]

Recollection is not yet the purposeful remembering of something (memory, *Gedächtnis*), for the thing of which we become innerly aware can be aroused without our trying to recollect it. The mere presence of something else that reminds us of it is sufficient to give rise to the object of recollection.

Recollection is, however, more than mere idea association, because we are conscious of the recollected object as familiar to us and of ourselves as familiar with it. Hegel writes: "Recollection posits alongside [the object recollected] the moment of the being-for-self—I have already seen or heard of this once: I recollect [myself to it]" (*G2* 173).[30]

The verb *to recollect* in German is reflexive. It is awkward to translate that reflexivity. Look, for example, at the following passage from the text we are considering:

> ich erinnere mich; ich sehe, höre nicht bloss den Gegenstand, sondern gehe dabei innerhalb meiner—erinner-mich, nehme mich aus dem blossen Bilde heraus, und setze mich in mich; ich setze mich besonders zum Gegenstande.

> I recollect [myself to it]; I see, hear not only the object, but go thereby inside what is mine—re-member myself, take myself out of the simple image, and put myself in myself; I posit myself in particular [relation] to the object. (*G2* 173–74)

This reflexivity is important. It differentiates us not only from mere idea association, but as well, at this level of cognition, from the animal. The animal is not capable of self-awareness in its imaginative conjuring of an edible thing. According to Hegel, we are. Kant advocated the same when he said that "[i]t must be possible for the 'I think' to accompany all my representations" (*CPR* 152; *KrV* B132, s. 140).

This self-awareness is the awareness of the Night. When the self recalls the familiar, what makes it familiar is not the presence of the thing being there again, so much as the fact that the thing there already stands in (relation to) the Night. If it stood only in relation to other things in the mind it would have its place, but when *ich erinnere mich*, I am accessing not only the memory—dreams do only that much—I am going into a space which I regard as my own, I am conscious of myself going about the representations in my mind. Nevertheless, I was drawn there in recollection, I did not go there looking for something I wanted to remember.

Recollection is reproduction out of the Night according to a similarity between an intuition and an image. As such, it provides the first building block for the creation of symbols and signs. In other words, it provides the basic movement that allows one thing to stand for another. But it does not provide of itself what is needed for symbolic mediation. The story of what else is needed is the story of how language comes about.

The story of the transition from recollection to language is a long one. Hegel's almost impenetrable 1805–06 notes make it difficult to follow. The fullest and clearest account comes later in Hegel's 1830 *Philosophy of Spirit*. Nevertheless, it is worth spending some time on this 1805–06 material.

(iii) To Mean (Bezeichnen), Signs

In the third moment, that of the sign (*Zeichen*), the object that stands before one in *Erinnerung* is the synthesis of the representation and being-for-me (*Fürmichsein*). While in *Erinnerung* the being for self was what gave the object familiarity, here Hegel writes: "In the sign, [the I's] being-for-itself as the essence of the object *is itself object*" (my emphasis). This requires explanation.

The dialectic of the imagination, in an earlier moment, gave being (*Sein*) to the inner image. At that point, the self was the object's *Sein*, as Hegel said. But here the self is not only the being of the thing, it is its essence: "[M]y being-for-me is the object as the *essence* of the Thing" (*G2* 174; my emphasis). What this means is that the internal relations within an image and between images, to which the self's originally capricious movement gives rise, are now consciously determined by the self. In other words, we have moved from recollection to intentional synthesis. The self applies one recollected image to another. Insofar as it so determines them, it is their essence, and not just their being. Essence is deliberative. It is consciously connecting the images in order to mean something with them.

Looking at the whole process from the start (intuition), we can see that at the level of sign making there have been two supersessions (*Aufhebungen*) of moments of consciousness. First, consciousness determines the object by inwardizing and thereby creating an image stored in the Night; this *aufheben* of intuition makes consciousness possessive; the image belongs to it. Second, that dialectical moment of possession is itself *aufgehoben*, possessed, and superseded. This is the consciousness that *recollects* something. It recollects what it owns, it recollects what is familiar to it. It also thereby comes to see its ability to repossess what it only capriciously owned in the first instance. In a further, third, *Aufhebung,* consciousness takes possession of its ability, through recollection, to familiarize; it does so by meaning something, intending something, intentionally exhibiting the relation of familiarity between images.

We can follow this same set of transitions focusing on negation and the Night. First, the imagination re-collects the image out of the manifold of the negative infinity (the Night), and thus gives it being (as image). But the object (the image) is not yet the essence of the self because the object does not have in it the moment of being for the self. It is as if one were traveling, as an explorer, from point A to a some unknown second point. The arrival at the second point, and the designation of it as point B, is the inwardizing of the place. We arrive, and our arrival point now belongs to our mental geography. But as a mere place of arrival it only has being. It does not exhibit my essence as a traveler or its essential relatedness to point A. It is only when I reflect on the arrival as a point on the route and draw a map indicating the relationship between point A and point B (and any other point I care to relate it to) that I have an object that reflects my essence as a traveler, and which itself is now part of a system of reference.

Drawing the map requires that I negate the traveling itself and the moment when I arrived at point B. I negate these in the sense that what was before a movement of arriving and the point of arrival (which gave rise to point B) is now determined as a line, and a point related to that line. I spatialize what was a temporal arrival and a temporal inwardizing of the place of arrival. I create a map of relations out of the history of my travels.

In order for the object to become the essence of the self, the movement must become a history. But it is not just a recollection of the route, it is an intentional mapping out, a retelling of the story of how one got there and how one could get there again.

In making the map, the history of my travel, I thus raise up, as a superseded dialectical moment, not just the thing (the arrival point), but the thing's negation into the Night where it became an image. I must own that movement, and to do so I negate the otherness of that moment; that is, I must take up the moment of inwardizing negation as a moment that is for me, that I can use. In other words, in sign-making imagination, interiorization becomes consciously used. Negation is *recognized, recollected,* and used to create a system of reference. Thus Hegel writes (rather cryptically!): "This, my being-for-me, which I add (*hinzusetze*) to the object, is that Night, that self, in which I sank the object" (*G2* 174).[31] Point B was sunk into my mental geography as an image; yes, in recollection I could haul it back out, but in sign making I do better: the very process of sinking point B and of recollecting it in relation to other places, is what I have now harnessed as an ability, and I reflect that harnessing in the object by representing point B in a map, a system of relations that are nothing other than my own recollections of my travels but this time put together consciously by me. I know myself to be the traveler and map maker.

The original negation expresses the thing's becoming mine, and as taken up this "becoming mine" or "being for me" is now itself also "for me." So the first negation is also re-collected as "being-for-me." The original negation is sublated into the new object: I *add* it to the object. Thus, "[t]his, my being-for-me, which I add (*hinzusetze*) to the object, is that Night, that self, in which I sank the object" (*G2* 174).

In signification, the image *stands for* its history, its re-collectedness. The sign is not only a reproduced content, it also bears the traces of, or has re-collected as part of its being, the previous re-collection. This entire process, held together objectively as the sign, is the *essential* nature of the self at this level.[32]

Signs are at first, however, only subjective characters. This is why sign making falls within the developments of "the dreaming spirit" and not of language. Let us briefly explore what it means to say it is merely subjective.

When the self relates to itself through signs, the objects it ponders (the signs) are essentially the self but only in a simple way. "[T]he content [the sign] is its [the self's] simple essence in general."[33] The content is only the *simple* essence of the self because the self is not yet objectively universal. For if we look to the object, *its* essence is only the self's self-relation: the essence of the sign is my being-for-me; its essence is that I am my content for me.

My being-for-me is not the same as the self that will become Spirit in and for itself. Here, the dialectic is between my being-for-me and the object, *not* between the self and the object in any objectively understandable sense. I am the one who determines what images stand for what, and this determination is purely subjective; while someone could understand that I was intending something, they could not understand what it was that I was intending. As yet, it is still subjective essentiality. In other words, we still have a ways to go before we have a map that makes sense to other people.

For the moment, all we have is a mental map, a personal history of the individual traveler.

If the sign making is to become universal, the inner must become outer: "[I]t (I) is first immediately innerward, it must also step into existence (*Dasein*), become object, as opposed to this inwardness it must be outward; return to Being (*Rückkehr zum Sein*)" (*G2* 174).

Hegel writes that the universal is characterized by the thing being posited as thing ("*das Ding als Ding gesetzt*" [*G2* 174]). At first this phrase sounds rather redundant. But what Hegel is focusing on is the posited, externalized "*gesetzt*" character of the universal sign. Also, he is making clear that we do not posit a new thing. It is the "thing" as what is being-for-me in my mind that must be externalized, not some new thing. We cannot let go of what we already have achieved; it must really be what I *mean* that is be posited. In other words, the thing has to be familiar and to have been consciously determined before it can make sense to others.[34] The problem now is to posit that thing as a thing for other people.

Once we begin discussing the sign as a thing for others we are in the realm of language (*Sprache*) and thus in the second major triad of the structure of the intellect.[35] We have therefore completed the section on "the Imagination in General."

Before moving to language, it is worth noting the following. For Hegel, the power of making signs falls under the heading of the third moment of "Imagination in General." Nevertheless, he has not explicitly discussed sign making as the work of the imagination. This changes by the 1830 lectures: there Hegel gives greater precision to sign making as an activity of the imagination. We are justified in discussing it explicitly as the work of the imagination here, not only because sign making falls within the section on imagination in general, nor because Hegel himself discusses it explicitly in this way later (in 1830). Rather, it is because it is the dialectical development of the imagination's moments of negation and possession that have given rise to the more complex forms of recollection and signs. Now let us turn to how that dialectic gets carried into the development of language.

In this change, the dreaming spirit is developed into the objective world. As with the developments so far, in the development of language the dialectical moments of the dreaming spirit develop in ever more complex, and therefore also, ever more encompassing and deeper ways, as it makes its way toward objective communication.

: "Rückkehr zum Sein"

Before looking at the individual moments of language, let me take a moment to discuss the general dialectic of the moments from Naming to Memory, and then from Memory to Understanding. The key point in this transition is Memory. Part of the purpose of analyzing this second triad is to show how the imagination is involved in higher cognitive activities.

The self has two relationships to its names, and each involves memory. The first form of the opposition between self and the name yields only repetition. It is a knowing in the sense of knowing something by heart—being able to recite the parts and relations by memory. The second form of opposition between self and name (in which the name is actually thought of by the self) is actual memory. Memory is fully itself only in this second relationship. It is actual memory because it is the process by which a thought is created; it is the inwardizing of the self in such a way that the relations established are not merely relations, they are actions of the self, and the self knows itself to be these actions. Unlike recollection, which *reestablishes* relations, actual memory is the *creation* of those relations. In this way the Night becomes thought, and the thing that is named is a set of relations according to the self's self-conscious making of them: they are thoughts of the object (*Gedanken*).

To use our map metaphor, the difference between sign making and name making is the following. Sign making gives us a personal map of our own historical journey. I can synthesize that journey and its resting points to myself in whatever order I want. But I cannot assume that anyone else has ever made the journey or seen those places. So I really have less than a private language. I have a schematic, consciously informed recollection, but no possibility of communication. With name making, however, I have the same structure, only now all the resting points are familiar. Even if I synthesize a story of possible routes of travel that have never been taken before, I can count on someone else knowing the relationships and being able to infer the connections to which I am referring. The subjective sign map has become an objective atlas.

Names

In my structural overview at the beginning of this chapter, I pointed out the different powers that Hegel thinks are operative in intelligence as a whole. Hegel brings these up again when he discusses names. These *Kräfte* are discussed as follows. The first power, "the [power of the] imagination[,] gives only empty form." While it is not entirely clear what Hegel means by empty here, we can assume that it is empty in the sense of possessing content without intentions to do anything with the content. To use our metaphor, it is the traveler going from place to place but without a map.

The second power is "the sign-making power." The self exhibits a degree of control over the syntheses. It does so insofar as the self tries to mean something, intends something by the synthesized signs.

The third power, the name-giving power, is the same as Memory (*Gedächtnis*), and as Creative power (*Schöpferkraft, G2* 174, note 3). In name-making, what is externalized is understood by the community.

What lays the ground for discussing memory in terms of knowing by heart versus knowing the thing actually, is the distinction between subjective and objective. A name, like a sign, retains a subjective side. It does so in the sense that I use a name in a specific context. It is also objective, in the sense that a name always invokes the communally memorized content. That objective side can be a hindrance to real communication insofar as it is mimetic and repetitive. It is the subjective side, the way the individual uses the name in a particular context, that makes name-use a practice of *wakened* spirit.

The dialectic between these gives rise to Spirit. Hegel writes, "This [language] is then the true being of Spirit as Spirit in general—it is there as the unity of two free selves" (*G2* 175).

Our identity is defined by names. And since they are nothing but established social usages, we are defined by social usages. We are inside them. They are just as much inside us, and through our use of them we are inside each other. Names make possible what Hegel refers to in the *Phenomenology of Spirit* as the "'I' that is a 'We' and 'We' that is 'I'" (*PoS* 110).

According to Hegel, this power is not abstract. Naming occurs in intuition. The name is a sound—a tone—my sound when I speak.

Spirit as language is concrete, but also, equally, concept. A name both represents and supersedes its immediate object. The name exhibits the character of sublation, of *Aufhebung*, and therefore it exhibits the character of the Concept. Hegel writes, for example:

> "Donkey" is a tone, which is wholly something other than the sensible being itself; insofar as we see it [the donkey], and feel and hear him, we are it, [we are] immediately one with him, filled [with him]; but stepping back, it is as name that [the donkey] is spirit [*ein Geistiges*]—[he] is something wholly other. (*G2* 175)

The name is a tone used, and anyone hearing it who speaks the language will have in themselves an appropriate reference. As a result, Hegel writes that the world is no longer a kingdom of images ("*Reich von Bildern*"). For images were only inwardly *aufgehoben* and possessed no external Being. Instead, the world is a kingdom of words ("*Reich der Namen*" [*G2* 175]).

Hegel refers to the first kingdom as the realm of the dreaming Spirit ("*der träumende Geist*") and writes that this world has "no reality, no existence" (*G2* 175). To wake up from this dreamworld is to enter the world of names. In this realm the self's images for the first time have truth (*G2* 175). The previously enclosed (*verschlossene*) being-for-itself (meaning) of the dreaming spirit now has the Form of Being in the name (*G2* 175–76). This would lead us to conclude that the being of the name is what makes it true, whereas the image only has the being that the self gives to it by virtue of the self's having mental possession of it. According to Hegel, the externality of names makes their production a wakeful, true production.

But Hegel also writes that "that is true, which is for him" (*G2* 176). Truth is a function of two selves communicating and does not exist in itself. There is no universality to names apart from their use. Names are the articulation of a Spirit in relation to itself, and such a relation is the true. Just as in the *Lectures on the Philosophy of Religion* Hegel will say that "God *is* spirit only insofar as God is in his *community*"(*Phil.Rel.* 90), the name only *is* insofar as it appears in the language of users for whom it has meaning, and only insofar as it is, is it true.

But why are two spirits in dialogue "awake"? This question concerns the order into which named experiences fall. Specifically, it concerns how the order is such that there is not only subjective meaning (as there was for the sign), nor only historically objective meaning (as there is in the natural relation of some names with others[36]) but also *actually* subjective-objective necessity to them (as when we truly *know* the Thing—*Sache*—that is before us). This last has to do with memory.

The third and last appearance of the term *imagination* (*die Einbildungskraft*) occurs here. Hegel compares the name's signification with the image. We saw earlier that the imagination "cuts out a piece of Space, interrupts, negates the continuity of Space" (*G2* 176). In so doing, it brings with the image, the images that are associated with it. "Imagination brings the object forth with its plurality, its nearest surroundings" (*G2* 176). A name, on the other hand, stands alone "without relation and connection" (*G2* 176). While images have their associative entourage, for a name to have context the self must put it in an order among other names. For this the negative moment is again needed. We no longer merely have an arbitrary re-collection, rather we have an intended activity of recollecting. (We are subtly moving toward the realization, as well, that theoretical intellect cannot really be thought apart from the activity of the will.)

This need for the negation in the derivation of objective order involves another venture into the subjective, this time to see how the negative moment (the Night, the self) is an *act* of the self *for* the self.

The sign failed to be language because it was *not subjective enough*: the subjective *act* of having one thing stand for another had not become objective to the subject; the synthesis was only imaginative in the sense of imagistic. In recollection (*Erinnerung*) the Night was witnessed reflexively, it was there alongside of and as part of the recollected, familiar thing. In memory we do not just come across the unity of the Night with the thing, rather, we reengage the activity of the negative itself as an act; we reenact it. Memory is not so much a question of the result (the thing recollected) as of the process.

In this transformation into a conscious act, inwardizing remains, therefore, central to the project of consciousness.

Memory: Order

Hegel's problem here is how to articulate the movement from appearance of order (which the imagination yields/is through signs) to real order (which the understanding yields/is through language).

The return of the negative in/as Memory is a higher spiritual order than in/as sign making. "The first real overcoming of intuition, of the animal, and of Time and Space occurs in naming" (*G2* 176). What is at issue here is not the order of words in a meaningful sentence considered in terms of the parts of language as modern linguists have divided them up (i.e., in terms of syntax[37]). Rather, what is under consideration is the mediation between the self, the name, and the thing signified.

According to Hegel, the self is the substance of names: "The I is alone the bearer, the space and substance of these names—it is their order . . . " (*G2* 177). The self must look to itself for the order. The self returns to the Night in order to discover (its) order there: "[the I] must (be)hold the names/the order in its Night, as useful, as belonging to the self" (*G2* 177).

The reason order arises is that the first subjective recollection is not stable, it is in fact still temporal, an active recollec*ting*. The moment that is *bestehende* is actually *vergehende*. In seeking to recollect these two together, the self is *verstehende*—the understanding. As language users, we are not just responsive. We are aware of our responsibility for how the world is characterized through language.

In the margins of his text, Hegel is musing over a problem (*G2* 178). At first he writes that the self is separate from names, and yet that their being is only possible in and through the singularity of the self. This is not unlike Kant's argument for the unity of apperception in any synthesis, here applied to the intention of a name. However, the question for Hegel then becomes: "How is Self their necessity or constraint (*Befestigung*) such that it is their Being?" This is a question about synthesis. Hegel settles on the answer that the I is the Being of names through self-mediation with the object: "[N]ow through mediation—it must become this through itself; its unrest must fix itself, it must itself—as unrest, as pure movement—become sublating movement (*aufhebende Bewegung werden*). This is the work; its unrest becomes object, as fixed Plurality, as Order;—the unrest becomes order precisely through this, that it becomes object" (*G2* 177, note 1). The ending here is noteworthy: through this process of self-mediation, the self becomes the object.

This happens in two ways. One way is a fixedness of order due to the work of memory holding the appearance of the images as they occurred in sense perception (*G2* 177). The other way is a fixedness of order due to the self's conscious use of memory. Here, the activity of consciousness is folding back on itself. The result is that "Memory holds the names in general, the free, arbitrary connection of these images, (the meaning) and the names, so that by the image the name appears, and by the name the image is there" (*G2* 178). While the first kind of memory gives an order of events, the second kind gives us a relation of signifier to signified (i.e., it allows us to relate and hold onto (*Bewahrung*) the two thoroughly distinct parts of a name—the sound or written form and its representation (*Vorstellung*) in an image (*Bild*) (*G2* 178).

These two kinds of fixing are not separate: name intention and events are interconnected. Memory allows us to give an account of events as they appear; the relations between the names are determined by their relation in sense perception. Hegel's example is that of thunder and lightning. "Lightning" and "thunder"—two words with different meanings—are used to describe a single sensible event (supposing they appear simultaneously in our experience). The order of these connections (here simultaneity) appears necessary, according to sense perception. But in such fixing, say, by a parent teaching a child, the language for that experience as it is happening, the arbitrary nature of the name-object relation is hidden. This is what Hegel will later call "mechanical Memory."

At a higher level, memory is that which allows us to connect names to each other in ways distinct from their relation in perception. This is what I take Hegel to mean by "freie Name" (*G2* 178). Here, the connection between event and linguistic expression is mediated through the speaker's thinking about the experience. The creative activity resulting from the imagination's sublating negation gives rise to something more than empiricism and less than pure idealism. It is a dialectic of linguistic ordering.

The creation of analogies and similes fits here, when, for example, we compare a cloud to a mountain or couple lightning with the idea of vengeance. The conventional associations are not lost, they are sublated, taken up into new, creative orders.

> The I is the power [*Kraft*] of this free—not yet posited as necessary—order[;]—it is the free holder, the free objectless order.—It is the first "I" to grasp itself as power; the I is itself the necessity, free from the picture-thought (*Vorstellung*)—the fixing and fixed order—the exercise of memory is therefore the first work of the awakened Spirit as Spirit. (*G2* 178)

We saw earlier that, according to Hegel, language is the "true Being of Spirit as Spirit" (*G2* 175). It is the immediate universal. But here Hegel declares that "the *exercise* of memory is the first work of the wakened Spirit as Spirit" (*G2* 178; my emphasis). With the exercise of memory, language ceases to be mechanical and becomes creative communication. The immediate universal has become an actual, mediated universal. As merely conventional, language is memorized. But it thereby does not have sight of the subjective depth necessary for Spirit to be fully what it is. The actuality of the Night is lost from sight. In awakened Spirit, language is actual: the Night of the other, their infinite otherness, is actual, engaged as the mediation of language by the language user.[38]

Hegel does not mention it, but we can see that the temporal-spatial dialectic is present here. The dominant moment of mechanical memory is the spatial moment: understanding is predominantly a fixing (*verstehende*); in real memory, however, time, the pure subject, negation, the Night, is the dominant moment, and the understanding is predominantly movement (*verstehende*: understanding).

But we are not out of the woods of revery entirely. There are levels of awakening. What we have so far is an incomplete awareness. The implicit component is the will. Only with the introduction of the will can we say self-consciously that we meant to create a given analogy as an analogy. That develops into the understanding as judgment making, and then to the conclusion of the section on the Intellect. In that account, we come to know that in the use of memory for full understanding, there is a *subjective genesis*. Even at the most awake, we still use the previous levels of creative convention to express ourselves.

We recall Hegel's earlier words, "one catches a glimpse of this Night when one looks others in the eyes—into a Night which would be frightful,—here hangs over against one the Night of the world" (*G2* 172). In awakened Spirit, this glimpse is a sustained gaze into the other, into the mediating genesis of Spirit. Without the spontaneity of subjective reflection, of the imagination's return, of the Night which is now reflected in the gaze of the other, there is no *true* language.[39]

Our business with this 1805–06 work ends here. We have traced the movement of the inwardizing imagination from its origins far enough into the practice of language, that we can see its necessity at every step.

CONCLUSION

The 1805–06 lectures reveal the imagination to be a power of inwardization. This is imagination's *für sich*, a separating from the immediacy of intuition that creates consciousness of an intuited other. This "pure subject," which is time, reappears in the preface to the *Phenomenology*, and has its "final" return in the final chapter of that work, in Absolute Knowing.[40] Its role is not to be underestimated.

However, the 1805–06 account gives an underdeveloped account of imagination's inwardizing activity. I sketched how important the depth and inwardizing moment of imagination is to language. But, even though the logic is evident, Hegel does not show it here. In the later 1830 version, however, this changes: memory-dependent sign making is the culminating moment of the imagination. This difference is due in part to the different role reflection, and therefore representation, begin to play in Hegel, particularly from 1807 onward. The inwardizing activity that is the hallmark here of the imagination, is that which makes that shift in Hegel's thinking possible. For it is the folds of the Night, the negative moment, the *für sich* that allows for a transition from the dovetailing dialectic of the dreaming spirit to the self-consciously creative, communicative one.

I have focused on the Night in order to bring out its origin and importance. Even once we have become subjects who understand each other's language, we never shake the original dialectic character of the Night and the light. Communication requires the negative movement and stored images of "the dreaming spirit" in order not to fall into mechanical orders. Our bodies, our unconscious inwardizings, our dumb animal state, our selves as sign makers and name users are the conditions of language. We need names and shared linguistic memories in order to make ourselves understood to one another. The story we tell cannot be separated from the dialectic development of negative inwardizing and positive externalizing. The inwardizing imagination, the Night time and space of the mind—the dreaming spirit with its storehouse of images—is crucial to reflective intelligence.

Inwardizing is the key to properly understanding the imagination and all higher forms of cognition. The discussion of the Night in the 1805–06 lectures give us insight into how inwardizing is operative when one is thinking imaginatively deeply. It is in these lectures that we begin to see what the imagination comes to mean for Hegel, and what its role will be in his later works. It is here that we begin to see the significance of the imagination for our own thought.

Nevertheless, for Hegel, the inwardized contents must be externalized into signs if Spirit is to be. It is therefore important to move on to Hegel's account of the imagination in his much later lecture series on the *Philosophy of Subject Spirit* (1830). That account leaves aside the discussions of inwardizing and focuses instead on the *communicative* imagination.

CHAPTER 5

The Communicative Imagination

(*Philosophy of Subjective Spirit* 1830)

The purpose of this chapter is to provide an exegesis of the 1830 *Encyclopedia Philosophy of Spirit* discussion of the imagination, and in the process to explain how the inwardizing imagination becomes a communicative one. I discuss the dialectical moments leading up to the imagination. These are Intuition, and then Representation and its first moment, Recollection. Then I discuss Representation's second moment, Imagination. After that general account, I look in particular at the transition from symbol-making imagination to sign-making imagination. That transition is one from subjective authentication to objective authentication. This reveals that objective authentication depends on the *system* of language. Central to the system is the abstract universal "I". That "I" is not the Kantian transcendental unity of apperception. Rather, as sign and as concrete reality, the "I" results from communication between two or more signifying consciousnesses. Hegel's (Eurocentric) privileging of the spoken tonal word of an alphabetical language belonging to any progressive civilization (as opposed to a "stationary civilization," which uses hieroglyphs) stresses the temporal character of the communicative system. This stressing of the temporal highlights the central role of the imagination in the system, since, as we have seen in the previous chapter, the imagination's inwardizing is identified with negation and with time. According to Hegel, the sign is saved from being merely the entombing "pyramid" by the inherent interpersonal dialectic of the communicative, sign-making imagination. It also becomes apparent in this discussion that what was missing in the earlier psychology lecture accounts of the imagination was some way of distinguishing between the phenomenological account and the speculative, genetic account of the imagination. By this 1830 text, that problem has been solved: a phenomenology, it turns out, is a propaedeutic to speculative science. It is such because in the phenomenology we properly think the imagination through to the end, thereby discovering *how* to think. By 1830, Hegel has learned to put a phenomenology prior to speculative psychology, rather than have its moments confusedly mixed into the psychology section.

Ironically, this clearer, 1830 account, presupposes the speculative system that his earlier psychology lectures helped him to figure out, and which the *Phenomenology of Spirit* prepares us to use.

Let us turn now to the 1830 text. The sections with which we are concerned are the following:

A) Subjective Spirit→ I) Anthropology

B) Objective Spirit   II) Phenomenology

C) Absolute Spirit   **III) Psychology→**   **a) Theoretical Mind (Intelligence)→**

b) Practical Mind

c) Free Mind

1) Intuition

2) Representation→   i) Recollection (Erinnerung)

3) Thinking   ii) Imagination→   **aa) Reproductive Imagination (¶455)**

iii) Memory   **ßß) Phantasy: Symbolizing, Allegorizing, Poetic Imagination (¶456)**

cc) Sign-making Phantasy: Signs, Language (¶457 intro, ¶458 Signs, ¶459 Language, ¶460 Names).

If we follow the middle term of each triad, we see that we are in Subjective Spirit, in the psychology section, concerned with the intellect. We also see that for Hegel in 1830, the moments of the intellect are different from what they were in 1805–06. Here they are *Intuition (Anschaung)*, *Representation (Vorstellung)*, and *Thinking (Denken)*. The middle term of the intellect is representation, *Vorstellung*, and if we look to its three moments we find the imagination (*Einbildungskraft*) to be the second. The Imagination follows from *Recollection (Erinnerung)* and develops into *Memory (Gedächtnis)*.

There are several facts about this breakdown that indicate that Hegel gives the imagination a more important role in 1830 than he has previously. To begin with, we arrive at the imagination by following the middle moments of the intellect. This was not the case in the earlier versions before 1807.[1] By making imagination the middle moment of representation, Hegel reveals it to be central to intellectual activity. Since for Hegel the middle term in a conceptual development is always negative, the fact that we arrive at the imagination through the middle moment of the intellect and of representation highlights the notion that the imagination's activity is a negative moment in any dialectical construction.

Secondly, we see that the imagination is playing a more central role in 1830 because sign making and name making have their place *within* the dialectical moment of imagination rather than being subsequent moments to the imagination as in 1805–06.[2] This is somewhat mitigated by the fact that Hegel names "this sign-making activity . . . 'productive' *Memory*" (*Enc.Phil.Spir.* ¶458; my emphasis). But we must conclude that his inclusion of it in the section of the imagination, and his referral to it as sign-making *Phantasie* means that the imagination is at play here.

These points now need to be investigated in the text. Since it is similar to his working through of these moments in the earlier psychology lectures there is some inevitable repetition in our exegesis here. But this is worthwhile in order to generate the whole picture and the differences of this text from those earlier works.

Before I begin, it is worth recalling how far Hegel has come in determining the moments of Reason since 1801. In 1801, he defined Reason as "intuition of the self-shaping or objectively self-finding Absolute" (*Diff* 171). Since then, his development of the notion of Spirit has made it possible to view the imagination as one moment of Subjective Reason instead of the principle act of the Sundering Absolute. Hegel has realized the necessary one-sidedness of this initial moment within a subjective system, and he has revealed its final moment to be the starting point of objective, phenomenological development.

EXEGESIS

I will now briefly go over the moments leading up to and including the imagination.

Intuition

There are three moments of intuition. (a) The first moment of intuition is the feeling Spirit. That is the Spirit that has some sensible object over against it.[3] (b) The second moment consists of a diremption of this feeling Spirit into two. On the one hand, there is *awareness* of the object. In awareness the object belongs to Spirit, is its own (*es ist "Seinige"*). This is an experience of possession. On the other hand, there is the determination of the feeling in the sense that the object is a being (*das "Seiende"*). In other words, there is here the experience of something Negative over and against Spirit (though nevertheless posited by Spirit). This is the moment of being. (g) The third moment of intuition is intuition proper (*eigentliche Anschauung*). It only occurs when the intellect has unified these two sides (awareness and being) on the side of being. It does this by casting the immediate object into space and time (*Enz.Phil.G.* ¶448, p. 249). Intuitions are, therefore, temporal-spatial castings.

But this third moment of intuition, intuition proper, is one-sided. It is so because we have gone over to the side of being (*des Seienden*) at the expense of the side of possession (*das Seinige*). The conclusion of the moments of intuition therefore is the reemergence of the moment of ownership (the moment "*des Seinigen*"). Because possession is also a moment of awareness, it is a reassertion of awareness. At this point the intuition belongs to the Intellect, is "its own" ("*Ihrige*"). Precisely because of this change, in this concluding moment Hegel no longer speaks of intuition. Rather, we are now in the realm of representation (*Vorstellung*).[4]

Representation (Vorstellung)

The three moments of representation are, as noted above, Recollection, Imagination, and Memory. To understand the imagination, we have to look at the moments preceding and following it. The moments following intuition and directly prior to the imagination are those belonging to recollection (*Erinnerung*).

Recollection

The three moments making up the concept of recollection[5] are the following: (a) The image (*Bild*), (b) the nightly (unconscious) mine ("*der nächtliche [bewusstlose] Schacht*") which is the universality of the intellect, and (g) a recollected image. This last is due to the presence of a new external intuition, which solicits the internal image; there is then a relating of the new intuition to the inwardized image, and a subsumption of that intuition under the recollected image. In this last moment the image returns to consciousness in a new way as a recollected representation (as opposed to a merely inwardized image). That is, the external intuition which solicits, and the internal image which is solicited, fall under a universal representation.

Let us now go through these moments in more detail. (a) The first moment is that of the image. An image differs from an intuition in that the image is inwardized ("*Er-innert*"). The nature of the image is that it is (potentially) a universal representation. The representation is universal in that the intuition does not belong to the abstract, outside space and time (*äußerlichen Raum und Zeit*), but rather to the universal, inner space and time of the subject—in its own space and time, its *"eigenen Raum und ihre eigenen Zeit"* (*Enz.Phil.G.* ¶452). The universality consists in the fact that the image is able to be brought forth again potentially at any time and in any relation. In the inner space and in the inner time subject and object are no longer determined (*bedingt*) through the transforming power of space and time as external and continuous. The image is "freed from its first immediacy and abstract singularity over against others" and "taken up into the universality of the I in general" (¶452).[6]

(b) The second moment of recollection involves what Hegel calls a mine (*Schacht*), in which there is an infinite number of images. This infinity (*Unendlichkeit*) is the formal universal of the I. The image is unconsciously taken up into this infinity. It no longer exists as something existing externally. Rather, it is held in the nightly mine, ready to be called forth, reformed into consciousness.[7]

(g) In order that it come out of this *Schachte* into consciousness, in order that it be recollected, a new intuition is necessary. An external intuition is that which solicits the internal one back. In this way, the image is no longer simply unconsciously possessed potential. The moment of being (*des Seienden*) comes again into play. This relation of the image to a new intuition is what Hegel calls recollection proper *"eigentlich Erinnerung."* Only when the image is recalled, is/has the image a recalled existence—*"[ein] erinnert(es) Dasein."*

It is important to note that it is the intellect and not the external intuition that is the power behind the return of the images to conscious existence. The external intuition is necessary for the recollection of the image, but it is not sufficient. In other words, Hegel does not believe that intuitions alone act on the nightly mine to elicit the corresponding or associated images out of it. The mind, with its nightly mine (*Schacht*) is a responsive agent.[8] But nor is it the mind alone that seeks out the reminder in order to elicit the associated image. There is a dialectic between the external intuition, the power of the mind, and the internalized image in the mind. Hegel writes generally that the dialectic here is that the intellect relates the external intuition and the internal image. We will see later, however, that the specific power of the intellect that is active in recollection is reproductive imagination. Self-consciousness of that power is not yet present—that only comes farther on in the dialectic, with the moment of Memory.

Returning to the text, we see that the external intuition becomes dispensable once the internal image has come into existence. What is important here is that the image has been given existence (*Dasein*) again. This produces what Hegel calls real representation ("*eigentliche(r) Vorstellung*").

We saw in 1805–06 that this unity of mind with its inwardized content produced something "familiar." I think we are safe in assuming that this is what is going on here as well. Hegel asserts that real representation is the synthesis of the inner image with the "recollected existence" ("*des innerlichen Bildes mit dem erinnerten Dasein*"). *Erinnertes Dasein*—recollected existence—is not just the image, it is its recollectedness, its inward being-there, *Dasein*, inward presence; this recollectedness is synthesized with the image.

The movement can also be recapitulated in terms of *Seiende* and *Seinige*. The moment of *Seiende* (Being) had been hidden since the image was unconsciously *aufbewahrt* in the mine; the image had no explicit being and the intellect was not determined through it. But when the intellect recollects the image, the moment of *Seinige* (the moment of being-for-the intellect) gives being back to the image: the image is being-for the intellect, and the intellect is determined through it. We can also say it the other way around: the moment of *Seinige* was hidden in the mine; the image was not properly possessed by the intellect because the intellect was not conscious of it. But when the image has being again, its existence is a recollectedness, and so it exists properly as that which is there for the intellect. The moment of the image's being (*Seiende*) make its being for consciousness (*Seinige*) explicit.

This repossession of the image is different from the original inwardizing into the unconscious. "The image, which in the mine of the Intellect was only its *property*, now that it has been endued with externality, comes actually into its *possession*" (*Enc.Phil.Spir.* ¶454).[9] This possession is different from awareness and unconscious harboring because the mind is conscious of its content as having been brought out of itself.

The moment of recollection is predominately characterized by the need of an external intuition (cf. ¶455Z). Something must be externally there as a reminder, in order for the image to become conscious and thereby properly in the possession of the Intellect. But if we focus on the power of the intellect rather than on the objective trigger for the recollection of an image, we uncover the activity of the imagination. "The intelligence which is active in this possession is the *reproductive imagination*, where the images issue from the inward world belonging to the ego, which is now the power over them" (¶455, p. 206). We can now begin to talk of the activity of the imagination.

The section on the imagination begins with Hegel's investigation into how the intellect is the power of determination or "reproduction" of an image.[10] The imagination is the moment in which the unconscious manifold that the image has become, is synthesized into an image that is then being-there for the intellect. The imagination is implicit in recollection, acting within it and for the purposes of the repossession of the image as representation. The work of the imagination is solicited in recollection in that the intellect actually reproduces the image of which it is reminded by the external intuition. In recollection, that act is involuntary. It is, however, an act that can be voluntary: as the imagination, reproduction stands on its own (¶455Z, p. 208). *In itself*, the imagination is a higher order of synthesis. Unlike recollection, it does not need the help of an external intuition in order to reproduce the image. This is what makes the imagination such an important moment: in it we begin to see the power of the intellect in distinction from its relation to the external world. At this juncture, one can see how some philosophers would find, in the productivity of the imagination, cause to make a transition from a mimetic theory of mental representation to a mind-first theory (as, for example, Fichte did). But Hegel never becomes a mind-first philosopher. Nonetheless, the productive power of the imagination, even within its reproduction of images, needs to be thoroughly understood if we are to understand his philosophy in general. For the imagination is the intellect's nascent in-itself.

Imagination

Imagination is "in general, the determinant of the images" (¶455Z, p. 208). It differs from recollection in that it actualizes (*verwirklicht*) the moment of the intellect's positing (*des Setzen*).[11] As in Kant, the imagination does not need the mnemonic help of an intuition in order to (re)produce its representation. Therefore, the reproductive imagination is "the coming-forth of the images out of the self's own inner, which is also their power" (my translation; *Enc.Phil.Spir.* ¶455).[12]

Hegel offers a general summation of the activity of the imagination: "Imagination fashions for itself a content peculiar to it by *thinking* the object, by bringing out what is universal in it, and giving it determinations which belong to the ego. In this way imagination ceases to be a merely formal recollection (inwardization) and becomes a recollection which affects the *content*, *generalizes* it, thus creating *general* representations or ideas" (¶451Z, p. 202). This general account needs to be broken into its moments.

Not surprisingly, Hegel divides the imagination into three moments: (aa) *Reproductive imagination* (¶455; (ßß) *Phantasy, symbolizing, allegorizing, or poetic imagination* (¶456; (cc) *Sign-making phantasy: Signs, Language* (¶457 intro, ¶458 signs, ¶459 language, ¶460 Names).

(aa) The first thing the imagination does, as we have seen, is bring forth images into existence. This is a formal (*formelle*) capacity, or one might better call it a forming capacity. It is synthesis. It is what is active in recollection's hauling of an image out of the nightly mine: "[I]ntelligence, emerging from its abstract inward being into determinateness, disperses the night-like darkness enveloping the wealth of its images and banishes it by the luminous clarity of a present image" (¶455Z, p. 208)

(ßß) The next level of the imagination is *Phantasy, symbolizing, allegorizing, or poetic imagination.* I will refer to it as *Symbolizing Phantasie* for short. It accomplishes a more complex task: it is the connecting of some images with other images, to form a universal representation. "Mental representation (*Vorstellung*) is the mean in the syllogism of the elevation of intelligence, the link between the two significations of self-relatedness—viz. *being* and *universality*, which in consciousness receive the title of object and subject" (¶455, p. 207). The creation of the universal repeats the forming activity of the imagination of giving existence to the image, but it is more complex because it also involves images already formed by the imagination, the relation of those images to one another, and their unity under a single representation. It is, therefore, a forming for the purposes of giving concrete existence to the universal representation: it is the creation of the symbol.

In the Zusatz it is written that "at this stage, imagination appears as the activity of *associating* images." But Hegel has earlier specified (in ¶455) that this is not the activity of mere association: "[T]he train of images and representations suggested by association is the sport of vacant-minded ideation" (¶455). And with regard to association causing general ideas, Hegel ridicules the notion of a "force of attraction in like images . . . which at the same time would have the negative power of rubbing off the dissimilar elements against each other" (¶455). He claims instead that "[t]his force is really intelligence itself—the self-identical ego which by its internalizing recollection gives the images *ipso facto* generality, and subsumes the single intuition under the already internalized image" (¶455). In paragraph 456, Hegel refers to this process of subsuming the individual under the universal and their consequent link. He writes that "intelligence is more than merely a general form: its inwardness is an internally definite concrete subjectivity with a substance and value of its own, derived from some interest, some latent concept or Ideal principle, so far as we may by anticipation speak of such" (¶456, p. 209). It is not clear here just what this latent concept or Ideal principle is. But what is key for our purposes is that it is the power of the intelligence which, according to some principle(s), does the synthesis. Hegel here refers to this power directly as the imagination:

> Intelligence is the power which wields the stores of images and ideas belonging to it, and which thus . . . freely combines and subsumes these stores in obedience to its tenor. Such is creative

imagination (*Phantasie*)—symbolic, allegoric, or poetical imagination—where the intelligence gets a definite embodiment in
this store of ideas and informs them with its general tone. These
more or less concrete, individualized creations are still "syntheses": for the material, in which the subjective principles and
ideas get a mentally pictorial existence, is derived from the data
of intuition. (¶456, p. 209)

In the Zusatz, Hegel specifies that regardless of the theory one holds about
the generation of abstract ideas, what he is concerned with here is "simply and
solely the *generality* of the idea" and its link with the image (¶456Z, p. 210).
The general idea "is the inward side; the image, on the other hand, is the
external side. . . . The truth of these two sides is . . . their unity" (¶456Z, p.
210). In an interesting echo of and contrast with Kant's analogy of chemical
union of the world of experience with the moral law in the *Critique of Practical
Reason*,[13] Hegel's claim here is that the unity of image and general idea is not
a chemical product.

[T]his unity, the imaging of the universal and the generalization of
the image, comes about not by the general idea uniting with the
image to form a *neutral*, so to speak, *chemical* product, but by the
idea actively proving itself to be the *substantial* power over the
image, subjugating it as an *accident*, making itself into the image's
soul, and becoming in the image *for itself*, inwardizing itself, manifesting its own self. (¶456Z, p. 210)

This unifying activity is the work of the productive imagination. "Intelligence,
having brought about this unity of the universal and the particular, of the
inward and the outward, of the idea (representation) and intuition, and in this
way restoring the totality present in intuition as now authenticated, the
ideating activity is completed within itself in so far as it is productive imagination" (¶456Z, p. 210).

In the move from recollection to imagination, we have moved not just
from an involuntary reproduction of images to a voluntary one. We have also
moved from recollecting images and connecting them with others in a way
that is inspired by the external world, to a more complex kind of recollection.
This latter is the recollection of singular intuitions from the external world
and singular images within the mind, *under* a voluntarily produced, general
idea that represents them all. In this activity of the productive, creative imagination, the mind knows itself to be this power, rather than being merely in
the grips of a recollection. Its ideas are "self-sprung" (¶457, p. 210).

What are essential to this second level of the imagination are the following. The imagination subsumes images under itself, gathering them up into a universal; the universal is nothing other than the power of the mind and is referred to here as the productive or creative imagination; the gathering under a universal is, therefore, a subjective process; but, since the imagination institutes a symbol or sign to represent the gathering into universality, the imagination moves toward being objective. Ironically, what gives a universal objectivity is individuality. We see this in the next moment, in the creation of signs.

(cc) This is the point at which the third level of the imagination, sign-making *phantasie*, is introduced. It must be introduced here, because so far, the spontaneity of the creative imagination is subjective (¶457, p. 210). That is, "intelligence has therein *implicitly* returned both to identical self-relation and to immediacy" (¶457, pp. 210–11), but it must do this return *explicitly*. Creative imagination needs to move from subjective authentication to objective authentication. To do this, it must create signs for its general ideas. Hegel explains:

> As reason, its first start was to appropriate the immediate datum in itself (¶445, 435) i.e. to universalize it; and now its action as reason (¶438) is from the present point directed towards giving the character of an existent to what in it has been perfected to concrete auto-intuition. In other words, it aims at making itself *be* and be a fact. Acting on this view, it is self-uttering, intuition-producing: the imagination which creates signs. (¶457, p. 211)

While intuition and recollection were themselves syntheses, "it is not till creative imagination that intelligence ceases to be the vague mine and the universal, and becomes an individuality, a concrete subjectivity, in which the self-reference is defined both to being and to universality" (¶457, p. 211). With the symbol and sign we enter into the arena of externalizing the imagination's content for others. We can therefore assert that here, the intellect is not just forming in an increasingly complex way, rather, this is the beginning of the intellect as *informing*—and the beginning therefore of its possession of information. The latter precision is the transition to memory. Thus, at this third level of the imagination, "[t]he image produced by imagination of an object is a bare mental or subjective intuition: in the sign or symbol it adds intuitability proper; and in mechanical memory it completes, so far as it is concerned, this form of *being*" (¶457, p. 211).

I want to focus in particular on the symbol-making and the sign-making aspects of the imagination. Technically, it is only when the image that is used to mean something differs radically from the meant object that we have a sign. Only then have we entered the third moment of the imagination: *Sign-making Phantasie*.[14] Unlike in his earlier *Philosophy of Spirit* lectures, Hegel here differentiates between symbol and sign.[15] Let us look at this distinction more carefully.

The distinction lies in that the symbol relies on something in the image to portray the meaning, whereas the sign is indifferent to its meaning. For example, in the symbol of Jupiter, "[t]he strength of Jupiter . . . is represented by the eagle because this is looked upon as strong" (*Enc.Phil.Spir.* ¶457, p. 212).[16] The sign does not rely at all on the character of the image it is using: there is a distinction between the immediate content that the sign is and that content of which it is the sign. In the sign, the matter (intuition) "does not count positively or as representing itself, but as representative of something else" (*Enc.Phil.Spir.* ¶458, p. 212). Thus, "[t]he sign is some immediate intuition, representing a totally different import from what naturally belongs to it; it is the pyramid into which a foreign soul has been conveyed, and where it is conserved" (*Enc.Phil.Spir* ¶458, Remark).

Hegel writes that the creative, productive imagination provides symbols. But to arrive at language we have to leave behind the symbol's dependence on images. Symbols have externality, but because that externality is rooted in images, symbols are merely "subjectively authentic" (¶457Z). They don't reach beyond my particular attempt at meaning, they don't signify anything to other people. In order to communicate, therefore, the intelligence "necessarily progresses from subjective authentication of the general idea mediated by the image, to its objective, absolute authentication" (¶457Z). This transition involves moving from symbols to signs. It is a transition in which the representation is "liberated from the image's content."

> Now the general idea, liberated from the image's content, in making its freely selected external material into something that can be intuitively perceived, produces what has to be called a sign—in specific distinction from symbol. The sign must be regarded as a great advance on the symbol. Intelligence, in indicating something by a sign, has finished with the content of intuition, and the sensuous material receives for its soul a signification foreign to it. Thus, for example, a cockade, or a flag, or a tombstone, signifies something totally different from what it immediately indicates. (*Enc.Phil.Spir.* ¶457Z, p. 212)

The transition from symbol to sign deserves yet more attention. The imagination, in its early moments, is only *generative* of universals. It is not capable of *recalling* universals. As merely generative, the imagination's production of a given symbol is a one-time event; further use of the symbol involves remembering the imagination's three-step path of generating the images, subsuming them under the universal, and generating an image that represents that universal. When this path is traversed a second or more times, we are traversing the imagination's activity. This traversing cannot be done without both the activity of the imagination and the activity of memory, for memory is what allows us to hold and synthesize the previous imaginings, as well as the activity involved in making those imaginings. This process generates signs rather than symbols.[17]

The analogy of the map that we used to explain the 1805–06 transition between *signs* and *names* can be used here to explain the difference now between *symbols* and *signs*. In both instances, we move from a map that is subjective to one that can be used to show others. Pointing to a line between two points in the sand provides a symbol, but not one that adequately conveys what we mean. If we repeat instances of the symbol in many contexts, we gather that symbol up into a new universal, the sign. Then the line, instead of symbolizing something incommunicable, signifies travel. The sign as convention is a result of a repetition of the work of the symbolic imagination, and a raising of what is recollected in that symbolic activity to a new universal, the sign. If we remained at the level of symbol-making imagination, we would have a production of a symbol that is both too determinate and not determinate enough because it is without context. We make the transition to a sign by repeatedly traversing the imagination's work and reproducing that pathway as itself a form that is conventionally determinate in a meaning system.[18]

The convention is not arbitrarily set up, it is the folding of the imagination's activity back on its previous sublations. The sign rises out of sublated symbols. A convention, before it becomes a dogma, arises from the desire to make the symbol intelligible. It is originally an act of self-consciousness. It derives necessity as much from that self-consciousness as from the recollections that are folded into the meaningful, universal, conventional sign. There is subjective and, now, communal history in the process. It is not an arbitrary product of a collective will. The sign grows. Recalling the earlier *Geistesphilosophien*, we can say the following. A convention arises from the dovetailing of time and space; since the dialectical imagination produces images that endure and disappear, and since the dialectical imagination is itself a consciousness that endures and disappears, the convention arises from imagination's *inwardizing,* that is, from its intuitions, its familiar recollections and its attempts at meaningful reproductions. Through further dialectical reproductions, these first attempts at meaningful reproductions are repeated and gathered into a new form; they become conventional reproductions, signs.

A conventional sign gets its systematic character from being a comprehensive dialectic. It is systematic because it takes up the earlier dialectical moments into itself dialectically, and is thereby determined by them. The system is the necessity and shape of the dialectic. To forget this origination is to lose the self-conscious character of language; communication would sink back into subjective symbolizings.

While the imagination gives rise to convention, it also prevents the system from becoming dogmatic. So its role in memory must be examined closely. I do so in the next chapter.

The characteristic of the sign is that it is much more mediated as a result of the activity of the imagination and memory, and therefore is not immediately dependent on images.

> The *sign* is different from the *symbol*: for in the symbol the original characters (in essence and conception) of the visible object are more or less identical with the import which it bears as symbol; whereas in the sign, strictly so-called, the natural attributes of the intuition, and the connotation of which it is a sign, have nothing to do with each other. *Intelligence therefore gives proof of wider choice and ampler authority* in the use of intuitions when it treats them as designatory (significative) rather than as symbolical. (*Enc.Phil.Spir.* ¶458, p. 213 my emphasis)

This mediating characteristic of objective authenticity needs now to be investigated further. The first thing that can be said is that objective authentication through signs takes shape as the system of language, or as what Hegel refers to as the "institution" of intelligence (¶459). In that system the intelligence has, as we saw above, "ampler authority."[19] The reason for that is on the one hand that representations are mediated not just through the imagination and its products, but through the imagination and memory. The other reason is that that mediation cannot happen in one psyche alone. For Hegel it is an interpersonal process.

Let us look therefore at the kind of self involved in the transition from symbol-making imagination to sign-making imagination, and why that self is ultimately interdependent with other selves.

Hegel asserts that the imagination's reproduced symbolic content is impressed (*geprägt*) with universality, and that that universality is the "I." The self finds itself as well as the image when it signifies. It is that difference which, when realized as a power of the intellect, makes it possible to be more free in choosing what image will represent the universal representation. The freedom lies in the difference between that which is represented and that which represents. It is this freedom that allows for the creation not only of repeated symbols, but of signs.

We are already familiar with this freedom, this self, this pure subject from the 1805-6 lectures. It is the inwardizing imagination. It was defined as time. Hegel declares this here as well: "The intuition . . . acquires, when employed as a sign, the peculiar characteristic of existing only as superseded and sublimated. Such is the negativity of intelligence; and thus the truer phase of the intuition used as a sign is existence in *time* . . ." (¶459). Part of this temporal character lies in the arbitrariness of the intuition used by the sign. This is why Hegel goes on to privilege alphabetical languages over hieroglyphic ones: the former are more versatile and show development of Spirit, whereas the latter remain stagnate because of their reliance on the symbolic. Another part of the temporal character of the sign lies in its being produced as a vocal note. The temporal character raises language to the "ideational realm" (¶459).

The negativity of intelligence is not limited to the domain of one self. The "ampler" range of options presented in sign making involves repetition and other selves. In fact, we cannot understand signs without looking at the interpersonal character of sign making. To have a "system" of associations implies a self familiar with the system. That inwardizing self must be familiar with a universal synthesis that has objective authentication. This involves learning, which involves repetition and communication. It is only with the consciousness of a fully developed communicative "I" that system can be attributed to recollection. Let me explain further.

For Hegel a conscious system, even for the most minimal system of I = I, requires consciousness of repetition. But the simple system of a person's identity also implies the radical alterity of another universalizing human being. It is one thing to say that for pragmatic reasons we abandon private associations in favor of social ones that work. But the issue is deeper: the very possibility of having a private, intentionally repeated association—a private symbol—could only be for the purposes of communicating identity. The desire for identity only arises when the symbol-image is recognized not to be the finite representation it was meant to be, not to be the singular association I mean, but rather a plurality of associations that were not meant. And such a revelation—that the symbolic image is a plurality of associations and not at all simple—arises through negation. That negation, if it is not to presuppose the repetition or self-consciousness which we are trying to explain, must come from other consciousnesses. It is another person's interpretation of the symbol,[20] another person's different interpretation or their perplexity—their different association with the same image, that causes the repetition necessary for identity.

Private language is impossible. So-called private meaning systems not only presuppose communication, but to be properly systematic (which means to *continue to be* systematic) they require *repeated* communication. The reason for repeating a symbolic association can only be for the purpose of ordering (an) experience according to an internal identity system. To be properly systematic, it has to be opened up to external exchange. (The artistic symbol is not different from the sign in this way.)

Thus, according to Hegel in the 1830 text, sign making is a necessarily interpersonal form of externalization: "The arbitrary nature of the connection between the sensuous material and a general idea occurring here, has the necessary consequence that the significance of the sign must first be learned. This is especially true of language signs" (*Enc.Phil.Spir.* ¶457Z, p. 212).

The beginning of *Vorstellung* is the moment of intuition inwardized and become mine. But it is only truly mine when I pull it out of the night. Prior to that it is unconscious. Its being mine is equivalent to its being universal, since the self is the form of universality—the self is that to which synthetic unity is referred. However, neither the self nor the universal representation has concrete universality until it becomes articulate(d). It must be part of a system before I can be properly conscious of it. As merely reproduced (once), it does not have the continuity needed for meaning.

When I give the universal external shape, it comes to be for others as well as for me. It becomes subjectively concrete in a public way. The key to the transition from a private into a public space is the self. In the *Logic* Hegel clarifies that "when I say 'I,' I *mean* me *as this one* excluding all others; but what I say ('I') is precisely everyone, an 'I' that excludes all others from itself" (*Logic* ¶20, p. 51). The "I" is also a universal. Hegel continues:

> Kant employed the awkward expression, that I "accompany" all my representations—and my sensations, desires, actions etc. too. "I" is the universal in and for itself, and communality is one more form—although an external one—of universality. All other humans have this in common with me, to be "I," just as all *my* sensations, representations, etc., have in common that they are *mine*. But, taken abstractly as such, "I" is pure relation to itself, in which abstraction is made from representation and sensation, from every state as well as from every peculiarity of nature, of talent, of experience, and so on. To this extent, "I" is the existence of the entirely *abstract* universality, the abstractly *free*. Therefore "I" is *thinking* as a *subject. . . . (Logic* ¶20, p. 51)

The move from *Vorstellen* to *Denken*, within philosophical *psychology*, is the move from imagination to language. In that transition, the imagination's associative pathways, and its subsumption of images under universals, become suffused with universality. But this process is also that by which the I becomes developed, determinate. Just as in symbol making we saw that the universal subjugates the image "as an *accident* . . . [and makes] itself into the image's soul," in language "thought is itself and its other . . . it overgrasps its other and . . . nothing escapes it. And because *language* is the work of thought, nothing can be said in language that is not universal" (*Logic* ¶20, p. 50).

Once we have this universality, and the communication that it is, we can go back to merely private symbols, but we cannot make sense to others with them. Hegel declares in no uncertain terms: "I cannot say what I merely *mean*. And *what cannot be said*—feeling, sensation—is not what is most important, most true, but what is most insignificant, most untrue" (*Logic* ¶20, pp. 50–51).

The self, then, is the form of universality. But it does not as such determine the content of the synthesis. For a communication system there has to be negation, and only another person can provide this at this level. Therefore, what is needed is not only one individual's inwardizing and externalizing; what is needed is the encounter of two inwardizing and externalizing consciousnesses. The communicative, sign-making imagination is the dialectic, in time and space, of two imaginations. In the development of consciousness, the sign is the first form of representation that captures this dialectic and brings Spirit into the world.

Hegel's use of the pyramid to symbolize the sign and its content highlights two things. It highlights both the death and the life that such an encounter between two individuals brings. On the one hand, convention entombs. Any reification, any identity, is fixity, non-movement. The imagination's association is fixed in the sign. On the other, the negative inwardizing activity of the interpreting other brings life, interpretation, difference. It introduces the necessary changeableness of each person's meaning.

Once we reach pure thoughts and their reproduction, we have moved well beyond the power of the imagination. According to Hegel, the power of the imagination is the reproduction of images, not of pure thoughts.[21] My claim that the imagination is at work in pure thought as well as in image and symbol formation is nonetheless true. For I am not claiming that the image-forming part of the imagination is at work in pure thought. Rather, it is the inwardizing activity, first seen in the imagination's activity in recollection, that remains central in pure thought. That is why we must think through the imagination first in order to do speculative philosophy: we have to learn not only conventional signs, but *how* to think. Thinking involves self-conscious use of the negative moment of the imagination. Only through that can we arrive at authentic communication. For this reason, despite the important role played by memory here, we are justified in referring to the 1830 theory of imagination as that of the *communicative* imagination. Logic is also something communicated.

COMMENTARY

There are three points I want to discuss that arise from what I have just elucidated in Hegel. The first concerns Hegel's claims about the difference of his theory from Kant's theory of the mind.[22] According to Hegel, Kant treats the mental process too much as a collection or powers.[23] This is a similar criticism to the one Hegel makes of the empiricists in the Skepticism essay. There Hegel writes: "As for the concepts, they stem from the sort of empirical psychology that disperses the spirit into mutually external qualities, and hence finds no whole, no genius and no talent among these qualities, but *describes them as if they were a sack full of faculties* . . . ."[24] In the *Philosophy of Spirit* lectures of 1830, Hegel criticizes faculty-oriented investigations in general for their "want of organic unity." In such approaches, he argues,

> [a]ny aspect which can be distinguished in mental action is stereotyped as an independent entity, and the mind is thus made a skeleton-like mechanical collection. It makes absolutely no difference if we substitute the expression "activities" for power and faculties. Isolate the activities and you similarly make the mind a mere aggregate, and treat their essential correlation as an external incident. (*Enc.Phil.Spir.* ¶445, p. 189)

Given these criticisms, one might well ask how Hegel's division of the imagination into three "parts" avoid this problem. Hegel's answer is that

> the *true satisfaction* . . . is only afforded by an intuition permeated by intellect and mind, by rational conception, by products of imagination which are permeated by reason and exhibit ideas—in a word, by *cognitive* intuition, cognitive conception, etc. The truth ascribed to such satisfaction lies in this, that intuition, conception, etc. are not isolated, and exist only as "moments" in the totality of cognition itself. (*Enc.Phil.Spir.* ¶445, p. 190; *Enz.Phil.G.* ¶445, s. 243)

The "truly philosophical grasp" of these forms of mind (the faculties of recollection, imagination, and memory) "just consists in comprehending the rational connection existing between them, in recognizing them as stages in the organic development of intelligence."

By 1830 Hegel has arrived at this truly philosophical grasp. We saw in his earlier versions of the *Geistesphilosophie* that Hegel had methodological problems. These problems made it hard for him to derive a convincing notion of the imagination and the interrelation of it to the other powers. By 1830, however, Hegel has written the *Phenomenology of Spirit* as a propaedeutic to Speculative Science, and rewritten it as that which precedes psychology in the

Philosophy of Spirit. In Hegel's discussion here, the *Phenomenology of Spirit* is presupposed, which means that one must already be at the standpoint of science to do philosophical psychology. It is the success of thinking the imagination through to the end in a phenomenology that allows Hegel to articulate a successful speculative psychology in 1830, one that neither makes the imagination into one mechanical-like faculty among others, nor runs into the methodological problems we have witnessed in the earlier lecture series. That is why an analysis of whether the *Phenomenology* actually succeeds is imperative to understanding Hegel's Speculative Philosophy.

Our task is to understand how the *Philosophy of Spirit* psychology lectures can help us understand how the imagination works in the *Phenomenology*. It might seem like a step in the opposite direction to find that the *Phenomenology* determined the success of his final account of the imagination in his 1830 psychology. But this makes even more sense of our claim that the *Phenomenology* is a working through of the imagination. With the *Phenomenology*, Hegel has finally successfully worked out the dialectical nature of representation. It is because he has thought through the imagination, and now *thinks* through it, that his "truly philosophical grasping" of the imagination, and of any other object, is now possible.

The second issue to discuss has to do with how reason and the imagination are linked. We recall that in *Faith and Knowledge* Hegel asserted alongside Schelling that the imagination *is* reason. It was reason as the self-sundering Absolute. In 1830 Hegel discusses their identity but in a different way:

> As reason, its first start was to appropriate the immediate datum in itself (¶445, ¶435), i.e. to universalize it; and now its action as reason (438) is from the present point directed towards giving the character of an existent to what in it has been perfected to concrete auto-intuition. In other words, it aims at making itself *be* and be a fact. Acting on this view, it is self-uttering, intuition-producing: the imagination which creates signs. (*Enc.Phil.Spir.* ¶457, p. 211)

Hegel writes that imagination is "only a nominal reason, because the matter or theme it embodies is to imagination *qua* imagination a matter of indifference; whilst reason *qua* reason also insists upon the *truth* of its content" (*Enc.Phil.Spir.* ¶457, p. 211; *Enz.Phil.G.* ¶457 An., p. 268). Such a claim suggests that speculative reason does move beyond the imagination's symbolic mediation of Spirit. It nevertheless does not prevent us from claiming that the negative movement of inwardizing and externalizing that characterizes the imagination remains in speculative logic. The *Logic*, while not symbolically mediated, is sign-mediated. We have discussed how conventional sign systems arise out of the dialectical imagination. A speculative understanding of the truth of that process and its content only brings the imagination into the light of reason, revealing reason's indebtedness to it.

A third point for commentary concerns how Hegel could refer to symbol-making imagination as that which is used in art. Hegel writes that "[productive imagination] forms the formal aspect of art; for art represents the true universal, or the Idea [Idee] in the form of sensuous existence, of the image" (*Enc.Phil.Spir.* ¶456Z, p. 210). There is a risk here of confusing Hegel's account of the development of symbol making imagination in the genetic development of thought, with the return to symbol-making for the purposes of art. Clearly, the latter involves a consciousness already fully equipped with language and sign making, for the return to art is a self-conscious attempt on the part of Spirit to represent itself through the socially recognized medium of art. Art is a form of Absolute Spirit according to Hegel. The genetic account of symbol-making imagination is not about artistic creation; Hegel indicates that symbol-making imagination is still only subjectively authentic. But it is that form which is returned to during artistic expression, and artistic expression, as a form of Absolute Spirit necessarily presupposes authentic objectivity. This is not to say that there are not different levels of self-conscious, authentic objectivity. This, and the artist's activity, are topics for the next chapter.

CONCLUSION

This final version of the *Philosophy of Spirit* presents more determinate moments of the imagination than either of the earlier Jena lecture series. Also, in the distinction between symbol and sign, Hegel has provided a clearer distinction between subjective and objective externalizations. The tension between a genetic account and an account of the self's return to these levels of consciousness is resolved, due, I will argue in Part Three, to the role that the *Phenomenology* plays in Hegel's thought.

It is worth taking stock as well, at this point, of the change in Hegel's terminology from the earliest Jena works to this final version of the *Philosophy of Spirit*. We have seen the "Night," the abyss of Reason gradually changed into the "nächtlicher Schacht"—the nightly mine. To recapitulate, in the *Differenzschrift* and in *Faith and Knowledge* the former was the return to the indifference point, the sinking of the finite into negation, a return to the Absolute's originary sundering. We have seen how in 1803–04 *Geistesphilosophie* this process is discussed as the time-space, dovetailing dialectic of the imagination; how later in the 1805–06 *Geistesphilosophie* the Night is a determining inwardizing movement of the imagination—time— the negation that places the world over against a subject, the dialectical repetition of which reveals it to be the power of reproducing images out of the inner self and synthesizing them; and we have seen how in 1830 the imagination is the nightly mine, in and through which communication arises. What in the earlier works was the absolute sundering imagination, remains here. But it remains with an important difference: the sundering becomes recognized by consciousness as the *aufhebende* movement of self-representing consciousness, a self-representing that finds its difference not only in the negative inwardizing, but just as necessarily in the determinate differences of communication through symbol and sign-making *Phantasie*. And sign-making *Phantasie* only works when two or more consciousnesses interact. In this way, the self that is the "I" of language, is the "we" of community, and the negation needed to create the symbol become the interpersonal otherness needed to create the sign.

In other words, in the earlier works, Hegel is mostly concerned with the genesis of the Absolute. The Absolute is therefore characterized in the more metaphorical terms of the "Night" and the "abyss." But in the following Jena years, Hegel develops his notion of Spirit. Gradually his concern lies not only with the genesis, but also with the *Spirit* of the Absolute. Community and language play an increasingly central role in the dialectic of the imagination. As we will soon see, this is important in understanding the role of *Einbildungskraft* and *Phantasie* in the *Phenomenology of Spirit*.

Hegel also turns to the metaphor of the *Schacht* or "mine." *Aufhebende* consciousness is thus a reflective process of "mining" experience, a mining that is also a development of it, and one that only makes sense as the activity of a community of selves. So we can see that his original concern with the Night of the Absolute, has been recognized as a concern for the depth of Spirit. Now we must look more closely at what that means for objective authentication.

PART TWO

Imagination in Practice:

"Objective Authentication"

CHAPTER 6

Memory, the Artist's *Einbildungskraft, Phantasie,*

and Aesthetic *Vorstellungen* (*Lectures on Aesthetics*)

The only place in which the word *Einbildungskraft* arises in the *Phenomenology of Spirit* is in a passage in which Hegel is explicitly distancing his philosophy from the celebration of creative artistic genius. His distancing is based on a Romantic movement's misuse of *Einbildungskraft* in their *Phantasie,* and on his belief that we must avoid such misuse when we are trying to understand the forms (*Vorstellungen*) of experience. Since the *Phenomenology of Spirit* is the science of experience, its concern is precisely the development of a proper grasp of these forms of experience and of how representing (*vorstellen*) works. Therefore, a close examination of the role of *Einbildungskraft* in *Phantasie,* and how the Romantics failed to understand that role in their poetic repre-senting (*vorstellen*) is essential for our subsequent discussion of the role of *die Einbildungskraft* and *das Vorstellen* in the *Phenomenology of Spirit.*

The first key player in this discussion is Memory.

MEMORY

We recall that in the 1830 *Philosophy of Spirit* lectures, representation (*Vorstellung*) has three moments: recollection, imagination (*Einbildungskraft*), and memory. Memory is the transition from representation to thought.

The paragraph in which Hegel discusses the objective, absolute authentication through signs is the same one in which he introduces memory (¶458).

> The right place for the sign is that just given: where intelligence—which as intuiting generates the form of time and space, but appears as recipient of sensible matter, out of which it forms ideas—now gives its own original ideas a definite existence from itself, treating the intuition (or time and space as filled full) as its own property, deleting the connotation which properly and naturally belongs to it, and conferring on it another connotation as its soul and import. This sign-creating activity may be distinctively named "productive" Memory (the primarily abstract "Mnemosyne"); since memory, which in ordinary life is often used as interchangeable and synonymous with remembrance (recollection), and even with conception and imagination, has always to do with signs only. (*Enc.Phil.Spir.* ¶458, 213)

Memory is the activity that (a) retains the meaning of names, (b) recollects the meaning of a given tone, and (c) is mechanical insofar as we can memorize a sentence and repeat it without understanding it.

Memory reenacts the earlier moments of recollection and imagination, but it also differs from these earlier moments. Memory repeats the activity of recollection in that we take into our mine (*Schacht*) a sensible intuition—the tone of voice expressing a name. Just as in recollection another external intuition can invoke the reproduction of the image in the mine, in memory an external intuition—the tone—solicits for memory representations from the mine.

There is however a difference between memory and recollection. Instead of the recollection of a simple image, memory recalls a name. A name, unlike an image, is complex in that memory's representations bear the trait of the imagination's work. Memory involves the repeated traversing of the associational pathways of the imagination. Hearing a word or a sequence of words causes the mind to reproduce universals. These are not images but orders of their association. What is called forth by memory, or what bodies-forth as a memory is not a temporally and spatially detached image, but a representation (*Vorstellung*). It is a synthesis that no longer necessarily depends on an image. As sign-making *Phantasie* it is still picture thinking (*vorstellen*), but as the creation of names, it is independent of images. Recollection, in contrast, always has to do with the reproduction of images.

Also, although recollection and memory are the same in the sense that in each the reproduced representation is familiar to me, recollection makes something subjectively familiar *to me* (and potentially *only* to me), whereas memory concerns socially accepted, objective universals. In memory, the sign is recognized by others. When something becomes familiar to me through memory, I am learning to communicate in my culture and language. What is remembered belongs to the world of intuited, shared utterances, and includes all the potential and actual particularizations of that universal sign into other people's particular experiences of it. I am a member of the waking Spirit. I belong to the community with a self-reflective, communicative imagination.

Recollection is private; memory is both private and public. The place of the image is in the mind, whereas the name can be uttered as a recognized tone. The tone occurs in time and space and is finite and fleeting when uttered. Yet the meaning persists for the individual to interpret. The two sides of the tonal word (outer and inner) as well as its presence and absence in time exhibits the dovetailing movement of the imagination we discussed in chapter 3.

Memory is also similar yet different from imagination (*die Einbildungskraft*). The first difference is that imagination does not synthesize by itself the difference between sign and signified. That requires repetition, and memory is precisely the repetition of imagination's synthesizing. It is for that reason that *Sign-making Phantasie* includes memory. The difference between sign and signified is the space of other people's particular syntheses/experiences of the expressed universal. Recognition of that space is Spirit awake to itself as such.

This multiplication of particulars under one universal occurs both in the individual's experience and by virtue of its being interpreted by many individuals. Because of it, even though the name requires associations provided by the imagination, the name exceeds the imagination's comprehension. The name is like Descartes' million-sided polygon that can be thought but not imagined: "Given the name lion, we need neither the actual vision of the animal, nor its image even: the name alone, if we *understand* it, is the unimaged simple representation. We *think* in names" (*Enc.Phil.Spir.* ¶462).

Memory is the transition to thought because it produces the kind of artifact that only thought can manage. While imagination produces images formed from intuitions, memory "has ceased to deal with an image derived from intuition . . . it has rather to do with an object which is the product of intelligence itself" (*Enc.Phil.Spir.* ¶462, 220). Memory can involve *Phantasie's* products in a system of reflected meanings so complex that they exceed containment within the symbolic image.

But memory also needs the imagination. Memory is limited to repetition of its signs and their appearance in certain orders. Memory is only the "outward and existing side" of intelligence (*Enc.Phil.Spir.* ¶462).[1] To be fully thought, memory must harness the inward side, which means making use of the imagination.[2] The merely outward and existing side of memory is evident in the third moment of memory. Hegel aptly calls it mechanical repetition.

> [T]his reception [by memory] has, at the same time, the meaning that intelligence thereby takes on the nature of a *thing* and to such a degree that subjectivity, in its distinction from the thing, becomes quite empty, a mindless container of words, that is, a mechanical memory. In this way the profusion of remembered words can, so to speak, switch round to become the extreme alienation of intelligence. (*Enc.Phil.Spir.* ¶462Z)[3]

A subtle but central problem arises here. Hegel is distinguishing between memorizing and *really* making sense. But what does it mean to really make sense? As we have seen already, on the one hand Hegel does not believe the answer lies in the ineffable:

> To want to think without words as Mesmer once attempted is, therefore, a manifestly irrational procedure which, as Mesmer himself admitted, almost drove him insane. But it is also ridiculous to regard as a defect of thought and a misfortune, the fact that it is tied to a word; for although the common opinion is that it is just the *ineffable* that is the most excellent, yet this opinion, cherished by conceit, is unfounded, since what is ineffable is, in truth, only something obscure, fermenting, something which gains clarity only when it is able to put itself into words. (*Enc.Phil.Spir.* ¶462Z)

Hegel offers the following explanation of the proper relation of words to things:

> Accordingly, the word gives to thoughts their highest and truest existence. Of course, one can also indulge in a mass of verbiage, yet fail to grasp the matter in hand. But then what is at fault is not the word, but a defective, vague, superficial thinking. Just as the true *thought* is the very thing itself, so too is the *word* when it is employed by genuine thinking. Intelligence, therefore, in filling itself with the word, receives into itself the nature of the thing. (*Enc.Phil.Spir.* ¶462Z)

The transition from mechanical memory to thinking is extremely difficult, as Hegel himself says (*Enc.Phil.Spir.* ¶464). However, we can make progress by focusing on three passages concerning mechanical memory and its failure.

Reading "Off the Tableau of Imagination"

In the following passage, Hegel criticizes the use of memorizing techniques on the grounds that they reduce memory to a superficial attachment to images:

> The recent attempts . . . to rehabilitate the Mnemonic of the ancients, consist in transforming names into images, and thus again deposing memory to the level of imagination [*Einbildungskraft*]. The place of the power of memory is taken by a permanent tableau of a series of images, fixed in the imagination, to which is then attached the series of ideas [*Vorstellungen*] forming the composition to be learned by rote.[4] Considering the heterogeneity between the import of these ideas and those permanent images, and the speed with which the attachment has to be made, the attachment cannot be made otherwise than by shallow, silly and utterly accidental links. Not merely is the mind put to the torture of being worried by idiotic stuff, but what is thus learnt by rote is just as quickly forgotten, seeing that the same tableau is used for getting by rote every other series of ideas, and so those previously attached to it are effaced. What is mnemonically impressed is not like what is retained in memory really got by heart, i.e. strictly produced from within outwards, from the deep mine [*Schacht*] of the ego [*Ich*], and thus recited, but is, so to speak, read off the tableau of imagination [*Tableau der Einbildungskraft*]. (*Enc.Phil.Spir.* ¶462)[5]

Though Hegel does not say it, the Mnemonic system is an inverse repetition of the moment of symbolizing: while symbolizing was the *externalizing* of a complex interior representation through the use of an image, the Mnemonic system is an *internalizing* (memorizing) of complex universal representations by using single images. Hegel rejects this because it is essentially a step backward from more complex to less complex; it is a regression from repetitions that are *Aufhebungen*—that is, which contain the path of increasing complexity—to repetitions that do not contain development because they are standardizations. In other words, in the proper development from imagination to memory to thought, the external articulation of the imagination's syntheses places synthetic representations in a complex system of meaningful exchanges; when these are internalized again they have new associative relations, a new infinity, a new indeterminacy—that of interpretation; memory is repetition of imagination's syntheses, and it is permeated with difference. This makes the content of remembered names and their relations rich. Mnemonic systems reduce that richness to standardized image association.

We are right to query, however, what Hegel means when in the above citation he writes that something can be "really got by heart, i.e. strictly produced from within outwards, from the deep pit of the ego." On the one hand, we can assume that the "within" out of which true communication is produced is the latent content to which Hegel referred in the *Philosophy of Spirit* lectures. The individual must turn to his/her (past) experience. On the other, the "within" is the inward movement of the inwardizing imagination; to produce from within outward is to engage in the movement of sublation (*Aufhebung*), and it is to make actual use of the sublated (*aufgehoben*) cognitive activities, activities that are hidden in the immediacy of language use. Thus, good communication makes use of the imagination.

In one sense it is true for Hegel that we need only look inward to our experience for the true meaning of the words we have learned, allowing our imagination to conjure up representations for otherwise empty words (even if a word is not, in the end, isolated to an image or images). But the content is fully mediated through the cognitive activities and through externalization and reinternalization: through intuitions, experience, and communication (*geistige* mediation).

Imagination is the middle moment in the triad constituting representation. It is the negative, determining moment (as all middle moments in Hegel are). Memory, in a meaningful recitation by heart, must make use of the imagination's negating and determining activity.

The imagination is spontaneity in the sense that it is the inception of differences. These differences are multiple: they are between images and the universal under which they are subsumed; between the universal and the symbolic image used to represent the universal externally; and between the universal and the remembered sign that represents it and invokes it. These differences are not fixed. As differences they announce the necessity of movement within the otherwise fixed order. Imagination is not just *comprehending* synthesis: it is also the *movement* of synthesis. Since mechanical memory merely repeats reified syntheses, the productive imagination is what is needed in order for something to be "really got by heart, i.e. strictly produced from within outwards, from the deep pit of the ego."

The mistake of Mnemonics consists in creating a path of associated images upon which to overlay other more developed associations. The depth that has been passed over is the depth of difference, of instability, of synthesis—of the need for synthesis. The latent content of ideas should unfold but does not because the signs are ordered and mechanical, not alive. The

Mnemonic image limits the idea to the level of imagistic presentation and does not let the idea spring forth in its complexity. Memory that properly takes up the communicative imagination produces thought that reflects this inherent complexity of words and phrases.

The Overly Familiar

> The more familiar I become with the meaning of the word, the more, therefore, that this becomes united with my inwardness, the more can the objectivity [*Gegenständlichkeit*], and hence the definiteness, of meaning, vanish and consequently the more can memory itself, and with it also the words, become something bereft of mind [*Geistverlassenem werden*]. (*Enc.Phil.Spir.* ¶462Z)

Here the problem is the repetition due to familiarity. In Mnemonics, it was the association with images that prevented the complexity of the word's meanings from being raised from within. Here, the word's newness, its differences and spontaneity, drown in familiarity.

With these two passages we have dealt with the repetition, the Scylla of memory. But something else "lurks below."[6] It is the Charybdis of romantic inwardness and self-certainty.

As we will see, the problem with romantic inwardness is favoring the imagination's productive capacity over memory. This occurs as a result of misunderstanding the nature of *Phantasie*. This happens quite innocently when people take children's uneducated, spontaneous connections to be acts of genius and insight. It also happens not so innocently in the Romantic effort to return to such unsullied imaginative creativity at the expense of cultural memory.

"The Child Is Father to the Man"

> The young have a good memory because they have not yet reached the stage of reflection; their memory is exercised with or without design so as to level the ground of their inner life to pure being or to pure space in which the fact [*die Sache*], the implicit content, may reign and unfold itself with no antithesis to a subjective inwardness. (*Enc.Phil.Spir.* ¶464, 223)

The latent content that the imagination synthesizes is this "implicit content" which unfolds in the minds of the youths. Through memory and education, the mind is exercised to the point where the self, the nightly mine with all its contents, is constantly in a condition of mediation. The mind is then the becoming of being, the historical unraveling of Spirit.

It takes longer still to realize that the logic of their thought is "God's thought before the creation."[7] That insight is not available to the spontaneity of a child. But we can see that their exercise of memory is the beginning of their objective world. In the genesis of Spirit, memory marks the transition from the subjective folds of symbolic expression to the objective institution of language and history. In memory "Subjective inwardness" is overcome in and through otherness, in the remembering(s) of Spirit. The romantic, subjective longings of youth are resolved into communicative life. Even in the solitary individual, it is the depth of Spirit, not of their limited self-reference, that is essentially communicative.

Hegel has added to the last remark that the youths' memories are exercised "with or without design." This suggests that the educational *direction* (design) is simply the implicit content itself unfolding in the mind.

We steer clear of the Charybdis of romantic inwardness by attending to the development of history. Historically, the child is the parent of the adult, but the differences of Spirit in communication parent the growth of Spirit in the child.[8]

There are thus two dangers between which the mind must sail in its use of memory. Memory is an Odyssey of returns: the latent content is past experience; that experience unfolds into new experiences that in turn are the implicit content for new experiences. The sequence has no beginning. To be genuine thought, the words we use must sail between the reified cliffs of representation and the whirlpool of appropriation by the self's familiarizing.

Now let us turn to Hegel's lectures on *Aesthetics*. The purpose of this discussion is, first, to show how *die Einbildungskraft* and *die Phantasie* get applied by the artist; and second to see more specifically how these are applied by the *poetic* artist. The latter is especially important because according to Hegel, Romantic poetry is the highest form of art. In that discussion I also distinguish between the German Romantic use of the imagination and Hegel's notion of Romantic poetry. Key to that distinction is Hegel's criticism of Romanticism's poetic irony. And that discussion is our segue into Hegel's critique of genius in the preface to the *Phenomenology of Spirit*.

Before I begin with the artist's use of imagination, *Phantasie,* and *Vorstellen,* however, we must take a moment to look at how these various German terms, mistakenly translated as "imagination" in Knox's translation of the *Aesthetics,* are actually being used by Hegel.

TRANSLATION OF *DIE EINBILDUNGSKRAFT, DIE PHANTASIE, AND DIE VORSTELLUNG*

It is clear from the *Philosophy of Spirit* lectures that *Einbildungskraft* is the set of moments including reproductive imagination, symbol, and sign-making

Phantasie. It is clear too, that *Vorstellung* is made up not only of *Einbildungskraft* and its three moments, but also of recollection and memory. In the *Aesthetics*, Hegel refers to *Einbildungskraft* predominately in terms of reproductive imagination (the first of the three moments), and thus he also speaks of it as a passive imagination, and contrasts it to creative *Phantasie*.

T. M. Knox, translator of the *Aesthetics*, makes the error of repeatedly ignoring these distinctions and persistently translating *die Einbildungskraft*, *die Phantasie,* and *die Vorstellung* as "imagination."[9] He explains why in two footnotes. In the first (5, n. 2), Knox explains that the terms *Phantasie* and *Einbildungskraft* are used synonymously by Hegel, and that the only reason both appear in a sentence or in a sequence of sentences is that "it is a trick of Hegel's not to repeat the same word" in such sequences, that Hegel will use "different words as synonyms, even if they are not exactly synonymous." Knox concludes that "[u]ntil this is realized, a translator may perplex himself unnecessarily to find two different English words, in fact synonymous to render the two different words used by Hegel synonymously." Knox then provides other "synonyms" used by Hegel.

Knox writes in the second footnote that *Vorstellung* should also be translated as "imagination." There the argument is that the kind of "conceiving" being done in poetry as opposed to prose is "imaginative" (1001, n.1). Thus, Knox translates the following heading "*Die poetische Vorstellung*" as "The Poetic Way of Imagining" (1001, s. 275, v.15).

But close attention to Hegel's texts shows that Knox is wrong to translate all these words as imagination. In the *Aesthetics* the imagination (*die Einbildungskraft*) is most often used by Hegel to mean the reproductive imagination, as opposed to the creative imagination, which he refers to as *Phantasie*. For example, Hegel distinguishes commonsense ingenuity from genuine insight in that ingenuity is based on a kind of imagination (*Einbildungskraft*) that consists merely of general reflections of his experience. (The German inserts are mine, not Knox's):

> [S]uch a kind of imagination [*der Einbildungskraft*] rests rather on the recollection of situation as lived through, of experiences enjoyed, instead of being creative itself. Recollection preserves and renews the individuality and the external fashion of the occurrence of such experiences, with all their accompanying circumstances, but does not allow the universal to emerge on its own account. But the productive fancy [*künstlerische produktive Phantasie*] of an artist is the fancy of a great spirit and heart, the apprehension and creation of ideas and shapes, and indeed the exhibition of the profoundest and most universal human interest in pictorial and completely definite sensuous form. (*Aesth.* 40; *Äst.* 63, v.13)

In that passage Hegel contrasts commonsense ingenuity (what Knox translates as) the "genuine mode of production [that] constitutes the activity of artistic imagination." The German here for "artistic imagination" is *künstlerischen Phantasie*. Hegel even italicizes the word *Phantasie* just to be clear. Thus, with *Einbildungskraft* and *Phantasie* Hegel is referring to different activities.

Furthermore, the distinction between *Einbildungskraft* and *Phantasie* is made explicit by Hegel in his discussion of the Artist: "[W]e must immediately take care not to confuse fancy with the purely passive imagination (*Einbildungskraft*). Fancy [*Phantasie*] is creative" (281, s. 363; see also *Aesth.* 961; *Äst.* 225 v. 15). Here Knox has preserved the difference in English, so it is puzzling that he does not do so elsewhere. We know from the 1830 *Philosophy of Spirit* lectures that *Phantasie* is the second and third form of *Einbildungskraft*. It is creative symbolizing and sign making. It is therefore different from the merely reproductive *Einbildungskraft*.

Hegel keeps the distinction between *Einbildungskraft* as reproductive imagination and *Phantasie* as creative throughout his lectures on *Aesthetics*. For example, he writes (note how Knox uses "imagination" in both cases; the German inserts are mine from the original text): "In imagination [*Phantasie*] we can readily transpose ourselves from one place to another; but, in the case of actual seeing, the imagination [*die Einbildunskraft*] must not be overtaxed to the extent of contradicting what we see" (*Aesth.* 1165; *Äst.* 483–84, v. 15). Also, Hegel discusses imagination in the context of the *reception* of art, not the creation of art, and he uses *Einbildungskraft*, not *Phantasie*: "The beauty of art presents itself to *sense*, feeling, intuition, imagination [*die Einbildungskraft*]" (*Aesth.* 5; *Äst* 18).

Furthermore, when Hegel is referring to artistic production in the lectures on *Aesthetics*, he never uses the term *Einbildungskraft*. He uses the word *Phantasie*, as for example in the expression "*dichterishe Phantasie*" (*Aesth.* 1007; *Äst.* 283, v. 15), and "*künstlerishen Phantasie*," which Knox translates badly as "activity of artistic imagination" (*Aesth.* 40; *Äst.* 62, v. 13).

With regard to poetic art in particular, Knox persists in using "imagination" everywhere. He translates "*Poesie als Dichtkunst*" (*Äst.* 237, v. 15) as "poetry as an imaginative art" when it should be "poetic art" (*Aesth.* 971; see also 1000).

Aside from those instances where Hegel refers to "*Dichtkunst*," Hegel refers to poetic activity as *Vorstellen* (and its products as poetic *Vorstellungen*). Knox translates that activity as "poetic imagination."[10] This translation of *Vorstellen* as "imagination" is not entirely wrong, since it is true that it is "picture-thinking" (as Miller often translates it in the *Phenomenology of Spirit*).

But it is *also* translated by Wallace as "Representation (or Mental Idea)" (*Enc.Phil.Spir.* 201). It is so translated because *vorstellen* is not *limited* to picture-thinking. The evidence for this is that memory and name making fall within its realm. So within representation we find not only picture-thinking but other forms of spirit's linguistic, cultural, political, and religious reflections.[11] The evidence of this is that all the forms of experience in the *Phenomenology of Spirit* are referred to as *Vorstellungen*, from the simplest experience of "here and now" to the French Revolution. It is toward a greater understanding of just what *Vorstellungen* are, and just what the role of the imagination in *vorstellen* is, that we are working in the present book.

To conclude, Knox's translation of all three terms (*die Vorstellung, die Phantasie*, and *die Einbildungskraft*) as "imagination" loses the following essential differences between them. *Vorstellung*, or representation, is always self-reflective, complex, using universals, and not always artistic; *Phantasie* (which I keep in the German) is always artistic; and *Einbildungskraft*, or imagination, can stand for the three moments of reproduction, symbol making, and sign making, and thus also as the middle moment of representation, or, as in the *Aesthetics*, it can refer specifically to merely reproductive imagination, which can be "passive." But *Einbildungskraft* is never creative or artistic.[12] In discussions below I have therefore amended Knox's translations and included the German words.

These distinctions become essential when we compare Hegel's praise of poetry and of poetic *Vorstellung* in the "Romantic Form of Art" with his criticism of Romantic irony. The difference between Hegel's "Romantic Poetry" and German Romanticism's poetic irony is the way in which the imagination (*Einbildungskraft*) is used in artistic creation (*Phantasie*) to produce representations (*Vorstellungen*). Unlike Romantic irony, which does not understand the imagination's role within the Concept, Hegel's "Romantic Poetry" does fully grasp the role of the imagination in *Phantasie* and thus creates *Vorstellungen* that are properly self-reflections of Absolute Spirit.

The Artist's *Phantasie* in the *Lectures on Aesthetics*

> In place of the strictness of conformity to law, and the dark inwardness of thought, we seek peace and enlivenment in the forms of art; we exchange the shadow realm of the Idea for bright and vigorous reality. (*Aesth.* 5; *Äst.* 18, v. 13)

In order to situate Hegel's discussion of the artist in the *Aesthetics*, and because my discussion of the artist eventually involves a brief account of a few of the different artistic forms discussed by Hegel, here is the general structure of the *Aesthetics*:

Part I: **The Idea of Artistic Beauty, or the Ideal**

    I. Concept of the beautiful as such

    II. The Beauty of Nature

    III. The Beauty of Art or the Ideal

        A) The Ideal as Such

        B) The Determinacy of the Ideal

        C) The Artist –*Phantasie*, Genius, and Inspiration

            –Objectivity of the Representation

            –Manner, Style, and Originality

Part II: Development of the Ideal into the Particular Forms of Art

    I. Symbolic art—Unconscious symbolism

    II. Classical form of art—The process of the shaping of the classical art form

    III. Romantic form of art—The religious domain of romantic art

Part III. The System of the Individual Arts

    I. Architecture—Independent or symbolic architecture

    II. Sculpture—The Principle of Sculpture proper

    III. The Romantic Arts—Painting

        –Music

        –Poetry   –epic

                    –lyric

                    –dramatic

Hegel's discussion of the artist's *Phantasie* occurs in the third section of chapter III (on the Beauty of Art or the Ideal) in Part I of the *Aesthetics*.

His account here returns us to the key opposition between mechanical repetition and expression from the heart. As with memory, there are two sides to artistic *Phantasie*. The artist must on the one hand deal with communal reality, and on the other deal with his or her own interiority. Let us look at each separately.

On the one hand, the artist deals with the configurations of the actual world, grasping what is really *there* and expressing it in the medium of his/her art; the artist's medium is "actual external configurations" (*Aesth.* 281). The artist should be spiritually developed (*durchgeistigt*) rather than free with his imagination: "[T]he artist is not relegated to what he has manufactured by his own imagination [*Einbildungen*] but has to abandon the superficial 'ideal' (so-called) and enter reality itself" (*Aesth.* 281). "Reality" is the interpersonal reality which memory and sign-making involve. It is the realm of communicative Spirit.

In this respect Hegel's differentiation between a passive imagination (*bloss passiven Einbildungskraft*) and *Phantasie*, which is creative (*Aesth.* 281), is important. We know from the *Philosophy of Spirit* that *Phantasie* is the symbol and sign-making, allegory and poetry-making, *Phantasie*. We conclude that the passive imagination is the first moment of the imagination—the reproduction of images in recollection. Even though it is re-*productive*, it is passive in the sense that intellect has not yet grasped itself as the power of synthesis, but is merely synthesizing. Like intuition, it is the merely epistemological requirement for memory and language. Imagination at that level has no conscious ability to make representations that will resonate meaningfully in someone else's head.

Since the first, reproductive imagination is passively in the service of recollection it produces merely unconscious imaginative displays with no conscious connection to Spirit. Therefore, it cannot be artistically creative. Hegel writes,

> It is therefore an absurdity to suppose that poems like the Homeric came to the poet in sleep. Without circumspection, discrimination, and criticism the artist cannot master any subject-matter which he is to configurate, and it is silly to believe that the genuine artist does not know what he is doing. (*Aesth.* 283)[13]

The artist's engagement with reality also differs from commonsense ingenuity. The former deals creatively with it, whereas the latter draws only on the use of the reproductive imagination (which Hegel refers to as *die Einbildunskraft* [*Aesth.* 40; *Äst.* 63, v. 13]).[14] What Hegel was trying to get at by using the term *die Einbildungskraft* with regard to ingenuity was the productive yet unreflective and unartistic moment of imagination in recollection. In this sense, then, even in commonsense ingenuity we are dealing with the "passive" imagination of recollection. This is a reason why Verene's claim[15] that recollection (*Erinnerung*) is central to the *Phenomenology of Spirit* is misplaced. (He would be right if by central Verene meant that recollection is the reproductive passivity that self-conscious Spirit overcomes through its labor throughout the book. But that is not what Verene means.) On the contrary, it is the inwardizing *and communicative* imagination *together* that are key to the dialectical labor of Spirit.

Phantasie (creative, symbol, and sign-making imagination) and not passive imagination (*Einbildungskraft*) alone, is involved in artistic production. The artist manipulates the community's reality. On the other hand, Hegel appeals repeatedly to a kind of "depth" and "inwardness" of the artist, which is essential to creativity. "[B]ound up with precise knowledge of the external form there must be equal familiarity with man's inner life, with the passions of his heart, and all the aims of the human soul" (*Aesth.* 282). "What therefore *lives and ferments in him* the artist must portray to himself. . . ." (*Aesth.* 282; my emphasis). The depth is not subjective inwardness, it is the depth of Spirit.

Because it is the depth of Spirit, this depth cannot really be discussed separately from the reality it embraces and transforms in the artist's *Phantasie*. When we consider these two together (real experience and the depth of inner life), it is evident that what we are considering is memory. Indeed Hegel indicates this: "[T]he artist must live and become at home in this medium. He must have seen much, heard much, and retained much, just as in general great individuals are almost always signaled by a great memory" (*Aesth.* 281).

For Hegel, artistic memory is profound and wide ranging. "[W]hat interests a man he engraves on his memory, and a *most profound spirit* spreads the field of his interests *over countless topics*" (*Aesth.* 281–82; my emphasis). The artist "must have pondered its essentiality and truth in its whole range and *whole depth* [*seiner ganzen Tief nach*]. For without reflection a man does not bring home to his mind what is in him, and so we notice in every great work of art that its material in all its aspects has been long and *deeply weighed* [*tief erwogen*] and thought over" (*Aesth.* 282; my emphasis).

Thus, in Hegel's conception of the artist's activity, "the task of *Phantasie* consists solely in giving us a consciousness of that inner rationality, not in the form of general propositions and ideas [as does philosophy], but in concrete configuration and individual reality" (*Aesth.* 282).

Now that we are clear on the two sides of the artist's *Phantasie*, we must look at how the artist executes artistic production. When we consider the balance of the depth and expression in the artist's use of imaginative reproduction and creative *Phantasie*, the key question for any individual artist in history is: How far back into the moments of the imagination can an individual artist go without losing her ability to express the content and thereby lose the audience?

If the artist were to descend into the passive imagination alone, he/she would be swallowed up by monstrous, repetitive imaginings; "The sleep of reason produces monsters."[16] The artist would be stepping down the phenomenological ladder to a less-developed consciousness (*Aesth.* 282).

Nevertheless, Hegel's focus in this *Aesthetics* passage on the artist's *Phantasie* does not preclude the reproductive moment of the imagination nor indeed the moments prior to imagination. For example, Hegel, in a remark about the artist's imagination, asserts that it is *feeling* that brings forth the fruit of artistic endeavor. The artist must absorb the material so that it becomes "his very own self, as the inmost property of himself as subjective being" (*Aesth.* 283). We recall that feeling and possession (the moment of *Seinige*) belong to the first moment of Theoretical Mind in the *Philosophy of Spirit*—the moment of intuition, which is prior to the imagination. The reason feeling is important is that "the pictorial illustration [*bildliche Veranschaulichen*] estranges every subject-matter by giving it an external form, and feeling alone brings it into subjective unity with the inner self" (*Aesth.* 283). Without feeling, art risks becoming merely imagistic. "[T]he artist must have drawn much and much that is great, into his own soul; his heart must have been *deeply gripped* [*tief ergriffen . . . worden sein*] and moved thereby; he must have done and lived through much before he can develop the *true depths of life* [*echte Tiefen des Lebens*] into concrete manifestations" (*Aesth.* 283; my emphasis)

This return to feeling and imagination is not a regression, not a romantic return to inwardness. The artistic ego has not dispensed with its development. The moments belong no longer to a subjective ego; rather, they belong to its mature form, to Spirit. The heart is the inwardness of Spirit.

The "inner," the "deep," is a felt difference, first arising in the reproductive imagination. It is the difference of determination in the recreation of an image out of the night, and then it is the many differences implied in the synthesis of a universal. These differences are what make imaginative comprehension inherently incomplete and therefore in movement. They make for a living Spirit. The content of Spirit is latent and becoming revealed. Through externalization of the imagination's products, through the external histories of artistic works and uttered words, through the internal histories of their reintegrations into the nights of many different people, and thus through the work of memory, these differences and determinations are Spirit. The depths and differences of artistic configurations are Spirit's self-interpretation though representation and its very process of becoming in time. The "inner rationality" (*Aesth.* 282) of the artist is the imaginative working of Spirit on itself. It is not the artist's imagination as a subjective activity, but the spirit of the time that is expressed in his or her *Phantasie*. Thus, Hegel writes:

> Now, in this its freedom alone is fine art truly art, and it only fulfils its supreme task when it has placed itself in the same sphere as religion and philosophy, and when it is simply one way of bringing to our minds and expressing the *Divine*, the deepest interests of mankind, and the most comprehensive truths of the spirit. In works of art the nations have deposited their richest inner intuitions and ideas, and art is often the key, and in many nations the sole key, to understand their philosophy and religion. Art shares this vocation with religion and philosophy, but in a special way, namely by displaying even the highest [reality] sensuously,

bringing it thereby nearer to the sense, to feeling, and to nature's mode of appearance. What is thus displayed is the depth of a suprasensuous world which thought pierces. . . . (*Aesth.* 7–8)

So the artist's *Phantasie* must delve into the depth of his subjective experience, for the artist cannot dispense with the earlier moments of the imagination (*die bloss passiven Einbildungskraft*) and of feeling. And yet that depth must be mediated by a good memory and much experience. Without it the artist would return to the earlier moments without the possibility of representing his or her experience or insight to others. *Phantasie* would be swallowed up in the depths. Praise of that as a mystical experience would be unacceptable to Hegel, for it would be making the imagination's spontaneity into an ineffable power. According to Hegel, there is no Spirit without communication.

THE ARTIST'S PRODUCTS: HOW INWARDIZING AND EXTERNALIZING MANIFEST AS/IN THE HISTORY OF ART

In turning to the artist's products, we find before us all the different forms of art (Parts II and III of the *Aesthetics*). It is not necessary or possible for us to look at all of these. It suffices to make two general points about the development of Spirit through the history of art as Hegel saw it.

First, Hegel's lectures on *Aesthetics* mirror Spirit's development in the *Philosophy of Spirit* from symbol to sign. This occurs in the progression from the Symbolic Forms of Art through the Classical Art Forms up to dramatic poetry, which is the final form of Romantic Art. But instead of being concerned with one consciousness' development, as in the *Philosophy of Spirit*, the *Aesthetics* is concerned with the different levels of a community's artistic *Vorstellungen*. These are produced through the artist's *Phantasie*. The artist's products reflect the community's level of development because the artist expresses the level of *Phantasie* at which that culture has arrived. In other words, a given form of art reflects the stage of Absolute Spirit's development. The historical progression of the kinds of art discussed in the *Aesthetics* is the history of Spirit's development in terms of art.

Thus, in the Unconscious form of symbolic art, the artist operates within an arena of shared cultural ideas that have not reached the complexity of a fully self-conscious Spirit. The Zoroastrian simply takes the sun to be the good (*Aesth.* 325). His art is barely even symbolic (*Aesth.* 329), since for the Zoroastrian artists the identity is real. Light *is* good. The art work is not understood by the artist or his culture to be a representation of its own essential creative identity, it is simply an expression of "what is true." It is thus unconsciously symbolic.

Hegel sees the Egyptian pyramids as a further stage in Spirit's development. The pyramid is not only a metaphor used by Hegel in the *Philosophy of Spirit* lectures to express the embedding of a signified in a signifier whose shape is indifferent to what it embeds. The pyramid as a form of art is Spirit's initial separation from pure symbolic identification and the beginning of its self-knowing in and through individuality (*Aesth.* 650). According to Hegel, the Egyptian concern for preserving the dead expresses Spirit's development of individuality: "[I]t is the rise of the individual concrete spirit which is beginning" (*Aesth.* 650). Hegel explains further:

> In this way the pyramids though astonishing in themselves are just simple crystals, shells enclosing a kernel, a departed spirit, and serve to preserve its enduring body and form. Therefore in his deceased person, thus acquiring presentation on his own account, the entire meaning is concentrated; but architecture, which previously had its meaning independently in itself as architecture, now becomes separated from the meaning and, in this cleavage, subservient to something else. . . . (*Aesth.* 653)

But while the Egyptians can pose the question of man, the shape of its query is the Sphinx, half human, half lion. Spirit has not quite woken up from its symbolic stage.[17]

This problem is solved later in Spirit's development, in the Classical Form of Art. There, individuality is expressed in and through the pantheon of gods. More importantly, the ancient Greek artist sculpts the gods in human form, and thus his *Phantasie* expresses Spirit's recognition of its human shape. Since this is a recognition of individuality in materiality, of the ideal in the real, it is for Hegel the "supreme expression of the Absolute" in art (*Aesth.* 438).[18] But what is missing in the Classical Art form as an expression of Spirit is modern subjectivity.

Only the Romantic Art Form, indeed only the Romantic *Phantasie* expressed in the temporal movement of spoken poetry, expresses modern Spirit's subjective complexity. Because it is thoroughly subjective and yet still seeking to express this in the form of artistic *Vorstellungen*, modern poetic *Phantasie* is inherently self-alienated. This is not just because we are no longer in the golden age of art in which ideal and real are classically unified. It is because art cannot fully reflect Absolute Spirit. The dialectic of poetry gives rise to drama, and its highest form is comedy. In comedy's dissolution of all fixity, art gives way altogether to religion and then to philosophy as a higher expression of Absolute Spirit's self-knowledge.

Second, Hegel's lectures on *Aesthetics* also mirror, at the level of Absolute Spirit, the dialectic of inwardizing and externalizing that we saw Subjective Spirit go through in the *Philosophy of Spirit*. We can therefore look at the development in art products in terms of the dialectic between the imagination inwardizing into its depth and externalizing its contents as artistic communications. The artist's dialectical *Phantasie* through the ages gives rise to the developing shapes of art, and these shapes are Spirit's self-presentation in the shape of *Vorstellungen* or mental ideas. In the transitions, the first moment of any triad is a form of externality such as intuition. It must then be inwardized in a second moment. In the third moment the inwardization is reexternalized in a way that reflects the two earlier moments.

Thus, the movement from Symbolic Art Forms to Classical Art Forms and then to Romantic Art Forms is organized, as usual, according to a dialectic. We begin with an unmediated identification: the symbolic form of art imagistically represents "this by that" (for example, the Zoroastrians take the light of the sun to be the Absolute Divine [*Aesth*. 325]); symbolic art concerns "indefinite, general, abstract ideas" (*Aesth*. 313). The second moment is a negation of that apparent immediacy. The symbolic "at once stops short of the point where . . . it is free individuality which constitutes the content and form of the representation" (*Aesth*. 313). This is a turn inward toward the subject, though only in the general shape of individuality. Thus, in the Classical Form of Art we find, for example, the plastic representation of the individual Greek gods. But that "peaceful reconciliation" between corporeality and individuality dissolves, in part because of the "deficiency in Inner Subjectivity" (*Aesth*. 504). The reconciling moment reunifies these opposites in the Romantic Art Forms of painting, music, and poetry. These arise as the most adequate form of Spirit's reconciliation with its artistic self-reflection, its *Vorstellung*. They manifest the mediating and mediated, changing, sublating character of Spirit in time and as time.

Within each of the larger headings of the *Aesthetics*, the developing dialectic between depth and externality, inwardizing and communication plays itself out until the next level, represented by the next heading, is reached.[19] The transition through the moments of painting, music, and poetry, as well as the transitions within poetry, likewise express the dialectic of inwardizing and externalizing. Most notable is that the necessity for music, the middle moment, is based on a need for the temporal, negative element of the pure tone. I look at these transitions more in the next section.

"THE POETIC WAY OF LOOKING AT THINGS *(DAS POETISCHE VORSTELLEN)*"

Hegel's discussion of Poetry in the *Aesthetics* makes up chapter III of the section on The Romantic Arts, which is in Part III of the system of the individual arts. The chapter takes up almost three hundred pages (*Aesth.* 959–1237) and a full account of what Hegel discusses there is beyond the scope of our investigation. But a look at what Hegel means by the phrase "*das poetische Vorstellen*" will help us clarify what the highest, most complex form of artistic activity is according to Hegel, and open the door to a discussion of how Hegel's notion of Romantic Poetry differs from the Romantics of the time.

From Painting to Music to Poetry

Painting is a movement inward from sculpture because it "reduces the real externality of the shape to a more ideal appearance in colour and makes the expression of the inner soul the centre of the representation" (*Aesth.* 959). Painting immerses the external, three-dimensional world into subjective inner life (*Aesth.* 794). Despite the fact that painting is "a pure appearance produced by the spirit," the content of painting is Spirit's visible reflection of "the forms of the external human figure and the whole of nature's productions in general" (*Aesth.* 795). Thus, painting is still focused on the "external shape of the spirit and things in nature" (*Aesth.* 959).

These spatial representations of painting do not adequately capture the subjective, temporal character of Spirit. Only with music do we enter the arena of pure subjectivity. In music we "withdraw from the foreign element in order to enshrine its conceptions in a sphere of an explicitly inner and ideal kind in respect alike of the material used and the manner of expression" (*Aesth.* 959). Music is thus a step forward. It makes the inner life and subjective feeling present to Spirit not in visible shapes, but in "the figurations of inwardly reverberating sound" (*Aesth.* 959) Thus, "[i]n place of spatial figuration, [Spirit puts] figurations of notes in their temporal rising and falling of sound" (*Aesth.* 795). For Hegel, sound is more idea than the visual because it is temporal. "[B]y reason of the negating of spatial matter . . . it corresponds with the inner life which apprehends itself in its subjective inwardness as feeling"; in the movement of notes we experience "every content asserting itself in the inner movement of heart and mind."[20]

But just as painting remains too much in the spatial, visual world, music goes to the other extreme. It takes us into "an undeveloped concentration of feeling" (*Aesth.* 795). Notes provide a pure symbolism of the inner world (*Aesth.* 959). What is lacking is the qualitative side of the spiritual content.

Since music "keeps firmly to the inner life without giving it any outward shape or figure" (*Aesth*. 795) it fails to be wholly representative of art. "[I]f it is to be adequate to the *whole* of its essential nature, art has to bring to our contemplation not only the inner life but also, and equally, the appearance and actuality of that life in its external reality" (*Aesth*. 795). Art has therefore to reexpress itself in an external shape more concretely complex than musical tones. It needs "the help of the more exact meaning of words and, in order to become more firmly conjoined with the detail and characteristic expression of the subject-matter, it demands a text which alone gives a fuller content to the subjective life's outpouring in the notes" (*Aesth*. 960). Thus, we move from music to poetry.

Poetry alone gives Spirit "an artistically adequate existence" (*Aesth*. 960). As the art of speech, poetry is the third term that unites the two extremes of painting and music "within the province of the spiritual inner life and on a higher level" (*Aesth*. 960). On the one hand, it is like music. It "contains that principle of the self-apprehension of the inner life as inner, which architecture, sculpture, and painting lack." And on the other hand, it reflects the outer world through ideas, perceptions and feelings, it captures the determinate character of sculpture and painting (*Aesth*. 960).

Hegel considers poetry to be the most complete form of Spirit's artistic *Vorstellen*. "[P]oetry is more capable than any other art of completely unfolding the totality of an event, a successive series and the changes of the heart's movements, passions, ideas, and the complete course of an action" (*Aesth*. 960). Thus, the highest form of Romantic art, poetry, is able to follow and represent the complex changes of the subject's reflections on itself and nature, in the most versatile medium of communication: spoken language.

Poetry is also the universal form of art. It owes its breadth in this respect to its appropriate use of *Phantasie*: "[P]oetry is adequate to all forms of the beautiful and extends over all of them, because its proper element is beautiful *Phantasie*, and *Phantasie* is indispensable for every beautiful production, no matter to what form of art it belongs" (*Aesth*. 90, my emended translation; *Äst*. 124). This does not mean that the beautiful springs forth from a creative *Phantasie* independent of Spirit and history: as we have seen, artistic *Phantasie* is mediated by Spirit's development; a proper use of *Phantasie* means an excellent memory. The beautiful *Phantasie*, and its beautiful artwork, therefore, keep in mind the historical components of the culture that finds the artwork beautiful. Thus, while poetry is on the one hand the most developed form of Spirit's artistic self-presentation because it is capable of expressing insight into the modern subject, it is also inherently present in all the other, previous art forms precisely as the genuine though limited exercise of Spirit's insights into itself at those levels. It is the turning of the artistic mind toward its own objective authenticity. We will discuss this further after outlining the difference between Hegel's account of Romantic Poetry and the poetry of German Romanticism in the next section.

The dialectic between inwardization and externalization into communication works its way through the moments of poetry as well. The highest form of poetry is dramatic poetry. However, we mentioned above that for Hegel Spirit only finds its ultimate satisfaction in thought, not in artistic *Vorstellungen*. It is not the beautiful that fully satisfies Spirit's quest for self-knowledge. Thus, despite the fact that poetry is the universal art, poetry itself nevertheless also passes over into the language of thought: "[A]t this highest stage, art now transcends itself, in that it forsakes the element of a reconciled embodiment of the spirit in sensuous form and passes over from the poetry of representation [*Vorstellung*] to the prose of thought" (*Aesth.* 89, emended; *Äst.* 123).[21]

Now that we have a general sense of where poetry fits in the Romantic Art Form, we can look briefly at how the poet's *Phantasie* works.

The Poet's *Phantasie*

The phrase "*das poetische Vorstellen*" is found in the chapter on poetry in the section that discusses the different genres of poetry (*Aesth.* 1035, s. 319 v. 15). There Hegel refers to poetic representation as the central element of *Vorstellung*. It is central because it is the "middle way between the extremes of what is directly visible or perceptible by the senses and the subjectivity of feeling and thinking." He explains in detail how it draws something "from both spheres":

> From thinking it takes the aspect of spiritual universality which grips together into a simpler determinate unity things directly perceived as separate; from visual art it keeps things juxtaposed in space and indifferent to one another. For representation [*Vorstellung*] is essentially distinguished from thinking by reason of the fact that, like sense-perception from which it takes its start, it allows particular ideas to subsist alongside one another without being related, whereas thinking demands and produces dependence of things on one another, reciprocal relations, logical judgements, syllogisms, etc. Therefore when the *poetic* way of looking at things makes necessary in its artistic productions an inner unity of everything particular, this unification may nevertheless remain hidden because of that lack of liaison which the

medium of representation [*Vorstellung*] cannot renounce at all; and it is precisely this which enables poetry to present a subject-matter in the *organically* living development of its single aspects and parts, while giving to all these the appearance of independence. In this way poetry is enabled to pursue its chosen topic by giving it a character now rather of thought, now rather of an external appearance. Therefore it can exclude neither the most sublime speculative thoughts of philosophy nor nature's external existence, provided only that it does not expound the former in the manner of rationcination or scientific deduction or present the latter to us in its meaningless state. For poetry too has to give us a complete world, the substantive essence of which is spread out before us artistically with the greatest richness precisely in its external reality, i.e. in human actions, events, and outbursts of feeling. (*Aesth.* 1035–36 emended; *Äst.* 319 v. 15)

Hegel goes on from here to explain that the expression must take place visibly, by means of the two kinds of visibility: print and the spoken words of someone present. The spoken words of poetry are more representative of Spirit than written ones. "Print . . . transforms this animation into mere visibility . . ." The printed word does not "actually giv[e] us the sound and timing of the word" (*Aesth.* 1036). According to Hegel, it is "the living man himself, the individual speaker, who alone is the support for the perceptible presence and actuality of a poetic production. Poetic works must be spoken, sung, declaimed, presented by living persons themselves, just as musical works have to be performed" (*Aesth.* 1036). It is in part for this reason that Hegel takes dramatic poetry to be the highest form of poetic art.

THE DIFFERENCE BETWEEN HEGEL'S CONCEPT OF ROMANTICISM AND GERMAN ROMANTICISM

Hegel's conception of Romantic poetry differs from that of the German Romantic movement of his day. Indeed, he is openly critical of that movement in the *Aesthetics*. That criticism, I will show, is largely a function of their differing views of the imagination. Although his criticism in the *Aesthetics* is not explicitly about their use of the imagination, the core of the difference has to do with the way in which each takes up the creative activity of the poet. To get a handle on this let us look briefly at the relation of the imagination to the German Romantic movement. Then I will turn to Hegel's critique of it in the *Aesthetics*.

The German Romantics and Their Imaginative Project

Imagination was important to the Romantics in general. But what this actually means is complicated, for at the end of the eighteenth and during the nineteenth-century Romanticism took root within Germany and in England, and later in France, and there are at least two generations of Romantics in Germany and England, each with its own spin. Thus, Romanticism encompasses many different movements and themes. Tracing the influences of one group of Romantics on another also complicates the matter. Our purpose is served by limiting our discussion to German Romanticism.[22]

The story of German Romanticism starts in the late eighteenth-century in Germany. It was predominantly a literary movement. The intellectual centers for Romanticism in Germany were Jena, Heidelberg, Berlin, and Dresden. Even though it was largely one generation, one can divide the German Romantics into the "old" Romantics and the "new" ones because there were two distinct phases in the development of the movement. The first articulated what Romanticism was to be about and provided the aesthetic theory; the second put that theory into the language of poetry.[23]

Our concern lies mostly with the "older" members who defined the aesthetic theory, since it is their work and concept of irony that Hegel criticizes in the *Aesthetics*. These were the Schlegel brothers, August Wilhelm and Friedrich Schlegel (1767–1845; 1772–1829); Friedrich von Hardenberg ("Novalis," 1772-1801); Wilhelm Wackenroder (1773–1798); Ludwig Tieck (1773–1853); Karoline von Günderode (1780–1806); and Caroline Schlegel (born Michaelis, 1763–1809.)[24] The Schlegel brothers, Novalis, and Tieck were the key players in the Jena circle of Romantics.

The project of Romanticism was announced and defined by Friedrich Schlegel in *Athenaum*:

> Romantic poetry is a progressive universal poetry. Its mission is not merely to reunite all separate genres of poetry and to put poetry in touch with philosophy and rhetorics. It will, and should, now mingle and now amalgamate poetry and prose, genius and criticism. The poetry of art and the poetry of nature, render poetry living and social, and life and society poetic. . . . It alone is infinite, as it alone is free; and as its first law it recognizes that the arbitrariness of the poet endures no law above him. The Romantic genre of poetry is the only one which is more than a genre, and which is, as it were, poetry itself, for in a certain sense all poetry is or should be Romantic.[25]

To understand the role of the imagination in this project, we must look to some of the sources of German Romanticism. On the one hand, German Romanticism begins with the *Sturm und Drang* movement and as a reaction against classical authors.[26] This movement emphasized "the original genius, independent from rules, and the feeling heart [and its members were] even more insistent on the autonomy of the artist in the aesthetic scheme."[27] I will pick up on this notion of genius later.

On the other hand, German Romanticism begins with Kant's theory of the transcendental productive imagination in the *Critique of Pure Reason* as well as his theory of the beautiful object in the *Critique of Judgment*. Let me deal with these two Kantian influences separately.

The first of these Kantian notions set the scene for subsequent German idealist and Romantic interpretations of the creative ego.[28] As I discussed in my introduction, Fichte interprets the Kantian transcendental ego as productive imagination and makes it the keystone of his epistemology: "[O]ur doctrine here is therefore that all reality. . . . is brought forth solely by the imagination [*Einbildungskraft*]. . . ." (*Sc.Kn.* I, 227); "The imagination [*Einbildungskraft*] gives the truth and the only possible truth" (*Sc.Kn.* I, 227); "[T]his act of the imagination [*Einbildungskraft*] forms the basis for the possibility of our consciousness, our life, our existence for ourselves, that is, our existence as selves . . ." (*Sc.Kn.* I, 227).

Fichte's view was adopted and reinterpreted as the creative act of the poetic imagination by both Schelling and the Jena Romantics (most notably Novalis). They did not like the alienating notion of nature being the "not-I" and sought to create a reconciliation with nature. This led some Romantic theorists to view the imagination as an organic, cosmic creator. For example, we saw in our introduction how Schelling reinterprets Fichte's Absolute creative Ego as the act of Divine Creation, an act he characterizes as that of an Absolute Sundering Imagination. For Schelling, nature and our unconscious creative impulses participate in that creative act; the poet, in the act of making poetry, participates consciously in that original creative sundering. The two are just different levels (*Potenzen*) of the original creative activity of the Absolute. Thus, Schelling claims that the imagination "is the poetic gift, which in its primary potentiality constitutes the primordial intuition, and conversely, what we speak of as the poetic gift is merely productive intuition, reiterated [repeating itself] to its highest power. It is one and the same capacity that is active in both, the only one whereby we are able to think and to couple together even what is contradictory—and its name is imagination [*Einbildungskraft*]" (*STI* 230; *Sys.Tr.I.* 297). So much for the epistemological force behind the poetry.

The other concern is with the product of the absolute creative act in nature, and poetry's productions of beautiful art through the same process. The beautiful object, be it in nature or poetry, is a symbol of divine creation. On the one hand it serves to unify the spiritual and the material, yet on the other hand the symbol can only ever do so imperfectly. Kant's notion of the beautiful object as an enticement of the cognitive faculties that does not allow them to settle on an adequate concept for that experience, captures the imperfection and the longing expressed by the Romantic aesthetic. Speaking generally of the Romantic movement Charles Taylor writes:

> This creative imagination is the power which we have to attribute to ourselves, once we see art as expression and no longer simply as mimesis. Manifesting reality involves the creation of new forms which give articulation to an inchoate vision, not simply the reproduction of forms already there. This is why the Romantic period developed its particular concept of the symbol. The symbol, unlike allegory, provides the form of language in which something, otherwise beyond our reach, can become visible. Where the allegorical term points to a reality which we can also refer to directly, the symbol allows what is expressed in it to enter our world. . . . [The symbol] can't be separated from what it reveals, as an external sign can be separated from its referent. . . .
>
> This concept of the symbol is what underlies the ideal of a complete interpenetration of matter and form in the work of art. . . .[29]

As Taylor goes on to point out, this is where Kant's notion of the beautiful object becomes important. "One of the sources for this conception of the perfect symbol was Kant's third Critique and his notion of the aesthetic object as manifesting an order for which no adequate concept could be found. This was an idea which deeply influenced Schiller, and through him the aesthetics of an entire generation" (*Sources* 380).[30]

These two concerns—the productive imagination and the symbol—are central to the aesthetic theory of the German Romantics. But there were others as well. There was an interest in the theosophy of Jacob Böhme,[31] and in the pantheistic thinking of Spinoza and Goethe, as well as an interest in, and sometimes actual return to, the Catholic Church.[32]

> [According to Novalis t]he poet more than other human beings has remained conscious of this exalted infinity of the human soul, and he alone knows of the secret paths that lead to the spiritual

truth that underlies all sense appearances. It is the task of the poet, therefore, to lead mankind from reason to faith, from philosophy to religion, through true self-knowledge to the mastery of the material and spiritual worlds whose motley forms and forces are mere hieroglyphics of the divine spirit. This "magic idealism" furnishes the key to the understanding of Novalis' unfinished novel, *Heinrich von Ofterdingen*, in which the broad realism of nature and history yield their secrets to the clairvoyant intuition of the poet. (*Germany* 476)

Other key notions were those of romantic love, described in Schlegel's *Lucinda,* and venturing far from home (*Wanderlust*) and then experiencing the yearning for a return home (*Heimweh*). This latter expresses the metaphysical view that our actual home is merely a symbol of the eternal one after which we strive but never reach. These themes are embodied in Eichendorff's tale *Pages from the Life of a Good-for-Nothing.*

Out of this disjuncture between the eternal and the real, between the universality of poetry and the fact that poetry can only give us symbolic approximations, arises another, central Romantic theme, that of irony. "[I]t was this consciousness of the relative and fragmentary character of artistic and literary forms that became the source of 'romantic irony'; the supreme effort on the part of the author to overcome the necessary limitations of human accomplishments by the sovereignty of the human spirit which rises above the contingencies of its own creations and ironically contrasts the absolute idea with the frailty of its symbolic representation" (*Germany*, 472). This is the theme Hegel picks up on most critically in the *Aesthetics*.[33]

Hegel's Critique of Irony

Despite the fact that both the Romantic poets and Hegel make bold claims about the universality of the poetic form of art, Hegel's conception of Romantic poetry differs from that of the German Romantic movement of his day. The difference is most marked in his criticism of their notion of Romantic irony. I want to show that that difference arises out of two different ways of conceiving the imagination. Let us begin with Hegel's critique of irony.

In three sections of the introduction to his lectures on *Aesthetics*, Hegel discusses the problems arising from bad theories about how to relate the subject and object in art. First, he addresses Kant's contributions to the effort to unite these two, especially in the *Critique of Judgment*. He ultimately criticizes Kant for placing any reconciliation within the subjective realm of Ideas, rather than making the reconciliation real. Next, Hegel congratulates Schiller for having executed a better reconciliation and for the depth of his philosophical understanding of art. Indeed, he claims that "the philosophical Concept is noticeable in many of his poems" (*Aesth.* 61). He praises Schelling for bringing the Idea to its absolute standpoint. Hegel criticizes Goethe for not doing so, and for instead being "steadily undisturbed by the Concept" (*Aesth.* 61). Hegel is most critical, however, of those philosophers who endorsed irony as their principle of art. So, while he praises the Schlegel brothers for "appropriat[ing] from the philosophical Idea as much as their completely non-philosophical, but essentially critical nature were capable of accepting" (*Aesth.* 63), he condemns them (especially Friedrich) for their development of artistic irony.

Hegel explains their notion of irony using three points. The first is that it is developed from the Fichtean ego, an ego that is "abstract and formal" (*Aesth.* 64); secondly, every content of experience is completely in the control of the ego, and has no independent existence: "Whatever is, is only by the instrumentality of the ego, and what exists by my instrumentality I can equally well annihilate again" (*Aesth.* 64). As a result of this separation between the ego and its products, the ego always transcends its products. The products are therefore only ever a "show," "a mere appearance due to the ego in whose power and caprice and at whose free disposal it remains" (*Aesth.* 64–65). The third point follows from the fact that earnestness is rendered impossible by the mere show. The artist develops a lofty disdain for the audience and anyone who is earnest. Audiences that find something earnest and serious in an ironic work of art are viewed as "simply deceived, poor limited creatures, without the faculty and ability to apprehend and reach the loftiness of my standpoint" (*Aesth.* 65).[34] This leads the ironist to even greater heights of self-praise and disdain for others, for it is evident to him that not everyone is as free as he is "to see in everything which otherwise has value, dignity, and sanctity for mankind just a product of his own power of caprice" (*Aesth.* 65). At its peak the "virtuosity of an ironical artistic life apprehends itself as a divine creative genius for which anything and everything is only an unsubstantial creature, to which the creator, knowing himself to be disengaged and free from everything, is not bound, because he is just as able to destroy it as to create it" (*Aesth.* 66).

Having thus explained the general characteristic of "this negativity of irony," Hegel goes on to express two possible outcomes of it. Both outcomes express the essential emptiness of the ironic stance. On the one hand irony leads to vanity, mere praise of a subjectivity that cannot have any content, for all content is mere show. On the other hand, it can lead to the experience of the "*morbid* beautiful soul" (*Aesth*. 67) who forever yearns for the substantial experience of concrete life that its own ironic stance forever precludes. This beautiful soul is distinguished by Hegel from the "*truly* beautiful soul" who "acts and is actual" (*Aesth*. 67).[35]

Hegel's Poetry of the Romantic Art Form and its Difference from German Romantic Poetry

In contrast to this criticism of irony, the *Aesthetics* offers a "good" form of Romantic poetry, poetry as a form of "Romantic Art." We have already discussed the characteristics of that kind of *Vorstellen*: it is the middle way between sense and thought; it is the expression of Spirit's subjective insights as well as insights into nature; it expresses the actual movement of Spirit because its medium is spoken words; and it is universal in the sense that poetic insight connects the artist's *Phantasie* to the historical self-representation (*Vorstellen*) of his or her culture. Now we need to look at the art form itself.

Poetry as a Romantic Form of Art has three different kinds: epic, lyric, and dramatic. The highest is dramatic poetry (*Aesth*. 1158 ff.). "Because drama has been developed into the most perfect totality of content and form, it . . . unites the objectivity of epic with the subjective character of lyric" (the latter are the two previous forms of poetry) (*Aesth*. 1158). Of the dramatists, Shakespeare is for Hegel the best: "For what creates a universal, lasting, and profound dramatic effect is what is really substantive in action—i.e. morality as specific subject-matter, and greatness of spirit and character as form. And here too Shakespeare is supreme" (*Aesth*. 1173).[36]

Hegel does not express his criticism of irony in terms of the imagination. But based on what has been discussed in this chapter, we can see that his critique concerns the German Romantic's appropriation of Fichte's transcendental imagination; their misunderstanding of the role of *Einbildungskraft* and of *Phantasie* in artistic creation; and their consequent lack of insight into and respect for historical and cultural *Vorstellungen*. The German Romantic poets took the imagination's negative power as the self's pure power to produce or dissolve any content while itself remaining unaffected. They failed to understand that *Einbildungskraft* is first of all reproductive and becomes *creative* only in the service of *Phantasie*, and *Phantasie* involves historical and cultural memory. Thus, they didn't grasp what for Hegel is essential, namely, that poetry is only "universal" when it reflects the depth and dialectical breadth of Spirit. As a result their "genius," unlike the genius of Shakespeare, could not produce real character or refinement.

Hegel's "good" poetry (of the Romantic Form) does express real character because it does delve into Spirit. As we have seen, for real character and nobility to be in the artist and the art work alike, imagination must be tempered by a good memory, and thus engaged in a socially complex way. This means that *Phantasie* is not only creatively but also *historically* self-conscious. Thus, Hegel praises Shakespeare for creating characters of "far reaching individuality" (*Aesth.* 1227; *Äst.* 561). This "far-reaching" is not merely formal construction: it is not the mere historical *forms* of character that make real character, for as forms alone they are subject to the mockery of ironic representation. It is rather the insight into how a given character and his or her situation has arisen, and a respect for the necessity of that dialectical development, that create real character. Thus, when Shakespeare presents us with a character such as Macbeth, he does not just present a formal structure of that character: according to Hegel, Shakespeare "actually gives his characters' spirit and *Phantasie,* and, by the picture [*Bild*] in which they can contemplate and see themselves objectively like a work of art, he makes them free artists of their own selves" (*Aesth.* 1227–28, emended; *Äst.* 561–62).

Thus, while it is true that art has to create the new and avoid crashing on the cliffs of repetition, for Hegel it cannot do so by forfeiting the Concept, for otherwise it is swallowed up by Romantic subjective capriciousness.

Transition to *Phenomenology of Spirit*: Poetic *Vorstellungen* versus Phenomenological *Vorstellungen*

Just as the various forms of art in the *Aesthetics* express the development of Absolute Spirit over time, from the symbolic to the most adequate form of *artistic* self-presentation, so the *Phenomenology of Spirit* expresses the ascent of consciousness up through progressively more adequate historical and phenomenological castings of the world until it reaches Absolute Knowing. How does *Vorstellen* figure differently in these two works, and how are the arrival points of these two works different?

The ultimate goal of consciousness for Hegel is speculative science (philosophy). To be able to do speculative science we have to understand how representation (*Vorstellen*) works, in the sense that we must understand how we as a community (Spirit) represent ourselves and our world to ourselves. According to Hegel we *represent* ourselves most completely through artistic and religious *Vorstellungen*. When we finally grasp how the Concept works in these *Vorstellungen*, we pass beyond art and religion to philosophy. We thus pass beyond being caught up in our representations to grasping the Concept that operates throughout all of them, that is, we pass on to actually, concretely grasping how and why these appear to us as they do.

To understand *Vorstellen* one has to understand the generative role of imagination in *Vorstellen*. One's insight into the imagination must not be a return to merely reproductive imagination, which only gives us common sense, or to the ahistorical, asocial imaginings of Romanticism. One has to grasp the historical necessity in the development of *Vorstellungen*, and the actual movement of representative thinking in that necessity. That means one has to grasp the inwardizing and externalizing movement of imagination as it arises in *Phantasie,* for only it uses memory creatively; only it reflects the depths of Spirit. Thus, in art, Shakespeare's *Phantasie* allowed him to represent dramatic characters. Not only was his *Phantasie* universal, even his characters' *Phantasie* is universal, for each character freely discovers itself within the limits of its living concept rather than being represented as a mere abstract form.

But how then does Shakespeare's dramatic poetry differ from the philosophical Concept? It would seem hard to distinguish them given the following considerations: The phenomenological moments are historical and phenomenological *Vorstellungen*, which is to say that, like dramatic characters, they are the shapes of conscious experience over time. Furthermore, the *Phenomenology of Spirit* is a kind of drama in that each shape is expressed in its free discovery of its own limited dialectic; while the *Phenomenology of Spirit* develops the character of experience at various different, increasingly complex levels, it is like Schelling's *Potenzen* in that the levels of experience in the *Phenomenology of Spirit* are increasingly developed forms of *creative* activity. So how does Hegel's phenomenology differ from poetic *Vorstellen*?

While the phenomenological moments are universal forms of experience, they are not poetic *Vorstellungen* of a dramatic kind nor *poetic* forms of the Absolute in Schelling's sense. Unlike dramatic characters, consciousness in the *Phenomenology* develops through the dialectic to ever more "far-reaching individuality." It thus progresses through self-consciousness and into the social forms of Spirit and self-conscious Spirit, until, as Absolute Spirit, it comes to know itself not only artistically and religiously, but philosophically. At that point it has grasped how the structure of the mind and of Spirit is operative in its representations of itself and the world.

So poetic *Vorstellen* and phenomenological *Vorstellen* are similar and yet different. On the one hand they are both universal and thus capable of "completely unfolding the totality of an event, a successive series and the changes of the heart's movements, passions, ideas, and the complete course of an action" (*Aesth.* 960). On the other hand, while poetic *Vorstellen* can and should give us philosophical insight into life, it remains an artistic representation of Spirit, whereas Hegel's progressive phenomenological *Vorstellen* is the dialectical deliverance of consciousness to the standpoint of philosophical Absolute Knowing and is thus the gateway to the *Logic*.

Finally, there is an important distinction to be made between the imagination as it works in the philosophical Concept, and the imagination as the Romantic ironists used it. Imagination as it works in the Concept must ultimately reach beyond art to philosophy. Thus, the representations (*Vorstellungen*) that *Phantasie* produces naturally progress from symbols to signs, to thoughtful prose and eventually to philosophy. Imagination as it works in Romantic irony, on the other hand, puts Spirit's art in the service of a capricious *Phantasie* whose products (*Vorstellungen*) are insubstantial.

In conclusion, it is only with this distinction between the bad German Romantic imagination and the good poetic representation that we can make sense, on the one hand, of Hegel's own theory of the Romantic Form of Poetry, and on the other of the role of imagination and *Vorstellen* in the *Phenomenology of Spirit*. When Hegel's applauds Romantic poetry in the *Aesthetics* he is not referring to irony. He is referring on the one hand to a Spirit that is complexly self-conscious as a result of a long history of dialectically "figuring" itself out. On the other hand, he is referring to that kind of *Vorstellen* that is universally present in all art forms in the sense that the *memory* of the culture figures in the *Phantasie* of the artist.

Given all of this, to translate Hegel's heading as poetic *Vorstellen* as "imagination" is misleading. Poetic *Vorstellen* carries all the weight of a historical development; it implies the use of memory, whereas "imagination" can be mistakenly understood to be what the Romantics understood by it, namely an all-powerful creative imagination, one disdainful of its history and audience. Finally, it is Hegel's crucial distinctions between imagination (*Einbildungskraft*), *Phantasie,* and *Vorstellen* that allows him to use the term *Vorstellen* throughout the *Phenomenology of Spirit* and to reserve the single use of *Einbildungskraft* in that book for a criticism of the a false, poetic way of understanding experience.

Let us now turn to a closer look at how these terms are operative in Hegel's *Phenomenology of Spirit.*

PART THREE

Synthesis and Disclosure:

The Phenomenology of Spirit

CHAPTER 7

Imagination and the Medium of Thought

(*Phenomenology of Spirit* "Preface")

The *Phenomenology of Spirit* is Hegel's science of *experience*. Therefore, his focus is not artistic *Vorstellen*. Rather, he is concerned with the more encompassing, phenomenological *Vorstellen*. While the former deals only with *Phantasie* and its products, the latter deals with all forms of representing experience including such forms as scientific paradigms and political revolutions. In all *Vorstellungen* prior to Absolute Knowing, the comprehending and disclosing movements of the imagination are central but they only manifest as the experience, as the content of thought, not as the self-realizing Concept. The Concept works dialectically through each new level in the *Phenomenology of Spirit*, but the imagination's sublating (*aufhebende*) work remains latent. What is revealed at each new level is a new shape of universal experience, a new phenomenological *Vorstellung*. When the Concept is finally realized to have been at work throughout the *Vorstellungen* and their transitions up the phenomenological ladder, the sublating work of the imagination becomes explicit, and we pass beyond merely *representing* our experience (*Vorstellen*) to full speculative comprehension of it.

In this sense, we already have an answer to the question why the imagination is not a chapter heading alongside sense-certainty, perception, understanding, and reason: Hegel's notion of imagination is so central to the whole book that it figures implicitly at every moment of the dialectic. But we need to look more closely at this.

The only passage in which the term *Einbildungskraft* arises in the entire *Phenomenology of Spirit* is in fourth last paragraph in the Preface (paragraph 68). In it we find a critique of genius and bad forms of philosophizing.

> In place of the long process of culture towards genuine phi-
> losophy, a movement as rich as it is profound, through which
> Spirit achieves knowledge, we are offered as quite equivalent
> either direct revelations from heaven, or the sound common
> sense that has never laboured over, or informed itself regarding,
> other knowledge or genuine philosophy; and we are assured that
> these are quite as good substitutes as some claim chicory is for
> coffee. It is not a pleasant experience to see ignorance, and a
> crudity without form or taste, which cannot focus its thought on
> a single abstract proposition, still less on a connected chain of
> them, claiming at one moment to be freedom of thought and tol-
> eration, and at the next to be even genius. Genius, we all know,
> was once all the rage in poetry as it now is in philosophy; but
> when its productions made sense at all, such genius begat only
> trite prose instead of poetry, or, getting beyond that, only crazy
> rhetoric. So, nowadays, philosophizing by the light of nature,
> which regards itself as too good for the Notion [Concept],[1] and
> as being an intuitive and poetic thinking in virtue of this defi-
> ciency, brings to market the arbitrary combinations of an imagi-
> nation [*Einbildungskraft*] that has only been disorganized by its
> thought, an imagery that is neither fish nor flesh, neither poetry
> nor philosophy. (*PoS* ¶68, 42; *PdG* 64)

In this passage, Hegel shows his disdain for the supposed philosophies and art forms that submit concepts to imaginative synthesis without attention to the Concept. The Concept is Reason, and central to it is the activity of sublation. I have argued that imagination is the inwardizing and externalizing activity at the heart of this sublating. So the failure of these "philosophers" and "artists" to concern themselves with the Concept is really a failure of their imagination. Just like the Mnemonic practitioners whom Hegel later criticizes in 1830, these "philosophers" and "artists" use the imagination in a misguided way. They have abandoned an interpersonally complex, systematic *Phantasie* in favor of immediate, "direct revelations from Heaven," and of arrogant common sense. Neither genius nor common sense re-members its content as and through the complexity of Spirit's self-interpreting development. Neither, therefore, generates the *Vorstellungen* that adequately express our experience.

There are a number of issues to be drawn out of this passage.

HEGEL'S CRITIQUE OF GENIUS

The notion of philosophical and artistic genius was a well-developed one in philosophy in Hegel's time: Kant discusses it in the *Critique of Judgment* (*CJ* 174–89) and Schelling refers to the creative genius in the last part of the *System of Transcendental Idealism.* Hegel too discusses it in an early *Critical Journal* essay of 1802 entitled "The Relationship of Skepticism to Philosophy"[2] and later in the *Anthropology* section of the *Encyclopedia Philosophy of Spirit* (*Enc.Phil.Spir.* 94ff and 100ff).

According to Kant, "*Genius* is the innate mental predisposition (*ingenium*) *through which* nature gives the rule to art. . . . [F]ine arts must necessarily be considered arts of genius" (*CJ* 174–75). Genius produces aesthetic ideas, that is, new artistic syntheses, which then serve as templates and standards for artistic production.

But for Kant the role of genius is limited *to* art (*CJ* 177). Furthermore, "Genius can only provide rich *material* for products of fine art; processing this material and giving it *form* requires a talent that is academically trained, so that it may be used in a way that can stand the test of the power of judgment" (*CJ* 178). In considering the respective merits of taste and genius, Kant holds that if something is to be sacrificed "then it should rather be on the side of genius" (*CJ* 188).

August Wilhelm Schlegel saw a contradiction in Kant's claim that genius provided the rule for art and yet needed to be formed through taste.[3] Schelling and the Schlegel brothers attributed a more important role to genius.

Schelling held it to be "absolute contingency in the highest form of self-intuition" (*STI* 236), and central to the work of the poetic. The poetic is the heart of all artistic creation. Genius resolves the most profound contradiction in man between his natural, unconscious impulse and his conscious freedom. It is that contradiction that is felt in the urge to create art, and the creative act is the resolution of the contradiction: "[T]he artistic urge also must proceed from such a feeling of inner contradiction. But since this contradiction sets in motion the whole man with all his forces, it is undoubtedly one which strikes at *the ultimate in him*, the root of his whole being" (*STI* 222) This "organic" notion of genius is central to Romanticism.[4]

Schelling describes genius as "other" to the conscious subject and likens it to destiny (*STI* 222). But he is careful to clarify that genius does not belong to the unconscious side any more than to the conscious side of man:

> Now again if art comes about through two activities totally distinct
> from one another, genius is neither one nor the other, but that

which presides over both. If we are to seek in one of the two activities, namely the conscious, for what is ordinarily called *art*, though it is only one part thereof, namely that aspect of it which is exercised with consciousness, thought and reflection, and can be taught and learnt and achieved through tradition and practice, we shall have, on the other hand, to seek in the unconscious factor which enters into art for that about it which cannot be learned, nor attained by practice, nor in any other way, but can only be inborn through the free bounty of nature; and this is what we may call, in a word, the element of *poetry* in art. (*STI* 223–24)

For Hegel, Kant's genius, the producer of aesthetic ideas, is Spirit reflecting itself in historical, concrete *Vorstellungen*.[5] Hegel relegates the term *genius* to the early stages of development of the soul. Hegel writes that "[t]he mother is the genius of the child" (*Anthropology, Enc.Phil.Spir.* 95).

[B]y genius we commonly mean the total mental self-hood, as it has existence of its own, and constitutes the subjective substantiality of some one else who is only externally treated as an individual and has only a nominal independence. The underlying essence of the genius is the sum total of existence, of life, and of character, not as mere possibility, or capacity, or virtuality, but as efficiency and realized activity, as concrete subjectivity.

Like Schelling, Hegel relates genius to destiny, but unlike Schelling that level of experience is likened to dreaming, not absolute insight.

By genius, we are to understand the particular nature of a man which, in every situation and circumstance, decides his action and destiny. . . . The genius, on the one hand, is the *self-like other* over against the individual, like the mother's soul in relation to the foetus, and on the other hand, forms an equally *indivisible unity* with the individual soul, as does the soul with its dream-world. (*Anthropology, Enc.Phil.Spir.* ¶405Z, 100–01)

For Hegel, the realm of genius has to do with transformation of, and conferring between individuals at the most subtle level of intuitions and feelings. It is therefore also the realm of magic. Genius is located in the movement of a merely subjective soul. Even if that aspect plays a role in Spirit, in itself it is not sufficient for a science of experience. For this reason, Hegel puts it and the imaginative products it generates in their place when he introduces his science of experience in the Preface of the *Phenomenology of Spirit*.[6]

WAVERING "TO AND FRO" VERSUS THE SPIRAL

Hegel's Preface explains that it is reflection, not genius, that is essential to the science of experience. Reflection is the key because it is the medium of Reason.

Reflection as the Medium of Reason

To understand this we must turn again to the role of imagination in picture-thinking (*Vorstellen*) and of picture-thinking in Reason. Reason is the science of experience when it fully comprehends its own reflection. To do that it has to understand imagination's sublating movement of internalizing and externalizing in the creation of *Vorstellungen*. The sign that it has comprehended this is that it is able to communicate its insights through language.

As long as reason is caught up in its *Vorstellungen* without awareness of reflection, it is not free. But as soon as it knows itself to be them, it has the same sort of "ampler authority" that the sign showed over the symbol: it both uses but is indifferent to its form of self-representation. It is aware of reflection as the medium within which it knows the world and itself.

Just as the sign makes no sense outside of the system of language, Reason cannot exist outside of the community of interpreters. Since the imagination is central to reflection and reflection is the medium of Reason, an undeveloped imagination leads to a confused community.

The Wavering Imagination of "Mere" Reflection

The critique of genius in the above passage can be understood in the context of a broader critique in the Preface of bad forms of reflection. These bad forms are typified by a "hither and thither" movement. In contrast to this movement, Hegel offers the spiral ascent of the dialectic up the phenomenological ladder.

Though he does not explicitly state that he is doing so, Hegel incorporates Fichte's idea of a "wavering imagination" into his *Phenomenology*. The wavering appears as the dialectic of reflection, inherent in all representation. More precisely, it expresses the temporal character of reflection, without which the synthesis of imagination yields only infinite relational modifications within a substantial, spatial plenum. But with only the temporal, the wavering remains "mere reflection" and is not recognized to be the medium of Reason. What is needed is a dialectic of space and time.

Mere reflection is characterized by a "to and fro" or "hither and thither" movement of the mind. Thus, in the Preface to the *Phenomenology of Spirit*, Hegel writes that the wrong kind of thinking is a "casual philosophizing that (*durch ein hin und her gehendes Räsonnement*) fastens on to this or that object relationship or thought that happens to pop up in the imperfect consciousness, or tries to base the truth on the pros and cons, the inferences and consequences, of rigidly defined thoughts" (*PoS* ¶34, 20; *PdG.* ¶34, 38).

Likewise, in the Preface, Hegel explains what True and False mean. We misunderstand these when we grasp them in a predominately spatial way, within which the wavering occurs. That is, "'True' and 'False' belong among those determinate notions which are held to be inert and wholly separate essences, *one here and one there* (*deren eines drüben, das andere hüben*), each standing fixed and isolated from the other, with which it has nothing in common" (*PoS* ¶39, 22 my emphasis; *PdG* ¶39, 40). For Hegel, the truth about the True and False are that they are only opposites insofar as they are held fixedly apart from one another; and they are only such insofar as we go back and forth between them, for the true as such a fixed point is only called true insofar as it is in relation to what is not true. From a substantive point of view, truth is a *movement*.[7]

We can understand this further by looking at Hegel's notion of a wavering "hovering over." In the *System der Sittlichkeit*, Hegel repeatedly uses this expression (e.g. "*über seinen Unterschieden schweben sollte*" *SPR* 487; "*über ihm schwebend*" *SPR* 486). What hovers over is that aspect that has not yet arisen before consciousness but which is nevertheless logically present. Mere reflection remains abstract and does not lose itself in its object. In *Faith and Knowledge*, Hegel was critical of the philosophies of reflection because their reflection never comes down to earth: "[T]hese philosophies of reflection cannot be prevented from fixating infinity, the Ego, and turning it into sub-jectivity instead of *letting it directly somersault* into the positivity of the absolute Idea" (*Faith* 190; my emphasis; *GW* 133–34). In that early work, the relationship between the logic and the phenomenal content he is discussing is often muddy. But by the time of the *Phenomenology* the structure of scientific knowledge which is the union of logic and phenomena has become clear. We therefore see a change in reflection from being a mere hovering above to being the element and aether of science (as Hegel describes in the Preface to the *Phenomenology*).[8] It is *within* that aether that incomplete reflective forms appear as superficial "to and fro" movements. In "mere reflection," the abstract moment "hovers over." But sublating, *Aufhebende* consciousness rises through the "aether" of reflection. The aether is the medium in the sense that it is the movement of self-conscious (*aufhebende*) reflection.[9]

In mere reflection, what is not recognized by consciousness is the identity of the object as reflectively constituted. Proper knowledge is a *spi-raling* motion. What is grasped (the *Begriff*), is not only the to and fro movement. Consciousness must experience the alienation (*Entfremdung*) of the self from itself as the self falls into the other and is defined by it. It must not just experience a Fichtean wavering between self and not-self. It is a question of Spirit's

> becoming an *other to itself*, i.e. becoming an *object to itself*, and suspending [*aufzuheben*] this otherness. And experience is the name we give to just this movement, in which the immediate, the unexperienced, i.e. the abstract, whether it be of sensuous [but still unsensed] being, or only thought of as simple, *becomes alienated from itself and then returns to itself from this alienation, and is only then revealed for the first time in this actuality and truth*, just as it then has become a property of consciousness also. (*PoS* ¶36, p. 21; my emphasis; *PdG* ¶36, p. 35)

Hegel writes that "[i]t is this coming-to-be of *Science as such* or of *knowledge*, that is described in this *Phenomenology* of Spirit" (*PoS* ¶27, p. 15; *PdG* ¶26, p. 29).

The *Aufhebende* Imagination: The Spiral

Hegel's second form of the wavering imagination is the "good," more developed form of sublating (*Aufhebende*) reflection. Fichte tried to get at this with the self's going beyond itself (and as a practical striving for the ultimate moral state). But Fichte's fixed notion of subjectivity and his lack of concern for memory made the self's act temporal but ahistorical and without content.[10] In Hegel's *Phenomenology of Spirit*, the wavering of imagination is developmental, historical, and content-rich. The dialectic is determined, but not by a subjective principle of self-striving. Rather, it is determined by substance and subject. It is determined, on the one hand, by the inwardized, "latent content" of interpersonal communication in which the imagining individual is embedded, and on the other by the expression of that content and its interpretation by others in communication with others. The *Philosophy of Spirit* psychology has shown that the latent content begins to be revealed in the subject through the moments of imagination and memory—in the externalization of imaginative syntheses in the form of symbols and signs (*Phantasie*) and in their being remembered as objectively *sign*ificant by memory. One does not get anything like this development or importance of memory in Fichte.

This double causation in Hegel is due to the dialectic being not just a temporal one as in Fichte. Hegel's dialectic is spatiotemporal. We saw in the 1803–04 *Geistesphilosophie* that the space-time dialectic is the dialectic of the imagination. In the *Phenomenology of Spirit*, that dialectic gives reflection the shape of a spiral.

This occurs in the following way. We begin with the "to and fro" imaginative motion of "mere reflection." In that form, consciousness does not capture, synthesize, or remember the movement in reflective space. It is instead immediately engaged in the back and forth movement. Ironically, because consciousness is so sunk in time, it is too much in that space. The spatial side becomes reflected when consciousness rises to a standpoint from which it watches the "to and fro" that makes up the shape of that time. It is then in a higher form of consciousness. The spiraling occurs because rising to the higher standpoint is a movement that gathers beneath it the opposing sides of the wavering imagination, and yet it is itself a movement. In the apparent stillness of its new vantage point, the wavering of its earlier position appears to happen in space, in the same way in which we can watch the trajectory of an ant across the floor. But the dialectic continues, for the higher standpoint itself is temporal in the sense that it has its own to and fro movement, whose development can only be grasped from a yet higher spatial standpoint in which the moments are enduring (bestehende), and so on.

This whole activity is of course that of Aufhebung.[11] It is the dialectic of space and time, substance and subject, as history. It is history because, although determinate negation first appears in subjective spirit as reproductive imagination, as we have seen that reproduction and all subsequent rememberings, including artistic ones, are not pure negation—not creation ex nihilo. Rather, reflection develops (according to) the "latent content" of the community into which the subject is born and according to which s/he recollects herself. So even at the beginning negation is not just subjective creative power of the imagination, as Fichte thought it to be, it is rather just as much substantial, belonging to what is (reflected). The whole movement is the natural unfolding of Spirit, its education.[12]

Just as the dialectic is not that of a subject alone, but rather of subject and substance, the science of experience is not something that the subject accomplishes completely alone. According to Hegel, it is not enough for consciousness to simply "make an attempt, induced by it knows not what, to walk on its head." The reconciliation is two-sided:

> The beginning of philosophy presupposes or requires that consciousness should dwell in this element [of reflection]. But this element itself achieves its own perfection and transparency only through the movement of its becoming. . . . Science on its part requires that self-consciousness should have raised itself into this Aether in order to be able to live—and [actually—ed.] to live—with Science and in Science. Conversely, the individual has the

right to demand that Science should at least provide him with the
ladder to this standpoint, should show him this standpoint within
himself. (*PoS* ¶26, pp. 14–15)

Science must "unite this element of self-certainty with itself, or rather show
that and *how* this element belongs to it" (*PoS* ¶26, p. 15).

So far we have looked at the passage in which the word *Einbildungskraft*
appears and discussed the reasons why Hegel takes issue with genius and
other bad forms of reflection. He has been trying to secure the correct view of
reflection as the medium of Reason. We have analyzed this with a particular
focus on the role of the imagination in these forms of reflection. Having done
this, we are now in a position to offer a general answer to our question about
the role of the imagination in the *Phenomenology*.

Imagination is at the heart of Spirit's development. It is imagination
that gives the *Phenomenology* its shape as a spiral. For it is imagination's synthesis of experience that is gathered into the shape of universality, into a
Vorstellung of consciousness. That universal experience appears at each level to
be circular, enclosed, a shape within which consciousness wavers back and
forth between the opposites contained in it. It is only when the imagination's
sublating activity is understood within representation that consciousness
moves beyond picture-thinking to Absolute Knowing. The key point is this:
it is the imagination—the spatiotemporal dialectical form of universality–that
in its very synthesizing both gives shape to consciousness, and pushes beyond
closure.

In *Faith and Knowledge,* Reason had to fall into its own "abyss" in order
to find the truth. In the Preface to the *Phenomenology*, Hegel writes something
similar: "[T]he life of Spirit is not the life that shrinks from death and keeps
itself untouched by devastation, but rather the life that endures it and maintains itself in it. It wins its truth only when, in utter dismemberment, it finds
itself" (*PoS* ¶32, p. 19). The question for us in the *Phenomenology* is, How does
Spirit find itself in this fragmentation? What kind of reflection works in the
face of *utter* dismemberment? What is this negation of negation?

Throughout the *Phenomenology*, consciousness is pushed dialectically to
ever more comprehensive levels of understanding its experience. But it does
not self-consciously and *freely* engage in its universalizing tendency until it
fully grasps the activity of the imagination in picture-thinking. This only
happens in two transitions of the book. The first is from the hard heart of
moral judging to forgiveness in chapter 6, and the second is from Religion to
Absolute Knowing at the end of the book. It is easiest to explain the former
through the latter.

THINKING THE IMAGINATION THROUGH TO THE END
OF THE *PHENOMENOLOGY:* THE TRANSITION FROM RELIGION
TO ABSOLUTE KNOWING AND THE TIME OF THE CONCEPT

There are two ways in which we can think Hegel's imagination through to the end: one is thinking it through in order to be at the beginning of the *Phenomenology of Spirit.* That is, to look at the imagination in his philosophical psychology and in others of his works in order to be able to understand (its role in) the *Phenomenology.* The central project of the present book has been just that. In the process we shed light on the *development* of Hegel's thought about the imagination up to the writing of the *Phenomenology.* These inquiries have revealed how fundamental the imagination is to the *Phenomenology* as a whole.

The other way to think the imagination through to the end is to delve into the *Phenomenology* chapters and to show how Hegel therein thinks *imagination through to its end* through the different forms of *Vorstellungen.* Particularly important in this is the final transition in the *Phenomenology* from religious imagination to Absolute Knowing. For it is in that "death of the picture thought" (¶785, p. 476) that imagination comes to be the medium of Reason, and in which Spirit reaches its teleological completion.[13]

The Transition from Religion to Absolute Knowing

The general difference between the most developed shape of religion—Revealed Religion (for Hegel, this is Christianity)—and Absolute Knowing is expressed as the sublation of picture thinking (*Vorstellen*) into Absolute Knowing. The dominance of content (in the content-concept dialectic) throughout the *Phenomenology* is finally balanced by a recognition of the Concept in the content.

That this grasping of the Concept is a proper grasping of the imagination is clear from the fact that we move from concern with created content to concern with the creative act. Revealed Religion has the Absolute—God—for its content, but Absolute Knowing is the recognition, in itself, of God's *activity:* "What in religion was the *content* or a form for presenting an *other,* is here the *Self's* own *act;* the Notion requires the *content* to be the *Self's* own *act*" (*PoS* ¶796, p. 485). This is the completion of what Hegel articulates in the Preface: it is the grasping of the truth as "not substance but just as much as Subject":

> For this Notion is, as we see, the knowledge of the Self's act within
> itself as all essentiality and all existence, the knowledge of this
> subject as substance and of the substance as this knowledge of its

act (*PoS* ¶796, p. 485). . . . Spirit which at the same time gives its complete and true content the form of the Self and thereby realizes its Notion as remaining in its Notion in this realization—this is absolute knowing. (¶798, p. 485)

Let us look at the moment of transition from Religion to Absolute Knowing. Hegel was a man of his time. Christianity was for him the form of religion involved in the transition to Absolute Knowing. The "other" represented in this "revealed religion" is Jesus. He is the incarnate Absolute Spirit. What must occur for Absolute Knowing to step on the scene, is as we saw above, that the "*content* or a form for presenting" this absolute other, must be recognized as "the *Self's* own *act.*" Jesus represents the completion of Spirit representing its absolute shape to itself. He is the culmination of Spirit's self-representation; his presence is the fulfilled prophecy, and he is the fulfiller of prophecy.

According to Hegel, consciousness' preponderance throughout the *Phenomenology* to determine its concept as other is, in Christianity, the one-sided recognition of the absolute as (only) other. For this preponderance to be overcome, for religious consciousness to recognize God as the activity of the Self, as absolute Spirit, the truth of Jesus the "Mediator" must be recognized by each of us as our own activity as Spirit.

The consciousness that does not recognize God in its own act, becomes an Unhappy Consciousness again when the external Mediator is no more. What dies is not just the representation of the absolute (for Hegel, Jesus). What is negated in that death is also the picture-thought (*Vorstellung*) of mediation as the responsibility of an other. "The death of this picture-thought contains, therefore at the same time the death of the *abstraction of the divine Being* which is not posited as Self. That death is the painful feeling of the Unhappy Consciousness that *God Himself is dead*" (¶785, p. 476). Hegel's description of this death reveals the negative moment of imagination that is inherent in representation:

> This hard saying is the expression of innermost simple self-knowledge, *the return of consciousness into the depths of the night* in which "I" = "I", a night which no longer distinguishes or knows anything outside of it. This feeling is, in fact, the *loss of substance and of its appearance over against consciousness*; but it is at the same time the pure subjectivity of substance, or the pure certainty of itself which it lacked when it was object, or the immediate, or pure essence. *This Knowing is the inbreathing of the Spirit, whereby Substance becomes Subject,* by which its abstraction and lifelessness

have died, and Substance therefore has become *actual* and simple and universal Self-consciousness. (¶785, p. 476)

In this death lies not only the experience of, but also the resolution of the Unhappy Consciousness. The one-sidedness of assuming mediation to be the responsibility of the other is overcome. This death negates the preponderance to be one-sided. It is the death inherent in any ideology, but told here with regard to the absolute Ideal. It negates the notion that a projected ideal communicator dominates actual communication.

The death of God is the negative moment inherent in representation. In it, we witness the imagination's negative moment of determination. The definitive recognition of this dialectic of negation is the beginning of proper mediation. For this death reveals the movement of (the) absolute representation—it is the "inbreathing of the Spirit, whereby Substance becomes Subject." It is the moment in which the Unhappy Consciousness hits the bottom of its despair, and gains in return the certainty it lacked—the certainty that the nature of consciousness is such that it can and does grasp itself as a member of a community of interpreters, that truth is not other than the movement of proper (self-)understanding. That truth is "not substance but just as much subject." In Absolute Knowing "[t]his letting-go is the same renunciation of the one-sidedness of the Notion that in itself constituted the beginning; but it is now its own act of renunciation, just as the Notion which it renounces is its own Notion. That *in-itself* [i.e., immediacy] of the beginning is in truth, as negativity, no less *mediated*" (¶796, p. 484).

The key difference between Revealed Religion and Absolute Knowing is thus Spirit's self-certainty, the certainty that in thinking it is knowing absolutely—that in thinking it is the movement of Absolute Spirit. Let us look, therefore, at this transition in terms of certainty.

We saw in the psychology that the movement of the imagination is the inception of the self; *certainty* of self is the determination of that power to determine—it is a dialectical repetition and development of time. If we go back to the chapter in the *Phenomenology* on "The Truth of Self-Certainty," we read that "[t]he determination of Life as it has issued from the Notion . . . [is] *independence* itself, in which the differences of the movement are resolved, the single essence of Time which, in this equality with itself, has the stable essence of Space" (¶169, p. 106). There, what was produced was a form of certainty that was not self-conscious; and the various levels of the *Phenomenology* provide the developing shapes of self, the various forms of the stable essence of Space. But we have seen the dialectical nature of Space and Time—that it is a dialectic of *bestehen* and *vergehen*. Thus, each time self becomes only *bestehende* it is one-sided: and if in its "final" shape it seeks to preserve itself as the shape of an absolute knowing self, it is the inversion of absolute knowing—it is evil. Insofar as this final shape, however, also gives up its stable shape, it is good (¶796, p. 484).

The self that has a proper self-certainty, and familiarity with its previous shapes—that is, the self that is as much *vergehende* as *bestehende*, and that has therefore a proper understanding of itself (that is, *verstehende)*—is an "absolute knower."

It must be kept in mind that *what* is going through the transition from Revealed Religion to Absolute Knowing is Absolute Spirit, not simply the individual. For Hegel, that has involved giving an account of the historical material developments of (Western) society: its culmination in the Reformation, the French Revolution, the Enlightenment, and completion in the philosophical grasping of the individual as Scientific Knower.

> [Absolute Knowing] is Spirit that knows itself in the shape of Spirit, or a *comprehensive knowing* [in terms of the Notion]. Truth is not only *in itself* completely identical with certainty, but it also has the shape of self-certainty, or it is in its existence in the form of self-knowledge. *Truth is the content, which in religion is still not identical with its certainty. But this identity is now a fact, in that the content has received the shape of the Self.* As a result, that which is the very essence, viz. the Notion, has become the element of existence, or has become the *form of objectivity* for consciousness. Spirit, *manifesting* or *appearing* in consciousness in this element, or what is the same thing, produced in it by consciousness, *is Science.* (¶798, pp. 485–86; my emphasis)

H. S. Harris writes that "our journey does not stop when we achieve the true consciousness of God. We go on beyond that point. The final object of our knowledge is not 'God,' but ourselves as *knowers.* Ours is not a 'journey of the mind to God,' but a transformation of philosophy (the *love* of wisdom) into the logical science of our own being in the world" (Harris, *Hegel*, 14).

This process of coming to know ourselves has required insight into the depths of Spirit. We have had to grasp the *aufhebende* activity of the imagination, and we have had to understand how it works in Spirit's most developed and revered picture-thoughts.

To summarize, the key to grasping the Concept is grasping the sublating role of the imagination (its inwardizing and externalizing activity in reproduction, *Phantasie*, and *Vorstellen*). Since the dialectic of the imagination is a spatiotemporal one, understanding how the imagination works within the production of representations (*Vorstellungen*) implies recognizing the historically necessary character of the memory-rich *Phantasie*. With that recognition, we find ourselves at the speculative end of history, and thus can enter the realm of *Logic*.

As we have seen throughout our investigation (especially in chapter 4), time, or inwardizing negation, is key to Hegel's definition of the imagination. In our conclusion to chapter 4 I noted that the "final" return of time is in the final chapter of the *Phenomenology of Spirit*, in Absolute Knowing. Therefore, to get a sense of the completion of imagination in the *Phenomenology*, let us look specifically at how time appears in Absolute Knowing, and show why a comprehension of this makes possible the highest form of ethical life.

The Time of the Concept

How then does Time appear in its final form in Absolute Knowing? Hegel writes:

> Time is the Notion itself that *is there* and which presents itself to consciousness as empty intuition; for this reason, Spirit necessarily appears in Time, and it appears in Time just so long as it has not *grasped* its pure Notion, i.e. has not annulled Time. It is the *outer*, intuited pure Self which is *not-grasped* by the Self, the merely intuited Notion; when this latter grasps itself it sets aside its Time-form, comprehends this intuiting, and is a comprehended and comprehending intuiting. Time, therefore, appears as the destiny and necessity of Spirit that is not yet complete within itself, the necessity to enrich the share which self-consciousness has in consciousness, to set in motion the *immediacy of the in-itself*, which is the form in which substance is present in consciousness; or conversly, to realize and reveal what is at first only *inward* (the in-itself being taken as what is *inward*) i.e. to vindicate it for Spirit's certainty of itself. (¶801, p. 487)

We can understand "Time" in three ways here: as a logical moment, as the individual moments of time (*Vorstellungen),* and as the chain of those representations, history. As a moment of consciousness, the description above is really the beginning of the *Logic*: for time that is absolutely empty is what we discover when we try to think Being pure Being. Since individual moments of time make up our experience, this "end" of time involves the end of history. The transition from Christianity to Absolute Knowing marks the end of experience as unthought-through *Vorstellungen* and the beginning of the Logical comprehension of time.

The history of Spirit is not complete without a consideration of the moral development of Spirit. The act that marks the moral completion of experience is forgiveness. The heading, "Conscience: The 'beautiful soul,' evil and its forgiveness," is the final moment of the *Phenomenology* chapter on Spirit. It shows how the inwardizing imagination, this self-sundering, is on the one side a necessary action of consciousness *for-itself*—each of us must act according to the dictates of our conscience: each of us acts in the interest of our limited knowledge of what "good" means. Thus, even if we are intentionally acting according to what we understand the good "in-itself" to be, in acting we cannot avoid (the possibility of) stepping on someone's toes. The possibility of negative consequences that is present in all action necessitates forgiveness. In it we express our capacity to take up the other side—someone else's viewpoint; we express the willingness to risk alienating ourselves from our own viewpoint.[14] Forgiveness is the *mutual* negation of "abstraction and lifelessness" between two (or more) people: the negation of the hard-heartedness of the judging individual, and of the negation of the unsociable self-interestedness of the other's cowardliness. Absolute Knowing is only absolution insofar as perpetrator and victim both recognize the evil, and negate it.[15]

As noted, in the *Phenomenology* we arrive at the moment of forgiveness before we arrive at the chapter on religion. But, "the spirit of the 'reconciling Yes' that comes to birth in the handclasp of the agent and judge who do perfectly understand each other is the Spirit of the God who dies as a man on the Cross" (Harris, *Hegel*, 78–79). In Absolute Knowing, this moral reconciliation is Spirit's recognition that forgiveness of the other is necessary to the process of self-knowledge. Science is set back by the "valet's eye view."

The act of forgiveness does not imply forgetting evil. Even if the negation is achieved, the negation has only served to determine the evil as something not to be repeated. The possibility of repetition is no less preserved in the *Aufhebung* than the moment of the categorical imperative—in fact, one necessitates the other. For a post-Holocaust Hegel scholar, the moment of the Categorical Imperative remains the operative response—that is, we must declare that such a thing as the Holocaust ought never occur again, and act against its repetition(s). But this does not mean that the logic of Absolute Knowing is impossible. It highlights its necessity. The absolution of Time does not take us out of history, it reveals what history demands of us. The willingness to attempt forgiveness may be what is meant by the meek inheriting the world, but it does not mean that the world they inherit is not hard-hearted, or incapable of engaging in forgiveness and transformation: indeed, absolute Spirit is for most of humanity, most of the time, an absolute labor.

The full reflection or full grasp of how we create *Vorstellungen* is the Time of the Concept. History is what we know the past to be through those *Vorstellungen*. If indeed the Spirit of our time is capable of producing absolute knowers, their self-certainty lies in that labor.

Since imagination is the middle moment of *Vorstellen*, the labor of engaging forgiveness is a labor of the imagination. Only by grasping the inwardizing and externalizing activity of imagination in the sublating, spiraling development of Spirit, can we think through the forms of Spirit's history and depth. Absolute morality is made possible only through that effort.

Progress is measured, on the one hand, in terms of the freedom from dogmatic ideology—freedom from ideology that represses our community's complex discussions with itself. On the other, it is measured in terms of the spontaneity of the manifold of cultural, artistic, and religious expression. Through such labor and self-expression "what is at first only *inward* is vindicated for Spirit's certainty of itself" (¶801, p. 487).

CONCLUSION

What, then, is the role of the imagination in Absolute Knowing? The *Phenomenology of Spirit* is the mine, the *Schacht* of the imagination, not unlike Dante's *Inferno*.[16] The pathways of that mine constitute the path of despair. The movement along that path is motivated on the one hand by the centripetal force of consciousness' inwardizing, a force that determines the world, but whose one-sidedness is also, on the other hand, worn out by the corresponding centrifugal power of its own expansion. Consciousness begins with the simple here and now as "mine," and it moves dialectically through ever more comprehensive spheres—through the maelstrom of French Revolution ideology, and beyond.

For reasons that Hegel could not have known, the final choice of the word *Schacht* is an excellent description—in its translation—of what is happening in the *Phenomenology*: the *Phenomenology* is the continuous "mining" of experience—the making mine, and the development of what is already there—of the latent content, of the language and community into and out of which the "I" is born. We recall from the *Philosophy of Spirit* that awareness in intuition divides into the moment of possession and the moment of being—into *das Seinige* und *das Seiende*. The *Phenomenology* is the process of bringing the predominance of the former into actual accord with the latter. It is the process of recognizing that what is "mine" is in fact "ours."

Thus, if the *Phenomenology* is the mine—Spirit's one-sided reconstructions, the mining of the mine—its conclusion is the emergence from mere reflection within that mine; it is the knowledge of the way in which that *Schacht* operates, and the proper operation of it. In other words, imagination's final *Aufhebung* is of picture-thinking (*vorstellen*) into absolute knowledge—into speculatively thinking one's representations through. That sublation is not only the subsumption of representation, it is also the *certainty* of the role and necessity of representation. If imagination is central to the movement of *Aufhebung*—if it is, indeed, the inception of it—then we never get beyond it. What the imagination holds, and what it *is* today, is the key to understanding the depth of our time. And if we have learned anything from Hegel, we must think it through carefully.

Notes

Preface

1. How this is so will become apparent in my discussion of the 1830 *Philosophy of Spirit*, my chapter 4. The Schema on p. xxxix is also helpful.

2. "[F]or although the common opinion is that it is just the *ineffable* that is the most excellent, yet this opinion, cherished by conceit, is unfounded, since what is ineffable is, in truth, only something obscure, fermenting, something which gains clarity only when it is able to put itself into words" (*Enc.Phil.Spir.* ¶462Z).

3. For further discussion of Magnus, see my Chapter 4 notes 2 and 38, and Chapter 5 note 19.

Introduction

1. "The story of imagination is as old as the story of creation itself. In *Genesis* it is suggested that the birth of the human power of imagining coincides with Adam's transgression of God's law . . ." Richard Kearney, *The Wake of the Imagination: Ideas of Creativity in Western Culture* (London: Hutchinson Education, 1988), 39.

2. See my article "Imagination in Vajrayana Buddhism: A Philosophical Investigation of Tibetan Thangka Symbolism in the Light of Hegalion Aesthetics and Kantian Epistemology," presented at "Writing Aesthetics" The International Association for Philosophy and Literature 27th Annual Conference, University of Leeds, England, May 26–31, 2003.

3. See Aristotle's *De Anima*, or Plato's *Republic*.

4. "Psychologists have hitherto failed to realise that imagination is a necessary ingredient of perception itself. This is due partly to the fact that that faculty has been limited to reproduction, partly to the belief that the senses not only supply impressions but also combine them so as to generate images of objects. For that purpose something

more than the mere receptivity of impressions is undoubtedly required, namely, a function for the synthesis of them" (*CPR* A121, p. 144).

5. David Hume, *Treatise of Human Nature*, ed. Selby-Bigge Oxford: Clarendon Press, 1888), 218; this is well paraphrased by Mary Warnock in *Imagination and Time* (Oxford and Cambridge, MA: Blackwell, 1994), 10.

6. See my Chapter 5 note 19 for a discussion of Kathleen Dow Magnus's critique of Derrida's critique of Hegel in her *Hegel and the Symbolic Mediation of Spirit* (Albany: State University of New York Press, 2001).

7. "*Imagination* is the faculty of representing in intuition an object that is *not itself present*" (*CPR* B151, p. 165; *KrV* B151, s. 166a).

8. See section A77/B102-A78/B104, just prior to the Deduction of the Categories.

9. I have separated and alphabetized them in order to discuss them clearly.

10. "Th[e] synthesis of the manifold of sensible intuition, which is possible and necessary *a priori*, may be entitled *figurative* synthesis (*synthesis speciosa*), *to distinguish it from the synthesis which is thought in the mere category in respect of the manifold of an intuition in general, and which is entitled combination through the understanding (synthesis intellectualis)*" (*CPR* B151; my emphasis).

11. In *Religion Within the Limits of Reason Alone* (trans. Greene and Hudson) Kant asserts that the postulates, upon which his moral worldview is grounded, are synthetic a priori practical judgments (New York: Harper and Row, 1960), note p. 7. Again, the issue here is how much Kant's moral picture depends upon synthesis of the imagination. See my article "The Moral Chemist if the *Corpus Mysticism:* Why Some Version of Kant's Practical Postulates is Necessary, Even for Hegel," presented at the Society for German Idealism Conference, Pacific American Philosophical Association Meeting, Pasadena, March 24–28, 2004.

12. There is a great deal of literature on the topic of the imagination in Kant. Cf. Lewis White Beck, "Did the Sage of Königsberg Have no Dreams?" in *Essays on Kant and Hume* (New Haven and London: Yale University Press, 1978), 38–50; H. Mörchen, "Die Einbildungskraft bei Kant," in *Jahrbuch für Philosophie und Phänomenologische Forschung*, B. XI, herausgegeben von E. Husserl (Halle: Max Niemeyer Verlag, 1930); W. Sellars, "The Role of the Imagination in Kant's Theory of Experience," in *Categories: A Colloquium*, ed. H. W. Johnstone, (College Park: Pennsylvania State University Press, 1978), 229–245.

13. He exhibits a peculiar bias against the small: ". . . we connect a kind of contempt with what we simply call small. . . . *That is sublime in comparison with which everything else is small*" (*CJ* 105).

14. Unbeknownst to Kant, he is here on the brink of something even greater, from the point of view of a Hegelian: the conflicting relationship of these two acts of the imagination—comprehension and apprehension—evokes as we shall see, not only Fichte's imagination, which wavers between the finite and the infinite, but also the dialectic of comprehension and disclosure at the heart of Hegelian *Aufhebung*.

15. By 1793 all three of Kant's *Critiques* had been published.

16. According to Fichte "Kant hat überhaupt die richtige Philosophie; aber nur in ihre Resultaten, nicht nach ihren Gründen." (*Briefwechsel*, Hrsg. Schulze, Bd. I 1930, S. 319, Brief Nr. 145; in; Gesamtausgabe, Hrsg. Lauth/Jacob, Bd. III 2 1970, S. 18, Brief Nr. 171.)

17. Cf. *Sc.Kn.* Second Introduction 1797, 38.

18. Daniel Breazeale has written a careful analysis of the check ("Check or Checkmate?" in *The Modern Subject: Conceptions of the Self in Classical German Philosophy*, ed. Karl Ameriks and Dieter Sturma [Albany: State University of New York Press, 1995], 87–114). His view is that, contrary to those who hold Fichte to a "productive theory" of the I (e.g., Dieter Henrich), Fichte's I is fundamentally opened onto otherness, and that otherness is a condition of the self being a self in the first place. Breazeale focuses on the role of the *Anstoss* (the check). The *Anstoss,* he claims, is the difference in the self without which the self would not be able to know itself. The *Anstoss* allows the self to know itself as determined and as free: without a check on the self's free positing, there would be no self determined to be there, and therefore no possibility of free reflection on the determined self or on the opposition within the self (arising as a result of the free positing being checked). I take it that without the check the self would unconsciously merge with its object, would be unaware of its own freedom from its object, a freedom expressed in positing.

But Breazeale does not argue convincingly, nor does he carry the analysis far enough: if he had, we would see that Fichte's position is not desirable. Breazeale writes of Fichte's modesty and circumspection (100), but this is not justified given the following passages from Fichte which Breazeale quotes, one of which I would like to comment on further. Fichte writes:

> As we also required, we have thereby discovered within the I itself the ground of the possibility of some influence of the Not-I upon the I. The I posits itself purely and simply, and thereby it is self-contained [*in sich selbst vollkommen*] and closed to all outside influences. But if the I is to be an I, it also has to posit itself as posited by itself, and it is by means of this new positing, which refers to an original positing of the I, that the I opens itself, if I may so express myself, to external influence. Simply through this repetition of positing it posits the possibility that there could also be something in the I that is not posited by the I. Both types of positing are conditions for the possibility of an influence of the Not-I: without the former positing there would present no activity of the I which could be limited; without the second, this activity would not be limited for the I and the I would not be able to posit itself as limited. Consequently, the I, qua I, stands in original reciprocity with itself and it is this that makes possible an external influence. (*J. G. Fichte—Gesamtausgabe der Bayerischen Akademie der Wissenschaften,* critical edition, ed. Reinhard Lauth and Hans Gliwitsky, vol. I/2 [Stuttgart-Bad Cannstatt: Frommann, 1964], 405. Cited in Breazeale, 110 note 36.)

Both Fichte and Breazeale would like to claim Fichte's philosophy is a kind of realism. Contra Breazeale and Fichte, I conclude that this is a one-sided privileging of the

Anstoss. That is, because it is the self positing a second time that "*makes possible* an external influence," that external influence is not really considered existent in any actual sense as something other than caused by the self. Fichte's statement, therefore, cannot be made into a realist's claim.

Admittedly, statements such as the following seem to suggest that the *Anstoss* is external or different somehow from the I. "*That* this [Anstoss] occurs, as a fact [Factum] is something that simply cannot be derived from the I, as we have often mentioned. However, it certainly can be shown that it must occur *if* any actual consciousness is to be possible" (408; SW, vol. 1, 275, cited in Breazeale, 111 note 40). But conclusions such as the following suggest again a failure to *really* take external influence as *really* possible. Breazeale writes:

> In an early letter to Niethammer, Fichte expressed his belief that "pure philosophy is acquainted with only a *single* I, and this one I ought not to contradict itself." Unfortunately—or rather, fortunately!—however, it always does. And, as Fichte came to see with greater and greater clarity, the I always *must* contradict itself, however much it may—and indeed *must*—struggle endlessly to overcome its own self-contradiction. In the end, the unity of the self is a necessary, infinite Idea of reason—nothing less, but also nothing more. Like the Sartrean "original project" of "striving to be God," which it so clearly anticipates, the original striving of the I is a striving after a self-contradictory goal.

It is no surprise that Breazeale brings in Sartre here and the notion of striving to be God. This striving and struggle is precisely what is the problem—the one-sidedness—in both Fichte and Sartre. To explain further, the "contradiction" mentioned above (which he says we fortunately cannot avoid) is only an epistemological contradiction, not an ontological one. If being were *actually* considered, there would be no such striving. The mistake lies in conceiving the self first and foremost as positing, and it is evident in the first citation above. The correct view is to realize the self is *ontologically* contradictory. This liberates one from the hold of a dogmatic self-conception.

19. "[T]he philosophy of Nature is the *theoretical* part of philosophy (where we contemplate necessity) and transcendental philosophy is the *practical* part (where we enjoy the consciousness of our own productive activity). But since this opposition is only an ideal one, and each of the two sciences is a conscious expression of the whole, each of them must strive away from its own ideal pole (necessity or freedom) towards the opposite one" (Harris, "Introduction." *Diff* 49–50).

Schelling's main assertions about the imagination prior to 1801 are in his *System of Transcendental Idealism (1800)*.

20. See *PoS* ¶68. ("Wortindex zu Hegels *Phänomologie des Geistes*," in Joseph Gauvin, *Hegel-Studien Beiheft* v.14. [Bonn: Bouvier Verlag, Herbert Grundmann, 1977]). Cf. my chapter 7 for the cited text. The word *Einbildung* comes up five times in the *Phenomenology of Spirit*, and while it is translated as "imagination," the correct translation, at least in Hegel's use of it (as well as in the *Wahrig* German dictionary) is as false presentation as in "*imaginary*," "*illusion*," or "*conceit*." Cf. my Key German terms

(page xli–xlii) for a list of places. What Hegel discusses in those passages is clearly not synthesis (in the aid) of understanding intuitions.

21. Francis Sparshott, "Imagination—the Very Idea," *The Journal of Aesthetics and Art Criticism* 48, no. 1 (Winter 1990): 7. I have taken the liberty of lifting Sparshott's line out of an article and passage that had nothing to do with Hegel; but the aptness of the phrase for describing Hegel legitimates, I feel, my use of it here.

Chapter One. The Sundering Imagination of the Absolute (Hegel's Earliest Works)

1. At the end the book Hegel summarizes: "We threw light earlier on the subordinate sphere of this intellect, where speculation can be found, i.e., upon the Idea of the transcendental imagination in Kant's philosophy. Then we had to pursue the intellect [in Fichte] into the reaches of what are for it the practical realities—the Ideals of the moral world order and of the End set by Reason—in order to show the absence of the Idea in them" (*Faith* 187).

2. My translation of: "Ideen sind nicht Begriffe, sondern reine Anschauungen, nicht diskursive, sondern intuitive Vorstellungen" (Kant, *Werke* XXI, 79). (Cited in Klaus Düsing, "Aesthetishe Einbildungskraft und Intuitiver Verstand," in *Hegel Studien* Band 21, heraus. F. Nicolin und O. Pöggeler [Bonn: Bouvier Verlag Herbert Grundmann,1986], s. 106, ft#33.)

3. We recall Kant's statement, "the power of the imagination, a blind but indispensable function of the soul, without which we should have no knowledge whatsoever, but of which we are scarcely ever conscious" (*CPR* A77/B103).

4. Cf. my introduction.

5. The question of freedom naturally arises when one reads passages such as these. A unity that posits, but that has original sundering as its principle, seems to exclude freedom. In other words, what choice is there, what individual will, when all division is fundamentally the sundering Absolute? One might answer negatively, that there cannot be any other kind of freedom. A self-understanding that takes itself to be free from division would be an abstract unity; it would be false because it would be static, incapable of developing. An argument for the false freedom that thinks it sees, would be an argument for a disembodied unity—a negation of the earlier *Potenzen*. Given that for Schelling and Hegel the original Identity of substance and subject is that unity from which all difference arises and from which all difference is ultimately not separate, such disembodied freedom would be an illusion. While the productive imagination is the unity "which is blind," false freedom would posit blindly, since the imagination would continue to be active even though such freedom declared itself free from the imagination. Blinded Gloucester sees the light in this respect when he says, "I stumbled when I saw" (*King Lear*, 4.1. 19–21). The proper freedom of theoretical positing (on the other hand) is the reflection of what *is*; and what is in reflection, is expressing its freedom as theorizing. However, I do not think that Hegel gets this story clear until he has changed his focus from the Absolute of the Identity Theory to that of the pro-reflection theory of his later Jena works. In this earlier work we are left to

deal with such phrases as: the intellect "posits the difference as identical but distinguishes itself from the different." This is indeed difficult to understand.

6. Hegel cashes out the moment of the negative in the *Phenomenology of Spirit*: it is the story of the overcoming of this preponderance. Throughout the book consciousness has the preponderance of dawning forms of subjective reason, which are one-sided, and of attempting to place the truth outside (beyond) itself, of attempting to name its truth. We are not reconciled with the sundering of reason (negation) until the negation of the negation in Absolute Knowing. Hence the description of the *Phenomenology of Spirit* as the "pathway of *doubt*, or more precisely the way of despair" (*PoS* Introduction ¶78, p. 49).

7. It is interesting to consider Hegel's view here in relation to happiness. Kant asserts that "happiness is an ideal not of reason but of imagination" (Kant, *Foundations for the Metaphysics of Morals*, trans. L. W. Beck [Indianapolis: Bobbs-Merrill, 1959], 36 [418 AK]). Since for Hegel, imagination is reason as it appears in empirical consciousness, this suggests that happiness is not only possible but also morally permissible. In what we can take to be a twist on Kant's repeated "as if" phrase in the *Critique of Judgment* and elsewhere, Hegel writes with some exasperation: "[A]s if the laws of nature were something quite different from rational laws! As if they were laws which a moral self would be ashamed to submit to, and as if obedience and subjection to them would make him indescribably miserable and bring him to despair!" (*Faith* 177).

8. Later, in the *Phenomenology of Spirit*, this is modified; Hegel has by that time integrated Fichte more positively. As we will see in my chapter 7, by 1807 the moment of *Wechselwirkung* becomes salient in reflection: in mere reflection as a "to and fro" movement, and in Speculative reflection as *Aufhebung*, the medium of Science. Thus, Hegel will say in the *Phenomenology* preface that "everything turns on grasping and expressing the True, not as *Substance*, but equally as *Subject*" (*PoS* 10 [with correction to Miller's translation: Miller writes "not only as *Substance* . . ." which is incorrect: ". . . das Wahre nicht als *Substanz*, sondern ebensosehr als *Subjekt* aufzufassen und auszudrücken" *PdG* 22–23]).

9. Cf. my introduction.

10. *Enc.Phil.Spir.* ¶445, p. 189. "Die Betrachtung des Geistes als eine Menge von *Kräften* . . . und der Geist auf diese Weise zu einer verknöcherten, mechanischen *Sammlung* gemacht" (*Enz.Phil.G.* ¶445, s. 241).

11. This is what Hegel accuses Jacobi of doing when he says that Jacobi takes the "copy" to be the real (cf. *Faith*, Fichte section). Thinking the faculties through properly is the task of the first five chapters of *Phenomenology of Spirit*. To give Fichte some credit, his "Deduction of Presentation" in the *Wissenschaftslehre* 1794 is an attempt to deduce the faculties. While it introduces the important dialectic process (the three principles) that are lacking in Kant's deduction, it remains, as far as I am concerned, unintelligible, largely due to the prerequisites which a deduction (as opposed to a phenomenology) place on the process. I discuss this more in chapter 3.

12. Cf. *CJ* Book I of the Analytic of the Beautiful (¶¶1–22).

13. "[T]he cognitive powers brought into play by this presentation are in free play . . . the mental state in this presentation must be a feeling . . . of a free play of pre-

sentational powers" (*CJ* ¶9, p. 62). The expression "free play" (*freies Spiel*) invites comparison with Fichte's wavering (*schwebende*) imagination. The wavering in Fichte is between the finite and the infinite, the ideal and the real. Kant's notion of play is in a sense between the finite and the infinite: for it is a play between the desire for conceptual definition (finitude) and the multitude of the beautiful object's attributes (infinite); the play is at the heart of a kind of judgment that by definition cannot come to rest but is spurred on by the seeming infinite possibilities presented by the beautiful object. It is a "quickening [*Belebung*] of the two powers to an activity that is indeterminate but, as a result of the prompting of the given presentation, nonetheless accordant . . ." (*CJ* 63). This is a precursor of Hegel's notion of *Aufhebung*.

14. As I discussed in my introduction, in the experience of the sublime, the agitated relation of comprehension and apprehension culminates in an idea of our supersensible vocation. This agitation and raising up to a higher level (though not its result per se) is likewise a precursor of Hegel's *Aufhebung*.

15. Some may disagree here. Klaus Düsing writes that "[a]ccording to Hegel, the structure of the absolute identity of opposed determinations was *veiled* in Kant's theory of the beautiful. But this absolute identity was *clearly expressed* in Kant's theory of intuitive Understanding. The structure of absolute identity characterized for Hegel the essence of actual and true Being, of the One substance. This structure is the All-One which [underlies] and is the thinking (*überlegene*) of finite consciousness. It is that in which we intellectually intuit and grasp any particular" (Düsing, "Aesthetische Ein." s. 118–19, my translation). But it seems clear that even if Kant expressed the same thing in his theory of intuitive Understanding, it did not mean the same to him as it did to Hegel.

According to Kant, completion of the relation between the subject and nature must be possible in the moral sphere. But even there, the morality of the willed event rests upon postulates, which are themselves "as if" structures. This is an interesting case, however. For a longer discussion of this see my article, "The Moral Chemist of the *Corpus Mysticism*: Why Some Version of Kant's Practical Postulates is Necessary Even for Hegel" presented to the Society for German Idealism Conference, APA Pacific Meeting, Pasadena March 24–28, 2004.

16. Hegel's eventual three-part *Encyclopedia System of Philosophy* is certainly a proper reconstruction. But part of what my book is about is showing that we have the first proper reconstruction in the *Phenomenology of Spirit*. That reconstruction is a proper view of the role of the imagination in all the possible levels of experience. The reconstruction is, therefore, what Hegel's original title of the book says it is: namely, "the science of experience."

My discussion in this chapter has been led to a degree by the structure of *Faith*: the development of Hegel's criticism in that work from Kant to Jacobi to Fichte takes us from the problems of the Speculative Idea in epistemology (in Kant) to the problem of the Speculative Idea in ethics (in Fichte). It is apparent in *Faith* that for Hegel reconstruction cannot be separated from the ethical. How this is so is not something I can get into here. For a phenomenological examination of why Hegel's epistemology implies morality and therefore ethical development, cf. John Russon's article "The

Metaphysics of Consciousness and the Hermeneutics of Social Life: Hegel's Phenomenological System," *The Southern Journal of Philosophy* 36 (1998):81–101.

17. Wolfgang Bonsiepen, *Der Begriff der Negativität in den Jenaer Schriften Hegels*, in *Hegel-Studien* Beiheft 16 (Bonn: Bouvier Verlag Herbert Grundmann, 1977), 29–31.

18. Cf. Fichte, *Sc.Kn.* I. 233, p. 207.

19. As we mentioned, while subjectively it *appears* as though we check the abstraction and move beyond it, the negation is part of the Absolute's self-development. Thus, whether the self perceives negation as self-determination, or as the self's undergoing a negation, a merely subjective encounter with absolute negation cannot but be an experience of loss.

20. *"und die Vernunft versenkt damit* ihr Reflektieren der absoluten Identität und ihr Wissen und *sich selbst* in ihren eigenen Abgrund, *und in dieser Nacht der blossen Reflexion und des räsonierenden Verstandes, die der Mittag des Lebens ist, können sich beide begegnen"* (*Differenz* 35; my emphasis).

21. See Søren Kierkegaard's "Preamble from the Heart," in *Fear and Trembling*, trans. Alastair Hannay (New York: Penguin, 1985), 68–82.

22. "Für die Spekulation sind die Endlichkeiten Radien des unendlichen Fokus, der sie ausstrahlt und zugleich von ihnen gebildet ist; in ihnen ist der Fokus und im Fokus sie gesetzt" (*Differenz* 43).

23. "indem in denselben das Denken als Unendlichkeit und negative Seite des Absoluten, welche die reine Vernichtung des Gegensatzes oder der Endlichkeit, aber zugleich auch der Quell der ewigen Bewegung oder der Endlichkeit, die unendlich ist, das heisst, die sich ewig vernichtet, aus welchem Nichts und reinen Nacht der Unendlichkeit die Wahrheit als aus dem geheimen Abgrund, der ihre Geburtsstätte ist, sich emporhebt,—erkannt wird" (*GW* 133).

24. As Harris explains:

> The light that shines in the primeval darkness is the light of Reason—the Logos that was "begotten not made"; and it seems that the nothing *out* of which God the *Father* made the world is to be *identified* with the creative might of the Father himself. We should note that there are two sides to the speculative interpretation of all this religious language. On the one side of the Philosophy of nature, "light" refers both to the physical principle of light (and heat) and to the principle of life, and "night" means not only darkness but that which, being impervious to light, is shown up by it, the heavy matter which is always inwardly dark till the higher light of life itself shines within it. On the side of transcendental Philosophy "light" stands for the reflective consciousness which discovers all the creative activity (of the Father?) that has already gone on in the "night" of unconscious nature; and "the nothing" means the mighty force of thought, the abyss out of which everything comes and into which it is hurled. God himself, when not identified with this abyss, which is both his creative power and his negative side, is identical with the life and order of the creative activity. Thus the night or the abyss is God the Father, while Reason in nature is God the Son, the Logos; and speculative Reason returning from the creation and reconciling it with its ground in the divine power

will be God the Holy Spirit, "proceeding from the Father and the Son" or "positing being in non-being as becoming [the Father], dichotomy in the Absolute as its appearance [the Logos], the finite in the infinite as life [the Spirit]" (Hegel 93–94). The trinitarian dogma of the Christian faith is a proper religious expression of speculative truth; while on the other hand, the Judaic creation story (in Genesis) expresses the truth from the "standpoint of dichotomy." (*Diff* "Intro." 22)

25. Cf. *Sc.Kn.* Introduction, 1797.

26. That Schelling is surreptitiously included in the scope of that loss will only become clear in the famous passage in the preface to the *Phenomenology of Spirit*. There the depth of Schelling's Absolute is measured in the shallowness of "the night in which all cows are black." A discussion of that leads us beyond the scope of this chapter.

27. "Das Wahre ist das Ganze" (*PdG* 24).

28. Contrast Hegel's general account of sundering above, with, for instance, its concrete phenomenological role in "Absolute Knowing" in the *Phenomenology of Spirit*: "[T]he pure knowledge of essence has *in principle* renounced its simple unity, for it is the self-sundering, or the negativity which the Notion is; so far as this self-sundering is the process of becoming *for-itself*, it is evil; so far as it is the *in-itself*, it remains good" (¶796, p. 484).

Chapter Two. Dialectical Beginnings
(Fragment 17 of *Geistesphilosophie* 1803–04)

1. While the first *Geistesphilosophie* is a concerted effort to hammer out the dialectic, and is thus both more intense and less skillful, by the time Hegel writes his 1805–6 *Geistesphilosophie* lecture notes he has developed enough ease to occasionally wax poetic, as we will see in chapter 4.

2. Robinson wrote the comment in German, this is my translation of it. The comment is cited in "Hegels Vorlesungen an der Universität Jena," by K. Düsing, in *Hegel-Studien* Bd. 26, Hrsg. von F. Nicolin und O. Pöggeler (Bonn: Bouvier Verlag, 1991), 15–21, see p. 23. (The citation was originally documented in *Hertha Marquardt: Henry Crabb Robinson und seine deutschen Freunde* Bd. 1 (Göttingen: Palaestra, 1964), Bd. 237; s. anme. 7, 84.) For one of Hegel's students' assessment see Gabler's accounts in *Dokument zu Hegels Jenaer Dozentätigkeit* (1801–1807), Hrsg von H. Kimmerle, in: *Hegel-Studien* Bd. 4 (1967), 53–56.

3. Düsing, "Hegels Vorlesungen," 23.

4. Düsing, "Hegels Vorlesungen," 23–24. My translation.

5. I. P. V. Troxler, *Schelling und Hegels erste absolute Metaphysik (1801–1802): Zusammenfassende Vorlesungsnachschriften von I. P. V.*, Hrsg., eingeleitet und mit Interpretationen versehen von K. Düsing (Köln: Jürgen Dinter, Verlag für Philosophie, 1988). Cf. pp. 63–77.

6. This is the standpoint that Hegel takes at the beginning of the 1812 *Science of Logic*: the first dialectical progression shows that Being is becoming.

7. Cf. Fragment 16.

8. Cf. Fragment 16. Given the explanation above of the shift in Hegel's view of logic, it would be wrong to assume that the logic referred to in Fragment 16 is that presented in his lectures on Logic and Metaphysics in 1801.

9. This version of the *Philosophy of Spirit* progresses dialectically out of the *Naturphilosophie*. What is being looked at is consciousness, but the same attitude of doing a philosophy *of* something natural is carried over in the analysis. So, although he doesn't express it this way, it is really the *nature* of consciousness which is under investigation. Hegel discusses consciousness in terms of *Potenzen*—levels or powers. For a discussion of *Potenzen* see Harris's Introduction to *FirstPhil*, 52–55.

Hegel provides a summary of the developments in the *Geistesphilosophie* as a whole in Fragment 19. It is important to have a sense of these developments in order to place our discussion of Fragment 17. Since our concern in this chapter is how the logic has become infinite, I merely summarized these developments of the *Geistesphilosophie* below. (Please also see my Schema of Imagination in Hegel's Works p. xxxix.)

The development is one from mere consciousness to its most developed form in *das Volk*. Hegel begins by describing the general character of the first power (*Potenz*): "The first form of the existence of spirit is consciousness in general, the concept of spirit . . . its pure theoretical existence" (*FirstPhil* 210; *G1* 195). We are, therefore, dealing first with consciousness *qua* theoretical (as opposed to consciousness qua practical). Consciousness in general is then determined to be the form of memory. The product of memory is speech. It is at this level of memory and speech that the imagination plays a role. (We will therefore be focusing on this later.) Through the process of understanding, speaking consciousness reflects upon itself. It thereby becomes absolute reflection in itself. At this point consciousness is able to recognize itself as emptiness. That is, it is able to recognize itself as the formal capacity for absolute abstraction (*G1* 195; *FirstPhil* 210).

At this point, the process evolves from a theoretical one into a practical one. This is the second *Potenz*. While the consciousness of the first *Potenz* had nominal command over nature, in the second it has real command over it: what stands over against consciousness is not merely named but is used as a tool. So while the first *Potenz* is an ideal mastery, the second is real mastery.

It is because of community (however small or limited) that language is possible, and the individual has a real existence only in that community. It is in part because of this that the raising of sexual desire to the ideal is possible: natural sexual desire is sublated (*aufgehoben*) into a sustained mutual desire (of one sex for the other). This gives rise to the family and the ethical system, which constitute the third *Potenz*.

The three *Potenzen* pass over into a still higher form. This final *Aufhebung* occurs for the following reason. The third *Potenz* is characterized by two sides: "[on the one side] the ideal constitution of consciousness as formal *Reason*, absolute abstraction, absolute emptiness [and] singularity, and [on the other side] its real constitution as the family . . ." (*FirstPhil* 211; *G1* 196). These two sides—formal Reason and the family—are ideal moments of the existence of spirit. This means that, regardless of their opposition, formal Reason and the family are both nevertheless on the same side with regard to nature: they are both organized over against nature. This opposition between spirit in its ideal forms and nature is, however, not a real opposition: it is an ideal one. This means that, considered thus far, the opposition between, on the one side, reason and the family, and on the other, nature, it is not an actual opposition: that is, the power of the community is organized upon a *theoretical, idealized* opposition of the community to nature. This idealized opposition is what is sublated in the move to the final form. In the final form the opposition becomes actual. The relation between the community and nature is therefore thoroughly dialectical. Thus, in the final section of the *Geistesphilosophie,* all the forms are contained within a self-determining (self-actualizing) totality. That form is *das Volk.*

To summarize, Hegel develops three *Potenzen*: (a) Speech, (b) the Tool, (c) Possession and the Family; and these three together pass over into the higher form of *das Volk.* The discussion of the imagination falls within the first *Potenz* (Fragment 20). That is, the imagination is directly involved in the development of language.

10. "Die einfache wesentliche Vielheit ist der soeben bestimmte Begriff, das unmittelbar in die positive Allgemeinheit aufgenommene Einzelne, das Einzelne als ein Sichselbstgleiches oder sein Anderssein, seine Ungleichheit, sich selbst, gleichgemacht. Das ihm Entgegengesetzte ist die Einheit als absolut ungleiche, als absolut ausschliessende, das numerische Eins; sich wohl selbst gleich, aber in seiner Sichselbstgleichheit das unmittelbar andre seiner selbst, als absolut nefierend oder die absolute Einzelnheit" (*G1* 186–87).

11. I am of course referring to Kierkegaard. "[P]eople unable to bear the martyrdom of unintelligibility jump off the path, and choose instead, conveniently enough, the world's admiration of their proficiency. The true knight of faith is a witness, never a teacher, and in this lies the deep humanity in him . . ." (*Fear and Trembling*, 107). Kierkegaard would himself never consider Hegel in this light: for Kierkegaard, Hegel was the archetypical systematizer who tried to make everything intelligible.

12. Leibniz, *The Monadology*, in *Leibniz Selections*, ed. Philip P. Wiener (New York: Charles Scribner's Sons, 1951), 533–551.

13. Dr. Daniels, a colleague of mine who is of the analytic school of philosophy, presented me with the following notion of identity. He claimed that, analytically conceived, a person's identity never changes from birth to death. Thus, it is true of the hairy, fifteen-year-old Danny that he will be bald at forty-five. And it is true of the forty-five-year-old Danny that at fifteen he had hair. It is also true of the forty-five-year-old that he is the fifteen-year-old with hair who had the future of becoming bald by forty-five. And it is true that the fifteen-year-old Danny is the forty-five-year-old baldy who has the memory of having hair at fifteen. According to this view of identity, the change from one property to another is not a change in identity. Even what we call substantial change does not change his identity—thus, it is true of Danny that at one hundred fifty he will be dead, and that before he was born he was going to be born on such and such a date and at such and such a time. This is a God's eye view of identity. According to this view, the fact that Danny himself didn't know when he was going to be born, go bald, or die (nor for that matter, did anyone else) does not mean that these facts about him only *become* true. They are always true. This is a view of identity that is a-temporal; it does not correspond to the view Hegel is presenting.

14. Hegel, *The Science of Logic*, 49.

15. Cf. Tom Rockmore's *Hegel's Circular Epistemology* (Bloomington: Indiana University Press, 1986).

16. "The most important and the most difficult step toward understanding the text as a whole is the comprehension of Hegel's theory of consciousness" (Harris, Introduction, *FirstPhil* 191–92).

Chapter Three. The Dialectical Imagination (*Geistesphilosophie* 1803–04)

1. Cf. my footnote summary of this, p. 164 note 9.

2. Our comparison with Kant brings up the difficulty of reading Hegel's text. It is difficult for the very reason that it attempts, as we pointed out earlier, to carry on the project of the philosophy of nature into an analysis of consciousness as the next "nature" under consideration, *while also* wanting us to go through a kind of phenomenological process, following the logic of *Aufhebung*, in order to experience what consciousness at the level of sensation, intuition, imagination, and memory *is*. The result is that there is no clear distinction—as there is in the *Phenomenology of Spirit*—between the "we" (the philosophers doing the philosophy of spirit) and the consciousness whose genesis "we" are experiencing. The seeds of the *Phenomenology* are in this text, as are those of the *Encyclopedia Philosophy of Subjective Spirit*. These seeds will fortunately drop into the more carefully tilled logic of Hegel's mature thought.

3. Consciousness is "das Hervorrufen in ihm selbst der ehmals oder an einem andern Orte gehabten Anschauungen" (*G1* 199).

4. Kant, *CPR* B151, 165.

5. I agree here with the translator that *ihrer* belongs to *Zeit* und *Raum*. Technically it might also be taken as "of the '*positive Allgemeinheit*,'" which means that what consciousness makes the self-opposite is the *positive Allgemeinheit*. The argument against this is that Hegel does not use *Allgemeinheit* but rather *Allgemein*, which is neutral.

6. Es [consciousness] schaut

        1) nicht Raum und Zeit als solche an —sie für sich sind allgemeine, leere, an sich höhere Idealitäten, Begriffe

A   2)—sondern sie nur als insofern allgemeine seiend und nicht seiend, als es sie als einzelne, besonderte setzt, erfüllte,

B   3) so zugleich, dass es ebenso, wie Raum und Zeit sein positives Allgemeines sind, es sie ebenso unmittelbar formal zum Gegenteil ihrer selbst macht und sie besondert;

A+B 4) jenes Sein des Bewusstseins ist ebenso theoretisch, passiv als praktisch; 5) jene Seite ist, dass es in der Form der positiven Allgemeinheit, dies, insofern es zugleich in der negativen Allgemeinheit ist und diese Allgemeinheit selbst besondert.

        6) Diese Form des Bewusstseins ist empirische Einbildungskraft,

        7) als positive Allgemeinheit ist die Anschauung in der Kontinuität der Zeit und des Raumes überhaupt, zugleich aber [als negative Allgemeinheit, praktisches Bewusstsein] sie unterbrechend und vere-

inzelnd, zu einzelnen bestimmten, d.i. erfüllten Stücken der Zeit und des Raumes machend. (*G1* 198)

7. For a discussion of Hegel's theory of time and space in his philosophy of nature, see Edward Halper's "The Logic of Hegel's *Philosophy of Nature*: Nature, Space and Time," in *Hegel and the Philosophy of Nature,* ed. Stephen Houlgate (Albany: State University of New York Press, 1998), 29–49. See also my chapter 4 notes 20 and 27.

8. The process can be expressed in terms of what Hegel later calls an "inwardizing" (*zurücktreten*). ("Inwardizing" is a translation of expressions such as *"in sich zurück-tretend,"* *"in sich zurückkehren"* and *insichseiend.*) Inwardizing is the process of deter-mining and taking up particular times and spaces into consciousness. It is what makes the reality of time and space as much mental as physical. The inward aspect is what gets neglected by Leibniz's view of the universe as a set of relations. According to Hegel, the very articulation of the existence of any relation cannot be distinguished from this inwardization. But to explain this passage in terms of inwardizing would be to borrow from Hegel's later thought. (See, for example, Hegel's description of Absolute Knowing, in particular the final two pages of the *Phenomenology of Spirit.*) I do not want to do that here in order to preserve our account of the development of Hegel's thought in his early works. So to make sense of the present passage, let us look at the two, dovetailing ways in which this particularizing of time and space occurs. Understanding this dovetailing will help us later when we do look at inwardizing.

9. This movement is evident in the opening two paragraphs of the *Science of Logic,* in the movement from Being to Nothing.

10. From one point of view, this argument seems problematic since negation is not an identity, it is a nonidentity. It is a return to ground, where there is no immediate ideational activity. ("Ground" can be equally used to describe the content of any pos-itive universality.) Empirical consciousness raises the ground to positive universality, thus giving rise to the identity "negative universality." In that way it is an identity. Since there is no way that negation qua negation is intuited, we can conclude that positive universality is equally the nonidentity of any identity. Positive universality turns out to be a negation of its identified intuition. Thus, positive universality is negative univer-sality, just as much as negative universality is positive universality.

Negation cannot be argued for except by pointing to contradictions in the coherence of any identity claimed to be inalienably true. This, as we will see, is one of the insights of *The Phenomenology of Spirit.* Indeed, this is what Hegel does throughout the *Phenomenology of Spirit.* It is also this which invites comparison between Hegel and some forms of Eastern thought, such as that of the Buddhist philosopher Nāgārjuna.

11. The German language allows us to follow the dialectic more easily because of the closeness of the words used: compare *Bestehende, Vergehende,* and *Verstehende.* (The last is the essentially fixed, and translates in English into "the understanding." We will encounter the latter shortly.)

12. This is an important point for anyone who wants to argue that Hegel's *Logic* takes place outside of time. I agree that the movement, for instance, from Being to Nothing to Becoming, *can* be analytically understood and thus appears outside of time.

But its *truth* is just as much temporal. Time and space are not just external, they are the very process of cognition. Becoming is equally disappearing, *vergehen*. There is no good reason to limit one's reading of the *Logic* to a purely analytic reading. Such a reading is one-sided and causes Hegel's philosophy to appear to have internal contradictions. The first movement from Being to Nothing to Becoming is evidently also a *synthetic* a priori truth. This is one of the reasons why we must understand the imagination even within the *Logic*, despite the *Logic* not being about images or picture-thinking. It is not the picture thinking that is so central to the imagination, it is the dialectical dovetailing of time and space in identity that is the basis of all cognition. Even though that dovetailing also appears to us in external, nonconscious matter, the dovetailing first appears in Hegel's developmental tale about cognition, in the movement of the imagination; and despite the fact that the dialectical dovetailing of time and space appears in nonconscious matter and therefore seems independent of cognition, the dialectical dovetailing imagination is the sine qua non of the dovetailing of time and space in nonconscious matter. It is that without which there would be no appearances at all. (See also my discussion below p. 96.)

13. It is ironic that, although *what* is being described is how subjective and confused the experience of empirical consciousness is, Hegel's description is far more readable than the passage with which we have just dealt.

14. See my chapter 4 note 20. For my refutation of Petry's argument that time and space are, for Hegel, external to the mind, see my chapter 4 note 27.

15. "Diese Besonderung ist zunächst dem Inhalt nach jene ersten sinnlichen Vorstellungen" (*G1* 198).

16. "das Allgemeine, das besondert wird, ist das allgemeine Element des Bewusstseins selbst, seine leere Unendlichkeit *als Zeit und Raum*, das Hervorrufen in ihm selbst der ehmals oder an einem andern Orte gehabten Anschauungen" (*G1* 198–99; my italics).

17. Cf. *Sc.Kn.* Second Introduction, 34.

18. "Imagination is a faculty that wavers in the middle between determination and nondetermination" (*Sc.Kn.* I 216, p. 194). "For Reason pure and simple, everything is simultaneous; only for the imagination is there such a thing as time" (Ibid. I 217).

19. "Begriff des Einsseins der Einfachen und der Unendlichkeit" (*G1* Frag. 15, 183).

20. See my discussion of Breazeale's view in my introduction note 18.

21. Hegel, "Preface," in *Hegel's Philosophy of Right*, trans. T. M. Knox (London, Oxford: Oxford University Press,. 1967), 10. I disagree with Knox's reading (see Knox's footnote 27, p. 302).

22. The three divisions of the *System der Sittlichkeit* are (1) Relation (2) Transgression, and (3) Ethical Life. The *Geistesphilosophie* divisions are (1) Consciousness, (2) the Negative, and (3) The People. One can make out in this work what would later be defined by Hegel as Subjective and Objective Spirit; this distinction is not however formalized in 1803.

23. Harris "Introduction," *FirstPhil* 190.

24. "We can see from the *Philosophy of Spirit* of 1803/4 that having once laid it down that '*Bewusstsein*' is the 'concept' of spirit, he was unwilling to abandon the standpoint of 'consciousness' at all" (Harris, "Introduction," *FirstPhil* 190).

Chapter Four. The Inwardizing Imagination (*Geistesphilosophie* 1805–06)

1. Hegel, *G2*. All translations of this work are my own. Leo Rauch provides a translation of the text in *Hegel and the Human Spirit* (Detroit: Univeristy Press Wayne State, 1993)—henceforth (Rauch p.-). But I prefer my own translations. The same must be said of working with this text as of working with the 1803–04 text. Because it consists of Hegel's posthumously published lecture notes, understanding Hegel is difficult. He often uses dashes rather than full sentences, and the dialectical moments are not always clearly marked in the text. As with *G1* however, the rewards of studying it are not to be underestimated.

2. This is similar to Kathleen Dow Magnus's claim, in *The Symbolic Mediation of Spirit*, that spirit is always symbolically mediated. See her discussion in her chapter 2 of the necessity of loss in memory's activity. She claims that the loss is necessary for there to be a transition from signs to thought. While there is some overlap in our views, there is still a difference of opinion here as to whether Hegel ever develops a speculative, systematic communication that is *not* symbolically mediated. I think he does, namely the *Logic*. But saying that symbols are not active in the *Logic* is not to say that the imagination is not central even to the *Logic*. (See my chapter 3 above, note 12). There is a difference between symbol and imagination that is key here. I take imagination to be central to *Aufhebung*, i.e., as essentially the negative moment *in* the symbolic but not limited *to* the symbolic. My reading therefore leaves open the possibility of the *Phenomenology of Spirit* arriving at a kind of system ("Absolute Knowing") that both knows how to read its experience symbolically, but also can read the fundamental categories of all experience speculatively (using dialectical logic). So while Magnus and I agree that the moment of loss or difference is essential to all communication (and therefore to spirit), I argue that Hegel wishes to limit *symbolic* mediation in the *Phenomenology of Spirit* to the moments prior to "Absolute Knowing." The *imagination's negative moment* is operative in speculative reason even in logic, but not as symbol-making *Phantasie*. Rather, the imaginative moment is cognitive difference within identity. That difference is temporal in essence. The difference is only *historical* when speculative reason is concerned with the symbolizing consciousness narrating its experience (i.e., only historical insofar as it is concerned, e.g., with the *Vorstellungen* of art, as in the *Aesthetics*, or of experience, as in the *Phenomenology of Spirit*. It is neither historical nor symbolic for speculative reason that is doing logic.) See my review of her book in *Philosophy in Review* (XXII, no. 5 (Oct. 2002): 336–38 and my chapter 5 note 19.

3. See my Schematic Breakdown of the Imagination (p. 29).

4. Much later (in Objective Spirit) Hegel provides a margin note in which the moments here are listed as: *Einbildungskraft*, *Erinnerung*, and *Zeichnen*. (Cf. *G2* 204, note 1). The second triad is essentially articulated by Hegel in his margins as follows:

a) *Namen geben, das Allgemeine dieser Sphäre; b) Tätigkeit, Fürsichsein, Gedächtnis; c) Anundfürsichsein . . . Verstand.* (*G2* 180, note 1).

5. Hegel does not articulate the moments of this section in the way with which we are familiar in his later works. But its general structure can be eked out of the text and out of what Hegel jotted down as structural plans in the margins of his lecture notes. I give it here as I have been able to extract it.

6. *Die Einbildungskraft: die "bezeichnende [kraft]"* (*G2* 174).

7. *Die Namengebendekraft, die "erste Schöpeferkraft, die der Geist ausübt"* (*G2* 175).

8. Petry, in his translation of the 1830 *Philosophy of Spirit*, writes that "by 1805/06, Hegel was already treating imagination in a way which was not so very different from that of the mature Encyclopedia" (*Hegel's Philosophy of Subjective Spirit*, ed. and trans. Vol. 3 [Dordrecht: D. Reidel, 1978], 408.)

9. That this is a beginning using the imagination is contentious, but see my chapter 3 note 12 for the justification.

10. The term *Geist* went out of fashion in the eighteenth-century. But Hegel chooses it rather than some cognitive term. Translating *Geist* as Spirit rather than as "Mind" works best. "Spirit" does lend itself to misinterpretations, but by using it we avoid the worse mistake of identifying the movement of consciousness with a faculty. That would happen if we used "Mind."

11. The passages are: *G2* 171, *G2* 174–75, *G2* 176.

12. We note in *Diff:* "[T]he task of philosophy consists in uniting these presuppositions [night and light], to posit being in non-being, as becoming" (*Diff* 93–94). The imagination's role in philosophy is that of spiritual genesis.

13. See below in this chapter, pages 66ff esp. p. 77.

14. "The books of Aristotle on the soul, along with his discussions on its special aspects and states, are for this reason still by far the most admirable, perhaps even the sole work of philosophical value on this topic. The main aim of a philosophy of mind can only be to reintroduce unity of idea and principle into the theory of mind, and so reinterpret the lesson of those Aristotelian books" (*Enc.Phil.Spir.* ¶378, p. 3).

15. Aristotle, *De Anima*, trans. W. S. Hett, (Loeb Classical Edition. Cambridge: Harvard UP, 1936). Cf. III iii. Henceforth (*De Anima* Bk-, p.-).

16. "It is a universal and ancient preconception that human beings are thinking beings, and that by thinking and thinking alone they distinguish themselves from the beasts" (*Phil.Rel.* 121).

17. We see this in Hegel's *The Difference Between Fichte's and Schelling's System of Philosophy.* The light is said to be "younger" than the night, which does not seem to be case in 1805. But the point is that even in this earlier, more Schellingian text of Hegel's, light is nonetheless essential. (See Hegel, *The Difference Between Fichte's and Schelling's System of Philosophy*, trans. H. S. Harris and W. Cerf [Albany: State University of New York Press, 1977], 93–04.)

18. John Sallis writes it thus: "Hegel will think imagination through to the end in the sense not only of filling out and completing the Aristotelian account but also of thinking it through to that point at which what was lost is recovered, to that end in which negativity comes to serve for reaffirmation, difference for self-identity, and

absence for the recovery of presence" (Sallis, "Imagination and Presentation in Hegel's Philosophy of Spirit" in *Hegel's Philosophy of Spirit*, ed. Peter G. Stillman. Albany: State University of New York Press, 1987. 66-88. p 71. Henceforth (Sallis p.—)). But one must be careful with such terms as reaffirmation. The wavering imagination is not of itself positive: it is essentially a movement of difference, of alienation as well as of mastery; and the moment of mastery is itself subject to further mediation.

19. This powerful description of inwardizing is lost in the 1830 account.

20. Willem A. DeVries claims that "although absolute knowledge has its roots in man's sensory encounter with the world, Hegel claims that this beginning is ultimately overcome, that true thought, free of any sensory admixture, is ultimately achieved" (DeVries, *Hegel's Theory of Mental Activity: An Introduction to Theoretical Spirit* [Ithaca and London: Cornell University Press, 1988], 69). I disagree. DeVries relies on the later *Encyclopaedia Psychology* discussion of sensation, and his reading relies on Hegel's use of the Aristotelian version of sensation without considering the inwardizing activity of the soul which I have just discussed. ("Hegel claims that, when he sees something red, his sensation is itself red" [69]. DeVries himself finds problems with his account of sensation in Hegel: "[I]n the system it is not until we reach the more sophisticated level of intuition that space and time are explicitly introduced and constructed. Hegel has not really thought out the way spatiality enters into our perceptual experience . . ." (DeVries, 69). And DeVries agrees that Hegel cannot be consistent if he leaves sensation out of the cognitive activity: "Perhaps the major source of disquiet in Hegel's treatment of sensation is the fact that he seemingly denies that sensations are cognitive while still attributing them content" (70.) I think we solve a great deal by using Hegel's earlier texts on space and time in intuition in order to generate a consistent reading of Hegel's genesis of cognition. In both the 1803 psychology (Fragment 20, *G1* s.197) and the 1805 psychology at which we are looking, Hegel jumps right into a discussion of space and time. No prior—noncognitive—levels come into the picture. On a consistent reading, absolute knowledge does have its roots in man's sensory encounter with the world, and true thought is not separate from it. Otherwise Hegel's unity of thought and being is limited.

This is not to say that Hegel himself always presents that consistent framework, or that there are not problems with the genetic account of how we come to have an image. With regard to the former, Hegel does repeatedly refer to space and time in a way that might be confused with the realist's claim that they exist outside of sensation. As I'll be discussing shortly, in our own text of 1805–06 he claims that, at the level of associative reproduction of images in the mind, the self's movement is "a completely other movement from the one of space and time, remaining free from the movement of mere being" (*G2* 173, note 3); and again in the 1830 *Encyclopaedia Philosophy of Mind* discussion of sensation Hegel writes, "This *natural* subjectivity is not yet a self-determining one, pursuing its own laws, activating itself in a necessary manner, but a subjectivity determined from without, bound to *this* space and *this* time, dependent upon contingent circumstances" paragraph 400, *Zusatz* as cited in DeVries, 68). With regard to the second issue (problems with the genetic account of how we come to have an image) see DeVries discussion of sensation, 69–70: DeVries concludes, "Our earlier analysis of the content of sensations, however, shows that Hegel need not be smothered by these problems. If a sensation has a certain content in virtue of occupying a position in a (mental) quality-space isomorphic in the essential respects to the quality-space applicable to the object by which it is typically caused, then some mental analogue of space suffices for us to be able to sense shapes" (p. 70). But as cited above, DeVries maintains that there is still a problem in not viewing the content of sensation as cognitive. I am proposing that the problem is solved by understanding the fundamental dialectic of Night and light as becoming (a becoming that is just as much substance as subject). See also my note 27 below.

21. "Dies Bild gehört ihm an, er ist im Besitz desselben, er ist Herr darüber; es ist in seinem Schatze aufbewahrt, in seiner Nacht—es ist bewusstlos" (*G2* 172).

22. W. Shakespeare, *A Midsummer Night's Dream*, ed. Wolfgang Clemen, (New York and Scarborough, Ontario: Signet Classic, 1963), line 14, p.109.

23. For a discussion of Hegel's concept of the body, see John Russon's *The Self and its Body in Hegel's Phenomenology of Spirit* (Toronto, Buffalo: University of Toronto Press, 1997).

24. The difference between this set of lectures and the 1803–04 ones is that here it is the mediation of *the Night* through language.

25. "It has been well said that the soul is the place of forms . . ." (*de Anima* 429a27).

26. Cf. Goethe's *Faust*, Part One, line 3835ff. This reference is in fact anachronistic since *Faust* Part One was only published in 1808 (after Schiller's prodding), three years after our present text. Hegel would certainly have known of (or even read) *Faust, ein Fragment* which came out in 1790. But the *Walpurgisnacht* is not in it.

27. De Vries, for example, appealing to the 1830 *Encyclopedia Psychology* lectures, asserts that for Hegel intuition finds a world, and the "found" world is spatiotemporal (112). De Vries writes, "In intuition the item found is found as an item (or as belonging to an item) in an external, spatiotemporal world. The structure of the connectedness among the found sensations is now completely specified. And it is only in intuition that adequate sophistication is reached to account for the experience of a spatiotemporal world as spatiotemporal." While this is certainly the way Hegel keeps coming back to the issue, I find it to be inconsistent with Hegel's dialectical account of the truth of the "given." Hegel did start out in our present 1805–06 lectures with the assertion that "I and the thing are in space" but he went on to say that we must understand the truth of that claim. And the truth is that "I" and "space" are in fact products of inwardizing and of much more complex levels of the dialectic coming into play (since to even distinguish the "I" from a thing requires a more advanced cognition than intuiting). Nevertheless, the inwardizing is *of* something. And whatever is inwardized becomes a spatiotemporal designate which can be reconstituted by the mind as image, and taken out of its "original" spatiotemporal matrix. But I reject the idea that the "original" spatiotemporal designates are strict re-presentations of what is outside us. The Night as Space is a reservoir filled with representations, but each representation is not a pure reflection of the outside world, it is a spatiotemporal configuration. Outside of the dialectical, dovetailing of imagination, the details of that original intuitive configuring remain unclear.

28. Miller translates it as recollection in his translation of the 1830 *Philosophy of Spirit*; Rauch translates it as "remembering," as "I remind myself"; he also suggests "'re-internalize' myself" (Rauch, 88).

29. "[S]chon bekannt; oder ich erinnere mich seiner. Oder ich habe unmittelbar das bewusstsein Meiner darin."

30. "Erinnerung setzt das Moment des Fürsich seins hinzu—ich habe es schon einmal gesehen oder gehört: ich erinnere mich."

31. "Dieses Fürmichsein, das ich zum Gegenstande hinzusetze, ist jene Nacht, jenes Selbst, worin ich ihn versenkte . . ." Hegel does not have the clear moments of the imagination demarcated which he will have by 1830, and so the next part of the dialectic is murky here. But I think we can nevertheless trace Hegel's meaning.

32. The bare logical structure evokes Fichte's three principles of the *Sc.Kn.*: in Fichte's second principle the Self posits a not-self over against the self (I, 104)—negation; then according to the third principle, "in the self I oppose a divisible not-self to the divisible self." (I, 110)—essentiality. It is clear that Hegel is thinking even more deeply than Fichte: Hegel expresses the dialectic from both the subject's and its object's side, i.e., the first principle does not remain unmediated by the process.

33. "*der Inhalt ist sein einfaches Wesen überhaupt*"—it appears syntactically that by "its" here Hegel means "the Self's." Though Hegel's reference remains unclear, I think this is the best way to read it.

34. Hegel's interpretation here of signs as primarily subjectively meaningful is in 1830 reserved for the symbol; by 1830, "sign" is the term Hegel uses to indicate the next step beyond symbols: it refers to the externalization of an image or tone which is conventionally understood.

35. Standing back from the text and comparing it with the 1803–04 *Geistesphilosophie*, we see that Hegel's focus at this point in his notes has been on essence, whereas in 1803–04 he does not discuss essence and focuses rather on how phenomenologically confused the merely subjectively imagining mind was. This is due in part to the fact that the logical moments are much more clearly articulated in 1805–06, the role of the negative (the Night) being explicitly developed.

36. As there is for example in the case of "thunder" and "lightning" (an example we will deal with more clearly later); or as there is in the recitation of a line from Shakespeare that we have learned by heart.

37. There is no question here of the twentith-century debate about whether syntax is innate—part of the genetic building blocks of the human mind—or learned. The learned-innate difference does not make sense if the rational part of us is fundamentally interpersonal to begin with: we don't learn syntax any more than we learn to interact: it is simply a function of reason. The inseparability of language, of interpersonal interaction and of reason, makes the innate-learned debate impossible in Hegel: for it would amount to asking whether we are innately rational or learn to be rational.

38. Kathleen Dow Magnus argues that this symbolic mediation of spirit is essential even to absolute spirit. See my Chapter 5 note 19. I agree that it is essential to spirit but not to speculative science since we leave the symbolic behind there. I claim rather that the inwardizing activity of the imagination is what is essential to all levels of Spirit.

39. Hegel realized well before Wittgenstein that there can be no private language.

40. Cf. *PoS* ¶801, p. 487. I discuss it in chapter 7.

Chapter Five. The Communicative Imagination
(*Philosophy of Subjective Spirit* 1830)

1. See my Schema p. xxxix.

2. This is due in part to the fact that Hegel has abandoned the separate triad headings of "Imagination in General" and "Language" (from 1805–06), and put all those developments under the heading "representation" (*Vorstellung*). This would suggest that the difference between the sleeping spirit and the waking one has changed. There has been a lot of scholarly investigation about the difference between Hegel's lecture notes and the *Zusätze* with regard to the placement of symbolizing and sign making within imagination (see Magnus, *Hegel and the Symbolic Mediation of Spirit*, note 7 of chapter 2, p. 258). But this discussion does not affect the fact that by this point Hegel has firmly placed this activity within the realm of the imagination. (See my note 15 below).

3. This first moment—*der fühlende Geist*—is also the first form of faith in the *Lectures on the Philosophy of Religion*. (The second form is representation, *Vorstellung*.)

4. Hegel explains the relation of intuition to Spirit in his lectures on the *Philosophy of Religion*:

> I have representations and intuitions, which constitute a specific content: this house, etc. They are my intuitions and represent themselves to me. But I could not represent them to myself if I had not grasped this content within myself. This entire content must be posited within me in a simple and ideal way. What constitutes spirit must have come into its own in such a way. Spirit must have been educated, must have traversed this circuit. These forms, distinctions, determinations, and finitudes must have been, in order for it to make them its own and to negate them, in order for what it is in itself to have emerged out of it and stood as object over against it, yet at the same time be its own.
>
> This is the path and the goal by which spirit has attained its proper concept, the concept of itself, and has arrived at what it is in itself. (*Phil.Rel.* 110)

5. See my discussion of *Erinnerung* (chapter 4). It is important to keep in mind the reflexivity of the German expression "*Ich erinnere mich.*"

6. It is "von seiner ersten Unmittelbarkeit und abstrakten Einzelheit gegen anderes befreit" and "in die Allgemeinheit des Ich überhaupt aufgenommen" (*Enz.Phil.G.* ¶452, s. 258).

7. "erinnert, ist das Bild, nicht mehr existierend, bewußtlos aufbewahrt" (*Enz.Phil.G.* ¶453).

8. For this reason it is not entirely right for Wallace to use the term *pit* as a translation for *Schacht* (see paragraph 462). That translation is picked up by John Sallis and others (Cf. e.g., the translated proceedings of Derrida's seminar *Hegel et la pensée moderne*, "The Pit and the Pyramid: Introduction to Hegel's Semiology," in *Margins of Philosophy*, trans. Alan Bass [Chicago: University of Chicago Press, 1982], 69–108).

The term *pit*, while not incorrect, obscures the determining power in the word *Schacht* and its translation as "mine." It is out of the dark that we forage and forge our meanings. I will be discussing this again in chapter 7.

9. The translation is Miller's (page 205): "Das Bild, das im Schachte der Intelligenz nur ihr Eigentum war, ist mit der Bestimmung der Äußerlichkeit nun auch im Besitze derselben."

10. "[Die Einbildungskraft] ist *überhaupt* das *Bestimmende* der Bilder" (*Enz.Phil.G.* ¶455Z, p. 264)

11. "Die zweite Entwickelungsstufe der Vorstellung ist . . . die *Einbildungskraft*. Zu dierser erhebt sich die erste Form des Vorstellens, die *Erinnerung*, dadurch, dass die Intelligenz, aus ihrem *abstracten Insichsein* in die *Bestimmtheit* heraustretend, die den Schatz ihrer Bilder verhüllende nächtliche Finsternis zerteilt und durch die lichtvolle Klarheit der Gegenwärtigkeit verscheucht" (*Enz.Phil.G* ¶455, p. 264).

12. "[D]as Hervorgehen der Bilder aus der eigenen Innerlichkeit des Ich, welches nunmehr deren Macht ist" (*Enz.Phil.G.* ¶455). I have used my own translation because I find Wallace's misleading: "[T]he images issue from the inward world belonging to the ego, which is now the power over them"—the problem is in the line "power over them" (*Enc.Phil.Spir.* ¶455).

13. Kant, *Critique of Practical Reason*, trans. Lewis White Beck, third edition (New Jersey: Prentice-Hall, Inc., 1993), 170–71 (AK 163) and 97 (AK 93).

14. "Zuerst tut sie [die Einbildungskraft] weiter nichts, als dass sie die Bilder ins *Dasein* zu treten bestimmt. So ist sie die nur *reproduktive* Einbildunskraft. Diese hat den Charakter einer bloss *formellen* Tätigkeit. Zweitens aber ruft die Einbildunskraft die in ihr vorhandenen Bilder nicht bloss wieder hervor, sondern *bezieht* dieselben *aufeinander* und erhebt sie auf diese Weise zu *allgemeinen* Vorstellungen. Auf dieser Stufe erscheint sonach die Einbildungskraft als die Tätigkeit des *Assoziierens* der Bilder. Die dritte Stufe in dieser Sphäre ist diejenige, auf welcher die Intelligenz ihre *allgemeinen* Vorstellungen mit dem *Besonderen* des Bildes identisch setzt, somit ihnen ein *bildliches* Dasein gibt. Dies sinnliche Dasein hat die doppelte Form des *Symbols* und des *Zeichens*, so dass diese dritte stufe die *symbolizierende* und die *zeichenmachende* *Phantasie* umfasst, welch letztere den *Übergang* zum *Gedächtnis* bildet" (*Enz.Phil.G.* ¶455Z, p. 264).

15. John Sallis notes that Hegel's ordering of the moments of the imagination differs in the *Zusätze* and the paragraphs. (Sallis notes as well the differences between the 1817, and 1827 editions on this matter.) He does this to highlight the difficulty he thinks Hegel had with these transitions in the imagination, particularly with regard to the second and third moments (Sallis 77). Sallis thereby opens up a space for his own interpretation of the imagination. But such differences may be due only to the fact that the *Zuzätze* belong to different periods of Hegel's thought than the paragraphs.

The difference in the ordering is more noticeable if one returns to the 1805–06 lectures. In those lectures, what Hegel discusses under the name of "sign" (*Zeichen*) is what he means in 1830 by "symbol." In 1805–06, the sign is the product of the imagination *par excellence*; only once names are introduced does Spirit have objective, universal exteriority. That transition from signs to names in 1805–06 was the weakest transition in that discussion of the intellect.

Whatever the outcome of the dispute over the ordering of the moments in 1830, Hegel has made an advance by 1830. In 1830, Hegel has inserted a division between symbols (which play the role signs did in 1805–06) and signs. The sign has the objective side, which the symbol does not, for with the sign we are in the world of conventional communication. (Magnus sides with the text claiming that the shift from symbol making to sign making is from associative imagination to creative imagination [see *The Symbolic Mediation*, note 7, p. 258].)

16. The example of Jupiter was used by Kant in the *CJ* 183 (AK 315). There Kant explains how aesthetic attributes give rise to an aesthetic idea, using as illustration: "Jupiter's eagle with the lightening in its claws is an attribute of the mighty King of Heaven." It would be interesting to compare Hegel's notion of symbol and Kant's notion of aesthetic idea (and of aesthetic attributes). But we do not have the time to go into that here.

17. Memory's activity itself only becomes apparent—or in-itself and for consciousness—at an even more developed stage: when the signs are detached from images altogether. That is when names are generated. An increasingly developed memory is an increasingly developed Spirit.

18. Hegel articulates this transition to sign making somewhat differently in 1830 than in 1805–06. In 1805–06 the advent of signs and names meant that we left the arena of the imagination and entered here into the realm of memory. In 1830, there is some question as to whether we leave the arena of the imagination or not. On the one hand, Hegel includes his discussion of the movement from symbol making to sign making within the chapter on imagination. But *within* that discussion Hegel writes that "This sign-creating activity may be distinctively named 'productive' Memory . . . since memory, which in ordinary life is often used as interchangeable and synonymous with remembrance (recollection), and even with conception and imagination, has always to do with signs only" (¶458). Given Hegel's placement of this discussion within the chapter on imagination, despite the fact that sign making falls under the rubric of memory we must nevertheless assume that the imagination is at work here in some way. As I go on to show above, I think that it is as inwardizing, as time, that it is at work.

19. For an interesting Hegelian reply to Derrida's critique of Hegel's theory of the sign, see Kathleen Dow Magnus's *Hegel and the Symbolic Mediation of Spirit*. See my chapter 4 note 2 above about her book and my review of it in *Philosophy in Review*. Since it is so close to my own argument I include an excerpt of that review here:

> [Magnus] offers a Hegelian counter to Derrida's charge that the sign dominates Western metaphysics (including Hegel's) and that metaphysics has failed to recognize its effacement of metaphor in its privileging of the sign. She counters that the symbol's lack of complete transparency is a necessary part of Hegel's idea of Spirit. "By interpreting Hegel's philosophy from the point of view of his theory of the symbol and his understanding of the symbolic, we can come to see how the contradictoriness, negativity, and "otherness" inherent to spirit is less an impediment to spirit's self-realization than *the condition for it* . . . serv[ing] the purpose

of *completing* spirit" (p. 31–32). She claims that "spirit is not just the act of trans-
parent self-knowledge, but also the intuitive, representing, artistic and religious
acts of expression, acts which contain significant *symbolic* components. . . . Spirit
cannot be or become *whole* without both elements [the sign and the symbol]" (p.
34–35). She offers a good metaphysical argument but her claim that this is Hegel's
view is not completely convincing. . . . The problem lies in the main argument. The
argument is that spirit needs the symbol as much as the sign because while the sign
gives clarity and comprehension to spirit so that spirit can know its objects
absolutely, spirit requires the ambiguities of the symbol in order negate itself and
experience itself as other. In this way it does not remain abstract but takes shape
and progresses. Progress is essential, she claims, since "[g]enuine self-determination requires that one was *not* 'always already' self-determining. For Hegel, there
is no such thing as simply *being* self-determining. Spirit must *become* self-determining" (p. 235). Self-difference is essential to that progress, so symbolic mediation is necessary. What she fails to see is that the idea that spirit can find its way
out of ambiguities in order to reach absolute spirit *presupposes* that the real was
always already rational and that spirit just had to mature into that realization.
Derrida's critique that Hegelian negation comes full circle in identity at the
expense of true ambiguity has itself not been touched. (This problem is particularly evident in her account of the necessity of loss in the move from mechanical
memory to thought in Chapter Two.) This is a problem not just for spirit's historical progress but for its ultimate, continuing self-genesis . . . (p. 238); once
absolute spirit *knows* itself to encompass all ambiguities in its totality there can be
no real loss or alienation.

   Her story would work if one thinks only in terms of the *Phenomenology of
Spirit* [not including the last chapter]. There alienation and ambiguity exist in the
distinction between absolute knowing and the natural consciousness making its
way toward it. But it is that distinction which is overcome by the end of the book
in order that consciousness now be able to do speculative science. Symbolic representation is the problematic of that work, not of the *Science of Logic.* Magnus'
claims are like claiming that Hegel never gets out of the *Phenomenology of Spirit*
into the light of speculative science. . . . Hegel wants us to move beyond the
Phenomenology of Spirit to speculative science, to thoroughly think through the
ambiguities and contradictions and consequent alienations which arise out of the
inadequate (symbolic) forms of self-reflection in order to gain the speculative
comprehension of the forms of experience. With all forms in hand at the end of
the *Phenomenology*, the process becomes one of the Word, the sign knowing itself
in and through any phenomenon. The sign has the upper hand, not the symbol.
We rise above the symbol even if the symbol is what we need to interpret.

   For Derrida the sign is still a symbol; there is no decidable absolute return to
spirit; no perfect self-reflection. Magnus, by keeping a distinction between sign and
symbol and arguing for the necessity of the symbol, does not address the key problem
Derrida poses. This does not mean that Derrida is right. But her book needed to
address that problem to successfully use Derrida as the foil. (Excerpted from my
review of her book in *Philosophy in Review* XXII, no. 5 (Oct. 2002): 336–38.)

Despite these points of contention, her book is important for Hegel scholarship.

20. That is the moment of *Seinige*: its being *theirs*.

21. "Zwar können auch reine Gedanken reproduziert werden; die Einbildungskraft hat jedoch nicht mit ihnen, sondern nur mit Bildern zu tun. Die Reproduktion der Bilder geschieht aber von seiten der Einbildungskraft mit *Willkür* und ohne die Hilfe einer unmittelbaren Anschauung. Dadurch unterscheidet sich diese Form der vorstellenden Intelligenz von der blossen *Erinnerung*, weche nicht dies Selbsttätige ist . . ." (*Enz.Phil.G.* ¶455Z, p. 264).

22. Hegel's three moments of the imagination contrast obviously with Kant's division of the imagination in *The Critique of Pure Reason*. In Kant's analysis there are three "kinds" or functions of the imagination: (1) reproductive (associative)(2) productive (figurative synthesis), and (3) transcendental. These are specifications of the imagination as the synthesis that joins intuition and the understanding. The specific differences between Kant's and Hegel's divisions would be too numerous to go into here, but generally I believe that Hegel changes Kant's transcendental imagination into *Sign-Making Phantasie*, transforming transcendental unity to system, moving from the subject toward interpersonal, dialectical communication.

23. Hegel critiques Fichte, too, for providing "nothing less than . . . a synoptic table like a skeleton with scraps of paper stuck all over it" (*PoS* ¶51, p. 31).

24. Hegel's 1802 *Critical Journal* essay "The Relationship of Skepticism to Philosophy" in *Between Kant and Hegel*, trans. di Giovanni and H. S. Harris (Albany, State University of New York Press, 1985), 311–62, (p. 354; my emphasis). Hegel's rhetorical critique is worth citing further: "The process lacks all the quickening vitality of an Idea of Reason; it carries on without the touch of fancy or of fortune in a resounding, sense-clouding, sleep-inducing, overwhelming tone, producing the same effect as if one was wandering through a field of henbane in bloom, the stupefying scent of which no efforts can withstand, and where one is not aroused by any enlivening beam, not even in the shape of an impending nemesis" (353–54).

Chapter Six. Memory, the Artist's *Einbildungskraft*, *Phantasie*, and Aesthetic *Vorstellungen* (*Lectures on Aesthetics*)

1. What is inwardized has the shape of something merely external. The memory is "such a *without-book* [memorized, *Auswendiges*] as remains locked up in the *within-book* [night, *Inwendiges*] of intelligence, and is, within intelligence, only its outward and existing side" (*Enc.Phil.Spir.* ¶462).

2. Kirk Pillow argues that "[i]n Hegel's genesis of mind . . . the imaginative power is born out of saving the soul from madness" ("Habituating Madness and Phantasying Art in Hegel's *Encyclopedia*," in *Owl of Minerva* 28, no. 2 [Spring 1997]: 183–216, 189). He claims that *Phantasie* overturns the abstract concepts to which imagination has habituated the sleeping soul, releasing habituation by allowing the associations to play a creative role in artistic production. I agree with Pillow generally but disagree that it is *Phantasie* alone that is the saving grace or that it is only the sleeping soul that can be habituated: his account of how the imagination informs creativity ought to have focused as much on the Night as a negative, inwardizing process, and on memory's relationship with *Phantasie*.

3. Earlier, Hegel notes in an introductory fashion that "[t]he image produced by imagination of an object is a bare mental or subjective intuition: in the sign or symbol it adds intuitability proper; and in mechanical memory it completes, so far as it is concerned, this form of *being*" (*Enc.Phil.Spir.* ¶457, p. 211).

4. An example is the Greek statesman who memorizes his speech by walking around the inside of the Parthenon connecting various ideas to various statues; later, while giving his speech, he walks through the Parthenon in his mind, arriving in sequence at the ideas he wishes to present.

5. Miller wrongly translates *Einbildungskraft* here as "Fancy" and *Schacht* as "pit." I have amended these. For justification of see p. 110 below and my note 8 chapter 5 p. 174–175.

6. Homer, *Odyssey*, Book 12, line 67, trans. Robert Fitzgerald (Garden City: Doubleday Anchor Book, 1963), 212.

7. Cf. Hegel, *The Science of Logic* (1812), trans. A. V. Miller (Atlantic Highlands, NJ: Humanities, 1969), 67–78.

8. "Consequently genius does burst forth in youth, as was the case with Goethe and Schiller, but only middle or old age can bring to perfection the genuine maturity of the work of art" (*Aesth.* 283).

9. Knox sometimes translates *Phantasie* as fancy, but this is not universally the case; he often translates it as "imagination."

10. Among other places, see Knox's translation in *Aesthetics* at pp. 89, 101, 162, 997–98, 1001, 1027, 1035, 1037. In each of these cases Knox translates "*die Vorstellung(en)*" or the verb "*vorstellen*" as imagination, imaginative, or to imagine.

11. Knox gives himself the lie when he fails to translate *Vorstellung* as imagination in the following case "the poetic *way of putting things (Vorstellungsweise)* stands in contrast to the *prosaic one* (s. 280, p. 1005; my emphasis).

12. Hegel clearly means them to be different when he writes that "the spirit does still nevertheless lead a full life in feeling [*Empfindung*], inclination [*Neigung*], imagination [*Vorstellung*], fancy [*Phantasie*] etc." (*Aesth.* 715; *Äst.* 368 v. 14). Knox translates *Vorstellung* and *Phantasie* differently here because Hegel lists them one after the other. But Knox does not keep up these distinctions. In any case, *Vorstellung* should be "representation."

13. Hegel says much the same in the *Enz.Phil.G.* (¶449, s. 255–56).

14. Since common sense appears to involve memory, one might conclude that the reproductive kind of imagination can in fact engage memory and represent things, just in a non-self-consciously and unartistic way. One might then suggest that it would have been better had Hegel referred to commonsense ingenuity as mechanical memory, as a form of *Vorstellung*, rather than *Einbildungskraft*. But that conclusion smudges the epistemological distinction between the reproductive imagination as pre-Spirit and sign-making *Phantasie,*which properly is Spirit. And the activity of commonsense ingenuity, while it may become mechanical, is in its origin really just a form of recollection, not mechanical memory. It works on the basis of stimulus from outside stirring up the recollection of something similar in the mind, not on the basis of knowing something by rote.

15. See my discussion above p. xix.

16. "El sueño de la razón produce monstruos." Goya, *Los Caprichos* (1799) Plate 43.

17. See Jay Lampert, "Hegel and Ancient Egypt: History and Becoming" in *International Philosophical Quarterly* XXXV, no. 1, No. 137 (March 1995): 43–58.

18. According to Hegel, Greek religion is therefore also "the religion of art itself, while the later romantic art, although it is art, yet points already to a higher form of consciousness than art can provide" (*Aesth.* 438).

19. One potential example to investigate for these moments is Hinduism, for Hegel refers to it in the *Aesthetics* as the "religion of *Phantasie.*" Hinduism, as Hegel understood it, expresses the moment of recollection without memory; it thus expresses the symbol-making, not the sign-making *Phantasie.* But since Hegel's view is not well informed, and since he, in his 1827 *Lectures on Philosophy of Religion*, decides against calling it the religion of *Phantasie*, and since a proper analysis would require a close look at those lectures, I have decided not to discuss it here.

20. Knox notes that "[f]or Hegel, time is the negativing of space. See e.g. *Philosophy of Nature* paragraph 257." It is an interesting *Zusatz*, in particular the last line: "In der Vorstellung is Raum und Zeit weit auseinander, da haben wir Raum und dann *auch* Zeit; dieses 'Auch' bekämpft die Philosophie" *Die Naturphilosophie* 48).

21. For Hegel's discussion of art as form of Absolute Spirit and as giving over to Religion see *Aesth.* 102ff. What gets added to art by religion is worship.

22. In any discussion of the Romantic interest in the imagination one must mention Blake, Wordsworth, Coleridge, and the influence of Transcendental Idealism on Coleridge, after 1801. (For Coleridge's distinction between imagination and fancy see Coleridge, *Bibliographia Lit.*, chapter XIII, p. 313). As fascinating as these thinkers are on the topic of imagination, an investigation of their work lies outside of our present concern.

23. Kurt Reinhardt, *Germany: 2000 Years*, vol. 1 and 2, revised edition (New York: Frederick Ungar, 1966), 470.

24. Reinhardt, *Germany: 2000 Years*, 470. Its "younger" members include "Clemens Brentano (1779–1842); Achim von Arnim (1781–1831); Jacob Grimm (1785–1863); Wilhelm Grimm (Jacob's younger brother, 1786–1859); Joseph Görres (1776–1848); Ernst Theodor Amadeus Hoffmann (1776–1822); and Joseph von Eichendorff (1788–1857)." For German Women Romantics, see Seyla Benhabib, "On Hegel, Women and Irony" in *Feminist Interpretations of G. W. F. Hegel,* ed. Patricia Jagentowicz Mills, Pennsylvania State Univeristy Press, 1996) (25–43) and Mary Hargrave, *Some German Women and Their Salons* (New York: Brentanto, n.d.).)

25. F. Schlegel, "Athenäum Fragmente" (Fragment 116), in *Dialogue on Poetry and Literary Aphorisms* (College Park: Pennsylvania State University Press, 1968), 140–41.

26. "But despite this seeming opposition they were still under the spell of Classicism to such an extent that they gave their first periodical a Greek name (*Athenäum,* 1798–1800) and considered Goethe's classical novel *Wilhelm Meister* as the incarnation of everything truly artistic and poetic" (Reinhardt, *Germany: 2000 Years,* 470).

27. Abrams, *The Mirror and the Lamp: Romantic Theory and the Critical Tradition* (London, Oxford, New York: Oxford University Press, 1953), 90.

28. For a discussion of the way in which Kant's theory of imagination was taken up by the Schlegel brothers, see Ernst Behler's chapter "The Theory of the Imagination," in *German Romantic Literary Theory* (Cambridge: Cambridge University Press, 1993), 74–87.

29. Charles Taylor, *Sources of the Self: The Making of the Modern Identity* (Cambridge: Harvard University Press, 1989), 379.

30. Taylor explains this further using the idea of "epiphany":

> [There is] the notion of the work of art as issuing from or realizing an "epiphany". . . . What I want to capture with this term is just this notion of a work of art as the locus of a manifestation which brings us into the presence of something which is otherwise inaccessible. . . .
>
> [In the kind of epiphany that dominated with the Romantics] the work does portray something–unspoilt nature, human emotion–but in such a way as to show some greater spiritual reality or significance shining through it. The poetry of Wordsworth or the paintings of Constable and Friedrich exemplify this pattern. (*Sources* 419)

31. For a discussion of this influence see Paola Mayer's *Jena Romanticism and Its Appropriation of Jakob Böhme: Theosophy, Hagiography, Literature* (Montreal: McGill-Queen's University Press, 1999). Mayer notes that the "demise of Jena Romanticism [occurred] (in 1805 for Schlegel, in 1809 for Schelling)" (7).

32. "While Tieck and Novalis professed a sentimental attachment to Catholicism, Friedrich Schlegel, F. von Stolberg, Zacharias Werner, and others actually embraced the Catholic faith, and Görres and Brentano returned in the end to the abandoned creed of their youth" (*Germany* 473).

33. Hegel's rejection of irony is important for feminist critiques of Hegel. For according to Hegel, "womankind—the everlasting irony (in the life) of the community—changes by intrigue the universal end of the government into a private end" (*PoS* 288). Hegel's view, according to Seyla Benhabib, makes him fail to recognize the emancipatory character of German Romantic women, and deny women an equal role in his historic dialectic. (See Benhabib "On Hegel, Women, and Irony" p. 34). I address this topic in "Tearing the Fabric: Hegel, Antigone, Coriolanus and Kinship-State Conflict" presented at the International Association for Philosphy and Literature, Syracuse May 19–25, 2004.

34. Hegel criticizes Tieck and others for a high-mindedness and disdaining disregard for the receiving public (*Aesth.* 1175, 1180):

> Since Tieck's time this contempt for the public has become the fashion, especially in Germany. The German author insists on expressing himself according to his own private personality and not making his works agreeable to hearers or spectators. On the contrary, German self-will requires that everyone shall be something different from everyone else in order to display his originality. For example, Tieck and the brothers Schlegel with their premeditated irony could not master the mind and spirit of their nation and time; they declaimed against Schiller especially and maligned him for finding the right note for the German people and gaining the height of popularity. (*Aesth.* 1175).

35. See also Hegel's *Philosophy of Right*, pp. 101–03 where he criticizes irony as a form of the Beautiful Soul. The Beautiful Soul is also a phenomenological moment in the *Phenomenology of Spirit*, pp. 400–409.

36. My book manuscript, *Cues: Hegel and Shakespeare on Moral Action*, is in progress.

Chapter Seven. Imagination and the Medium of Thought (*Phenomenology of Spirit* "Preface")

1. Miller translate "*Begriff*" as "Notion." I prefer to use the word *Concept* as I have consistently done above.

2. It is in *Between Kant and Hegel*, translated by Di Giovanni and H. S. Harris (Albany:State University of New York Press, 1985), 311–62.

3. August Wilhelm Schlegel, *Kritishe Ausgabe der Vorlesungen*, ed. Ernst Behler in collaboration with Frank Jolles, 6 vols. (Paderborn: Schöningh, 1989-), I, 243 paraphrased by Behler in *German Romantic Literary Theory* (Cambridge: Cambridge University Press, 1993), 81.

4. See Philippe Lacoue-Labarth and Jean-Luc Nancy's discussion of romantic genius in *The Literary Absolute: The Theory of Literature in German Romanticism*, trans. Philip Barnard and Cheryl Lester (Albany: State University of New York Press, 1988), 55. They cite the following: "'Understanding is mechanical spirit; *Witz* is chemical spirit; genius is organic spirit" (cf. A[thenäum fragment] 426)'" (55).

5. Cf. Düsing's discussion of the *Genieästhetik* in "Aesthetishe Einbildungskraft und Intuitiver Verstand," in *Hegel Studien* Band 21, heraus. F. Nicolin und O. Pöggeler (Bonn: Bouvier Verlag Herbert Grundmann, 1986), 102–03.

6. See also my discussion of Hegel's critique of irony and Romanticism in chapter 6.

7. "Subject and object, God, Nature, Understanding, sensibility, and so on, are uncritically taken for granted as familiar, established as valid, and made into fixed points for starting and stopping. While these remain unmoved, the *knowing activity goes back and forth between them, thus moving only on their surface.* ['*mit allem Hin— und Herreden kommt solches Wissen*' (*PdG* 35)]" (Preface, *PoS* ¶31, p. 18; my emphasis).

8. Hegel uses the word *aether* in his *Geistesphilosophie* of 1803–04. That *Geistesphilosophie* was written between the *System der Sittlichkeit* and the *Phenomenology*. In it Hegel develops *Aufhebung* in terms of a sequence from *Luft* to *Erde* to *Äther* (*G1* 1803–04, Frag. 18, p. 192). But it is only in the *Phenomenology of Spirit* that we get aether as an expression of proper reflection.

9. The rising up is nonetheless concrete. Hegel's use of "somersaulting" certainly evokes a down-to-earth activity, one that lends itself to the historical-material progression which the *Begriff* really is. The expression suggests that Karl Marx's desire to put Hegel on his head is always already occurring!

10. One has only to turn to Fichte's abstract "Deduction of Presentation" in the *Science of Knowledge* to see this. See my note 11 in Chapter 1, p. 160.

11. The process of *Aufhebung* is what is watched/experienced throughout the *Phenomenology*. Hegel's *description* of how this works can be found in the Preface (¶¶29–35), in his overview of the transition which the *Phenomenology* as a whole takes

us through. That transition is from *Vorstellen* to *Denken* to *Begriff*. In the description, Hegel is concerned with the *Erhebung* of consciousness, not its activity or *Aufheben*. Hegel seems to use the word *Erhebung* when he describes the raising of consciousness to a new *Potenz* or level, whereas *Aufhebung* is the process by which that happens. In one *Erhebung* to a new level there could be any number of *Aufhebungen*, since *Aufhebung* is what consciousness *is*: it is its essential movement or *Begriff*. "We" as speculative scientists watch the transitions, the *Erhebung* of consciousness at each level in the *Phenomenology*. We watch how science is this raising of consciousness. On the other hand, the reader's experience of the process of consciousness moving through the *Phenomenology*, goes through the continual *Aufhebung* of what is familiar to it (*das Bekannte*) to knowledge (*das Erkennen*), and finally to its knowledge of itself as *aufhebend*. The latter is consciousness as *der (absolute) Begriff*.

12. Hegel refers to *Erhebung* as consciousness' education (*Bildung, PdG* ¶29, p. 33. Cf. also ¶28, p. 33, ¶33, p. 36). But Erdmann warns against reading the *Phenomenology* strictly as a history of consciousness' education: "[Es] könnte . . . nun scheinen, als werde die Philosophie von Hegel zwar nicht psychologisch, aber historisch begründet, durch eine Bildungsgeschichte nämlich des Geistes. Da würde aber vergessen, dass die Phänomenologie nicht die Geschichte, sondern die begriffene Geschichte darstellen, dass sie nicht erzählen will, wie der Geist sich entwickelt hat, sondern wie er sich entwickeln musste" (Erdmann, "Die Phänomenologie des Geistes" 59.) For a more detailed investigation of the concept of *Bildung* in Hegel see Otto Pöggeler's essay "Hegels Bildungskonzeption im Geschichtlichen Zusammenhang" in *Hegel-Studien* Band 15, heraus. F. Nicolin und O. Pöggeler [Bonn: Bouvier Verlag Herbert Grundmann, 1980], 241–69.)

13. This allows for the move on to the *Logic*, or for the phenomenologist, a return to sense-certainty in a new way, to a consciousness of experience that thinks its moments through absolutely. Or again, the end of the *Phenomenology* dawns the beginning of the *Encyclopedic* attitude toward intuition. See also *Enc.Phil.Spir.* ¶449Z, p. 200.

In one way we have already reached this end of the imagination since our work of thinking the imagination through in order to explain its role in the *Phenomenology* required grasping the end of the *Phenomenology*. It required grasping the *Phenomenology's* aim, its goal. However, a phenomenologically rich investigation of how Hegel thinks the imagination to the end in that work requires investigation of the moments in the *Phenomenology*, as well as looking closely at the final chapters of the *Lectures on the Philosophy of Religion*. That is a task that exceeds the scope of the present inquiry. Nonetheless, it is appropriate to develop the general theory in order to complete the argument I have been developing throughout the book.

14. "Forgiveness is the only moral duty that is truly *absolute*, for the willingness to enter even into the standpoint of the coward who saved his own life in the battle is the condition of truly human communication. This is the reality of moral respect" (Harris, *Hegel* 78–79). But the act must be accomplished on both sides: "The coward must, of course, confess that he was a coward and that he needs forgiveness if the communication is to become perfect."

15. Forgiveness "cannot be conditional. Reciprocity is looked for, but it cannot be demanded" (Harris, *Hegel* 78–79).

16. Although its complete message bears a secular resemblance to the entire *Divine Comedy*.

Bibliography

Adelman, Howard. "Hegel's *Phenomenology*: Facing the Preface." *Idealistic Studies* xiv, no. 2 (1984): 159–70.

Abrams. M. H. *The Mirror and the Lamp: Romantic Theory and the Critical Tradition.* London, Oxford, New York: Oxford University Press, 1953.

———. *The Correspondent Breeze: Essays on English Romanticism.* New York: W.W. Norton, 1984.

Aristotle. *De Anima.* Trans. W. S. Hett. Loeb Classical Edition. Cambridge: Harvard University Press, 1936.

———. *Nicomachean Ethics.* Trans. Rackham. Cambridge: Harvard University Press and William Heinemann LTD, 1975.

Bates, Jennifer. Review of *Hegel and the Symbolic Mediation of Spirit* (Kathleen Dow Magnus) for *Philosophy in Review*, Volume XXII no. 5, October 2002. 341–434.

Bates, Jennifer. *Cues: Hegel and Shakespeare on Moral Action.* (Working manuscript).

———. "Imagination in Vajrayana Buddhism: a Philosophical Investigation of Tibetan Thangka Symbolism in the Light of Hegelian Aesthetics and Kantian Epistemology." Paper presented at "Writing Aesthetics" The International Association for Philosophy and Literature 27th Annual Conference, University of Leeds, England, May 26–31, 2003.

———. "The Moral Chemist of the *Corpus Mysticism:* Why Some Version of Kant's Practical Postulates is Necessary, Even for Hegel." Paper presented at the The Society for German Idealism Conference, Pacific American Philosophical Association Meeting, Pasadena March 24–28, 2004.

———. "Tearing the Fabric: Hegel, Antigone, Coriolanus and Kinship-State Conflict." Paper presented at the "Virtual Materalities," the International Association for Philosophy and Literature 28th Annual Conference, Syracuse, May 19–25, 2004.

Beck, Lewis White. "Did the Sage of Königsberg Have no Dreams?" In *Essays on Kant and Hume*, 38–50. New Haven and London: Yale University Press, 1978.

Behler, Ernst. *German Romantic Literary Theory*. Cambridge: Cambridge University Press, 1993.

Benhabib, Seyla. "On Hegel Woman and Irony." In *Feminist Interpretations of G.W.F. Hegel*. Ed. Patricia Jagentowicz Mills. 25–43. Pennsylvania: Pennsylvania States University Press, 1996.

Bodammer, Theodor. *Hegels Deutung der Sprache. Interpretationen zu Hegels Äusserungen über die Sprache*. Hamburg: Felix Meiner Verlag, 1962.

Bonsiepen, Wolfgang. *Der Begriff der Negativität in den Jenaer Schriften Hegels*, in *Hegel-Studien* Beiheft 16, 29–31. Bonn: Bouvier Verlag Herbert Grundmann, 1977.

Breazeale, Daniel. "Check or Checkmate?" In *The Modern Subject: Conceptions of the Self in Classical German Philosophy*, ed. Karl Ameriks and Dieter Sturma, 87–114. Albany: State University of New York Press, 1995.

Burbidge, J. "Man, God, and Death in Hegel's *Phenomenology*." *Philosophy and Phenomenological Research*, VXLII, no. 2 (December 1981).

Coleridge, Samuel. *Bibliographia Literaria*. In *The Oxford Authors: Samuel Taylor Coleridge*. Oxford, New York: Oxford University Press, 1985.

Cook, Daniel. "Commentary on 'Imagination and Presentation' by J. Sallis. In *Hegel's Philosophy of Spirit*, ed. Peter G. Stillman, 89–93. Albany: State University of New York Press, 1987.

Cook, Daniel. *Language in the Philosophy of Hegel*. The Hague: Mouton, 1973.

DeMan, Paul. "The Intentional Structure of the Romantic Image." In *Romanticism and Consciousness: Essays in Criticism*, ed. Harold Bloom, 65–77. New York: W. W. Norton, 1970.

Derbolav, Josef. "Hegel und die Sprache." In *Sprache—Schlüssel zur Welt*. Festschrift für Leo Weisgerber. Düsseldorf: Pädagogischer Verlag, 1959.

DeVries. Willem A.. *Hegel's Theory of Mental Activity: An Introduction to Theoretical Spirit*. Ithaca and London: Cornell University Press, 1988.

Dokument zu Hegels Jenaer Dozentätigkeit, (1801–1807). Hrsg. von H. Kimmerle. In *Hegel-Studien* Bd. 4, 53–56. Bonn: Bouvier Verlag, 1967.

Düsing, Klaus. "Aesthetishe Einbildungskraft und Intuitiver Verstand." In *Hegel-Studien* Bd. 21, hrsg. F. Nicolin und O Pöggeler, 87–128. Bonn: Bouvier Verlag, Herbert Grundmann, 1986.

———. "Hegels 'Phänomenologie' und die Idealistische Geschichte des Selbstbewusstseins." In *Hegel-Studien* Bd. 28, hrsg. F. Nicolin und O. Pöggeler, 103–126. Bonn: Bouvier Verlag, 1993.

———. "Hegels Theorie der Einbildungskraft." In *Psychologie und Anthropologie oder Philosophie des Geistes: Beiträge zu einer Hegel-Tagung in Marburg 1989*. Hrsg. Franz Hespe und Burkhard Tuschling, 297–320. Frommann-holzboog, 1991.

———. "Hegels Vorlesungen an der Universität Jena." In *Hegel-Studien* Bd. 26, hrsg. F. Nicolin und O. Pöggeler, 15–21. Bonn: Bouvier Verlag, 1991.

Erdmann, J. E. "Die Phänomenologie des Geistes." In *Materialen zu Hegels "Phänomenologie des Geistes,"* hrsg. H-.F. Fulda und Dieter Henrich, 54–64. Frankfurt am Main: Suhrkamp Verlag, 1973.

Feminist Interpretations of G.W.F. Hegel. Ed. Patricia Jagentowicz Mills. Pennsylvania: Pennsylvania State University Press, 1996.

Fichte, J. G. *The Science of Knowledge.* Ed. and trans. P. Heath and J. Lachs. Cambridge: Cambridge University Press, 1982.

———. *Grundlage der gesamten Wissenschaftslehre (1794).* Einleitung und Register von Wilhelm G. Jacobs. Hamburg: Felix Meiner Verlag, 1988.

Fulda, H.-F. "Vom Gedächtnis zum Denken." Sonderdruck aus *Psychologie und Anthropologie oder Philosophie des Geistes: Beitrage zu einer Hegel-Tagung in Marburg, 1989,* hrsg. F. Hespe und B. Tuschling, 321–360. Frommann-holzboog, 1991.

Gauvin, Joseph. "Wortindex zu Hegels *Phänomologie des Geistes.*" In *Hegel-Studien Beiheft* Bd. 14. Bonn: Bouvier Verlag, Herbert Grundmann, 1977.

Gibbons, Sarah, L.. *Kant's Theory of Imagination: Bridging Gaps in Judgement and Experience.* Oxford: Clarendon Press, Oxford University Press, 1994.

Goethe. Johann Wolfgang von. *Faust.* Trans. W. Arndt and C. Hamlin. New York and London: Norton Critical Edition, 1976.

———. "Dichtung und Wahrheit." *Goethes Werke.* Hamburger Ausgabe. Bd. 9. München: C. H. Beck, 1974.

Halper. Edward. "The Logic of Hegel's *Philosophy of Nature*: Nature, Space and Time." In *Hegel and the Philosophy of Nature,* ed. Steven Houlgate. Albany: State University of New York Press, 1998.

Hargrave, Mary. *Some German Women and Their Salons.* New York: Brentano, n.d.

Harris, H. S. *Hegel: Phenomenology and System.* Indianapolis: Hackett, 1995.

———. *Hegel's Ladder.* Vol. 1 and 2. Indianapolis, Cambridge: Hackett, 1997.

Hegel, G. W. F. *Ästhetik.* Bd. 1 und 2. Nach der zweiten Ausgabe von H. G. Hothos (1842). Hrsg. F. Bassenge. Frankfurt am Main: Europäische Verlagsanstalt GmbH, 1955.

———. *Vorlesungen über die Ästhetik. (Hegel: Werke 13–15.)* Frankfurt am Main: Surkamp Verlag, 1970.

———. *The Difference Between Fichte's and Schelling's System of Philosophy.* Trans. H. S. Harris and W. Cerf. Albany: State University of New York Press, 1977.

———. *Differenz des Fichteschen und Schellingschen Systems der Philosophie.* Frankfurt am Main: Suhrkamp Verlag, 1974.

———. *The Encyclopaedia Logic.* Trans. T. F. Geraets, W. A. Suchting, H. S. Harris. Indianapolis, Cambridge: Hackett, 1991.

———. *Encyclopaedia Philosophy of Mind.* Trans. W. Wallace. With *Zusätze in Boumann's text (1845),* trans. A. V. Miller. Oxford: Clarendon Press, 1971.

———. *Enzyklopädie Philosophie des Geistes* (1830). Redaktion E. Moldenhauer und K. M. Michel. Frankfurt am Main: Suhrkamp Verlag, 1970.

———. *Faith and Knowledge.* Trans. Walter Cerf and H. S. Harris. Albany: State University of New York Press, 1977.

————. *Geistesphilosophie (1803–04)*. In *Jenaer Systementwürfe I: Das System der Spekulativen Philosophie*, hrsg. K. Düsing und H. Kimmerle. Hamburg: Felix Meiner Verlag, 1986.

————. *Glauben und Wissen, Jenaer Kritische Schriften*. Hrsg. H. Brockard und H. Buchner. Hamburg: Felix Meiner Verlag, 1986.

————. *Lectures on Aesthetics*. Vol. 1 and 2. Trans. T. M. Knox. Oxford: Clarendon Press, 1975.

————. *Lectures on the Philosophy of Religion—the Lectures of 1827*. Ed. Peter C. Hodgson. Trans. R.F. Brown, P.C. Hodgson, J. M. Stewart, with the assistance of H. S. Harris. London: Univeristy of California Press, 1988.

————. *Naturphilosophie und Philosophie des Geistes (1805–6)*. In *Jenaer Systementwürfe III*, hrsg. R.-P. Horstmann. Hamburg: Felix Meiner Verlag, 1987.

————. *Phänomenologie des Geistes*. Redaktion E. Moldenhauer und K. M. Michel. Frankfurt am Main: Suhrkamp Verlag, 1970.

————. *The Phenomenology of Spirit*. Trans. A. V. Miller. Oxford, New York, Toronto, Melbourne: Oxford University Press, 1977.

————. "The Relationship of Skepticism to Philosophy." in *Between Kant and Hegel*, trans. di Giovanni and H. S. Harris, 311–362. Albany: State University of New York Press, 1985.

————. *Schriften zur Politik und Rechtsphilosophie*. Hrsg. Georg Lasson. Leipzig: Verlag von Felix Meiner, 1913.

————. *The Science of Logic* (1812). Trans. A. V. Miller. Atlantic Highlands, NJ: Humanities, 1969.

————. *The System of Ethical Life (1802/3) and First Philosophy of Spirit (Part II of the System of Speculative Philosophy 1803/4)*. Trans. H. S. Harris and T. M. Knox. Albany: State University of New York Press, 1979.

————. *Vorlesungen*. Bd. 13. Hrsg. F. Hespe und B. Tuschling. Hamburg; Felix Meiner Verlag, 1994.

Hegel and the Philosophy of Nature. Ed. Steven Houlgate. Albany: State University Press, 1998.

Heidegger, M. *Poetry, Language, and Thought*. Trans. A. Hofstadter. New York: Harper and Row, 1971.

Homer, *Odyssey*. Trans. Robert Fitzgerald. Garden City: Doubleday, 1963.

Hume, David. *Treatise of Human Nature*. Ed. Selby-Biggs. Oxford: Clarendon Press, 1888.

Hyppolite, J. "Note sur la preface de la Phenomenologie de l'esprit et le theme: l'absolu est sujet." In *Hegel-Studien Beiheft*, Bd. 4 (Hegel-Tage Urbino 1965), hrsg. H.-G. Gadamer, 75–80. H. Bonn: Bouvier Verlag, 1969.

Kant. *Critique of Judgment*. Trans. W. Pluhar. Indiana: Hackett, 1987.

————. *Critique of Pure Reason*. Trans. N. Kemp Smith. London and Basingstoke: MacMillan, 1983.

————. *Critique of Practical Reason*. Trans. Lewis White Beck. Third Edition. New Jersey: Prentice-Hall, 1993.

————. *Foundations for the Metaphysics of Morals*. Trans. L. W. Beck. Indianapolis: Bobbs-Merrill, 1959.

————. *Kritik der reinen Vernunft.* Hrsg. R. Schmidt. Hamburg: Felix Meiner Verlag, 1990.

————. *Kritik der Urteilskraft.* Hrsg. W. Weischedel. Frankfurt am Main: Suhrkamp, 1957.

————. *Religion Within the Limits of Reason Alone.* Trans. Greene and Hudson. New York: Harper and Row, 1960.

Kearney, Richard. *The Wake of the Imagination: Ideas of Creativity in Western Culture.* London: Hutchinson Education, 1988.

Kierkegaard, Søren. "Preamble from the Heart." In *Fear and Trembling,* trans. Alastair Hannay, 57–82. New York: Penguin, 1985.

Kimmerle, Heinz. "Zur Chronologie von Hegels Jenaer Schriften." In *Hegel-Studien.* Bd. 4. Hrsg. H. Kimmerle. Bonn: Bouvier Verlag, 1967.

Labarrière, Pierre-Jean. "La Phenomenologie de L'esprit comme discours systematique: Histoire, Religion et Science." In *Hegel-Studien.* Bd. 9. Hrsg. F. Nicolin und O. Pöggeler. Bonn: Bouvier Verlag Herbert Grundmann, 1974.

Lacoue-Labarth, Philippe, and Jean-Luc Nancy. *The Literary Absolute: The Theory of Literature in German Romanticism.* Trans. Philip Barnard and Cheryl Lester. Albany: State University of New York Press, 1988.

Lampert. Jay. "Hegel and Ancient Egypt: History and Becoming." *International Philosophical Quarterly,* XXXV, no. 137 (March 1995): 43–58.

Leibniz. *The Monadology.* In *Leibniz Selections,* ed. Philip P. Wiener, 533–51. New York: Charles Scribner's Sons, 1951.

Magnus, Kathleen Dow. *Hegel and the Symbolic Mediation of Spirit.* Albany: State University of New York Press, 2001.

Mayer. Paola. *Jena Romanticism and Its Appropriation of Jakob Böhme: Theosophy, Hagiography, Literature.* Montreal: McGill-Queen's University Press, 1999.

Marx, Werner. *Hegel's Phenomenology of Spirit: A Commentary Based on the Preface and Introduction.* Trans. Peter Heath. Chicago and London: The University of Chicago Press, 1975.

Mörchen, H. "Die Einbildungskraft bei Kant." In *Jahrbuch für Philosophie und Phänomenologische Forschung.* Bd. XI. Hrsg. E. Husserl. Halle: Max Niemeyer Verlag, 1930.

Pillow, Kirk. "Habituating Madness and Phantasying Art in Hegel's *Encyclopedia.*" *The Owl of Minerva* 28, no. 2 (Spring 1997): 183–216.

Piper, H. W. *The Active Universe: Pantheism and the Concept of Imagination in the English Romantic Poets.* London, New York: The Athlone Press, University of London, 1962.

Plato. *Phaedo.* In *Plato, the Collected Dialogues,* ed. E. Hamilton and H. Cairns, 40–98. Princeton: Princeton University Press, 1961.

Rauch, Leo. *Hegel and the Human Spirit.* Translation of the 1805–6 *Geistesphilosophie* text. Detroit: Wayne State University Press, 1993.

Reinhardt, Kurt F. *Germany: 2000 Years.* Vol. 1 and 2. Revised Edition. New York: Frederick Ungar, 1966.

Rockmore, Tom. *Hegel's Circular Epistemology.* Bloomington: Indiana University Press, 1986.

Russon, John. "The Metaphysics of Consciousness and the Hermeneutics of Social Life: Hegel's Phenomenological System." *The Southern Journal of Philosophy* 36 (1998): 81–101.

———. *The Self and Its Body in Hegel's Phenomenology of Spirit*. Toronto, Buffalo: University of Toronto Press, 1997.

Sallis, John. "Hegel's Concept of Presentation: Its Determination in the Preface to the Phenomenology of Spirit." In *Hegel-Studien*. Bd. 12, 129–156. Bonn; Bouvier Verlag Herbert Grundmann, 1977.

———. "Imagination and Presentation in Hegel's Philosophy of Spirit." in *Hegel's Philosophy of Spirit*, ed. Peter G. Stillman, 66–68. Albany: State University of New York Press, 1987.

Schelling, F. W. J. *System of Transcendental Idealism (1800)*. Trans. P. Heath. Charlottesville: University Press of Virginia, 1993.

———. *System des transzendentalen Idealismus*. Hrsg. H. D. Brandt und P. Müller. Hamburg: Felix Meiner Verlag, 1992.

Schellings und Hegels erste absolute Metaphysik (1801–1802): Zusammenfassende Vorlesungsnachschriften von I. P. V. Troxler. Hrsg. K. Düsing. Köln: Jürgen Dinter, Verlag für Philosophie, 1988.

Schlegel. August Wilhelm. *Kritische Ausgabe der Vorlesungen*. Ed. Ernst Behler in collaboration with Frank Jolles. 6 vols. Paderborn: Schöningh, 1989-.

Schlegel. "Athenäum Fragmente" (Fragment 116). In *Dialogue on Poetry and Literary Aphorisms*, 140–141. University Park: Pennsylvania State University Press, 1968.

Sellars, W. "The Role of the Imagination in Kant's Theory of Experience." In *Categories: A Colloquium*, ed. H. W. Johnstone, 229–45. University Park: Pennsylvania State University Press, 1978. 229–245.

Shakespeare. W. *A Midsummer Night's Dream*. Ed. Wolfgang Clemen. New York and Scarborough, Ontario: Signet Classic, 1963.

———. *The Tragedy of King Lear*. In *The Norton Sharkespeare*. Based on the Oxford Edition. General ed. Stephen Breenblatt, Walter Cohen, Jean E. Howard, and Katharine Eisaman Maus, 2319–2554. New York and London: W. W. Norton, 1997.

Simon, Josef. *Das Problem der Sprache bei Hegel*. Stuttgart: W. Kohlhammer Verlag, 1966.

Solomon, Robert. "A Small Problem in Hegel's *Phenomenology*." *Journal of the History of Philosophy* XIII, no. 3 (1975): 399–400.

Sparshott, Francis. "Imagination—The Very Idea." *The Journal of Aesthetics and Art Criticism* 48, no. 1 (Winter 1990): 1–8.

Stevens, Wallace. *The Necessary Angel, Essays on Reality and Imagination*. London: Faber, 1942.

Taylor, Charles. *Sources of the Self: The Making of the Modern Identity*. Cambridge: Harvard University Press, 1989.

Tuschling, B. "Hegels Vorlesungen zur Philosophie des Subjektiven Geistes." In *Hegel-Studien* Bd. 26, hrsg. F. Nicolin und O. Pöggeler, 54–63. Bonn: Bouvier Verlag, 1991.

Verene, Donald Philip. *Hegel's Recollection: A Study of Images in the Phenomenology of Spirit*. Albany: State University of New York Press, 1985.

Warnock, Mary. *Imagination*. Berkeley and Los Angeles: University of California Press, 1976.

———. *Imagination and Time*. Oxford and Cambridge, MA: Blackwell, 1994.

Wordsworth, W. "My Heart Leaps Up." In *Norton Anthology of Poetry*, ed. A. Allison, C. Blake, A. Carr, A. Eastman, H. English Jr., 600. New York and London: W.W. Norton, 1975.

Index

Absolute, 6–7, 9, 14, 20, 24–25, 100. *See also under* Fichte; Schelling
  Kant on the, 10
  synthesis of the, xxxvii
absolute, imagination as the sundering, 3–9, 55
absolute Concept, xxvi
Absolute Knowing, xiii, xxvi, 29, 80, 131, 132, 137, 145, 146, 153, 160n6, 163n28, 167n8, 169n2, 171n20, 177n19
  role of imagination in, 152
  transition from religion to, 146–52
absolute singularity, 28
Absolute Spirit, xi, xiii, xxxix, 82, 99, 113, 118–20, 131, 132, 147–49, 152, 173n38, 177n19, 180n21
aesthetics. *See under* Kant
Aesthetics (Hegel's lectures on)
  artist's *Phantasie* in the, 113–18
  Hegel's critique of German Romanticism in, 128–31
allegorizing, 88
animal state, inwardizing as, 61–63
animal *vs.* human cognition, 62
animals, imagination in, 62, 65
Anstoss. See under Fichte

apprehension, 156n14
Aristotle, xxiii, 61–63
art, 9, 99, 114
  Classical Form of Art, 119
artistic genius, 139–40. *See also* genius
artistic memory, 116
artistic *Vorstellen*, 137. *See also* representation (*Vorstellen*)
artists, 115–18
artist's products, 118–20
association, 88
Aufhebende imagination, 143–45
Aufhebung (sublation), xiii, 16, 36, 37, 52, 71, 75, 107, 108, 143, 144, 151, 153, 156n14, 157n14, 160n8, 161nn13–14, 164n9, 166n2, 169n2, 182n8, 182–83n11, 183n11
authentication, subjective *vs.* objective, 90, 91, 93, 94
awareness, 79. *See also* consciousness

beautiful object, Kant's theory of, 126, 127
beauty, 12, 114. *See also under* Kant
being-for-me, 70, 72
Being (*Sein/Seiende*), 8, 62, 86

193

knowledge
    Kant on synthesis of imagination
        and, xxviii–xxx, xxxviii, 4,
        156nn11, 14
    proper, as spiraling motion, 142–43
    systems of, xiv–xvi
Knox, T. M.
    translation of *Aesthetics*, xii
        terms translated as "imagination,"
        xi, 111–13

language, 37, 56–57, 73–75, 77–79, 96
Leibniz, Gottfried Wilhelm, 24, 167n8
light, 16, 62, 162n24
linguistics, 78. *See also* language; names
logic, 19, 21, 98–99
Logic, 168n12, 169n2
loss, logic of, 14–17

Magnus, Kathleen Dow, xviii–xix,
        155n3, 156n6, 169n2, 173n38,
        176–78nn15, 19
Maimon, Salomon, xxxiii
mediation, xxvii
memorizing *vs.* really making sense, 106
memory, 73–77, 103–6, 109–10. *See also*
        recollection
    artistic, 116
    Fichte and, 143
    identity and, 31
    imagination without, 45
    from intuition to imagination to, 45
    Kant and, 36
    "mechanical," 78
    order, 77–79
    and the overly familiar, 109
    as reading "off the tableau of imagi-
        nation," 107–9
    as superficial attachment to images,
        107
Mesmer, Franz Anton, 106
metaphysics, 20–21. *See also* reality
Miller, A. V., 112
Mind. *See Geist*
mine (*Schacht*), 85, 86, 95, 100, 152–53
mnemonic systems, 107–9

Mörchen, H., xxix
multiplicity
    as the "determined concept," 22–24
    simple essential, 22, 23
music, 121–22

name-giving power of the imagination,
        57
name-making power, 75
name making *vs.* sign making, 74
names, 37, 74–77, 92, 104. *See also* lan-
        guage
natural consciousness, 40
Nature, philosophy of, 158n19
negation (*Anstoss*), 14, 15, 41, 45–46, 52,
        66, 68, 71–72, 76, 157–58n18,
        167n10
    Fichte on, 15, 52, 144
    moment of, 28, 160n6
negative moment, 33, 54–56, 59, 60, 69,
        76, 80, 83, 96, 98, 147–48,
        169n2
negativity. *See* Night
Nietzsche, Friedrich Wilhelm, xxv
Night
    early interpretations of, 14–18,
        162n24, 163n26
    later interpretations of, 52, 55, 59,
        61–72, 74, 76–77, 79, 80,
        88, 95, 99, 100, 117, 147,
        170nn12, 17, 172nn20, 24,
        27, 173n35, 178nn1–2
nightly mine, 54, 84, 85, 88, 99, 100,
        109
Notion, 29, 146–50

objectivity, 49, 54, 75
oneness with absolute life, 9
oppositions, 57–58
original principle, 3
originary principles of self, 23
originary sundering (imagination), 3, 8

painting, 121
paradigms, xiv
particularity, 39–40

Made in the USA
Middletown, DE
19 February 2019